THE GREATER RIDGEWAY

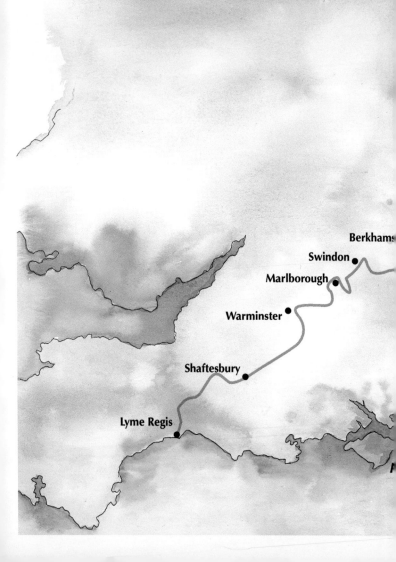

Berkhams

Swindon

Marlborough

Warminster

Shaftesbury

Lyme Regis

The Greater Ridgeway

ABOUT THE AUTHOR

Ray Quinlan is a scientist by profession, and escapes onto his local stretch of the Ridgeway over the Berkshire Downs in order to refresh both mind and body. He finds the contrast between the noise and bustle of modern southern England and this ancient landscape an endless source of wonder and enjoyment. The pubs are good, too! The Ridgeway, therefore, was a natural choice for this, his sixth, walking guide. Ray's previous books have focused primarily on routes along the canals of England and Wales.

THE GREATER RIDGEWAY

A WALK ALONG THE ANCIENT ROUTE
FROM LYME REGIS TO HUNSTANTON

by
Ray Quinlan

2 POLICE SQUARE, MILNTHORPE, CUMBRIA, LA7 7PY
www.cicerone.co.uk

British Cataloguing-in-Publication Data.
A catalogue record for this book is available from the British Library.
ISBN 1 85284 346 2

To Ellie – this is your book

Advice to Readers

Readers are advised that while every effort is taken by the author to ensure the
accuracy of this guidebook, changes can occur which may affect the contents. It is
advisable to check locally on transport, accommodation, shops, etc, but even right
of way can be altered.

The publisher would welcome notes of any such changes.

CONTENTS

ROUTE SUMMARY

Day	Distance km (miles)	Start	Finish	OS Map No	Terrain
1	31.7 (19.7)	Lyme Regis	Beaminster	193	Hilly & long
2	22.5 (14)	Beaminster	Sydling (for Cerne Abbas)	193, 194	Hilly
3	29.8 (18.5)	Cerne Abbas	Shillingstone	194	Hilly & long
4	23.3 (14.5)	Shillingstone	Ludwell	194, 195, 184	Easy country
5	27.3 (17)	Ludwell	Heytesbury	184	Easy but long
6	21.6 (13.5)	Heytesbury	Coulston	184	Easy country
7	24 (15)	Coulston	Devizes	184, 173	Hilly then country
8	16.8 (10.5)	Devizes	Avebury	173	Hilly
9	25.7 (16)	Avebury	Fox Hill	173, 174	Remote country
10	25.6 (15.9)	Fox Hill	Scutchamer Knob	174	Remote country
11	24.5 (15.3)	Scutchamer Knob	Mongewell	174, 175	Remote country
12	24.1 (15)	Mongewell	Chinnor	175, 165	Easy country
13	18.2 (11.3)	Chinnor	Wendover	165	Easy country
14	18.5 (11.5)	Wendover	Ivinghoe	165	Some hills
15	20.9 (13)	Ivinghoe	Luton	165, 166	Country & town
16	21.3 (13.3)	Luton	Letchworth	166	Town & country
17	23.4 (14.7)	Letchworth	Royston	166, 153, 154	Town & country
18	20.9 (13)	Royston	Great Chesterford	154	Easy country
19	28.9 (18)	Great Chesterford	Stetchworth	154	Easy but long
20	27.3 (17)	Stetchworth	Icklingham	154, 155	Easy but long
21	26.5 (16.5)	Icklingham	Knettishall	155, 144	Easy but long
22	23 (14.3)	Knettishall	Little Cressingham	144	Easy country
23	19.2 (12)	Little Cressingham	Castle Acre	144, 132	Easy country
24	22.5 (14)	Castle Acre	Sedgeford	132	Easy country
25	14 (8.7)	Sedgeford	Hunstanton	132	Easy country

INTRODUCTION

It's hard to imagine a world without roads. Not roads with tarmac and speed cameras, but *routes*; interconnecting tracks or ways that link people with people, or people with places.

PREHISTORIC ROADS

There have probably been roads for as long as there have been people. In the earliest times, these would have led to watering places or hunting sites, and may have followed routes of animal migration. Then, perhaps, lines of human migration developed into lines of contact between peoples, maybe for purposes of trade or worship. Neolithic farmers (c. 4000 BC) traded stone axes throughout the country, and also dealt in agricultural products, salt, tools, clay for pottery, and pottery itself. These early Britons built barrows, henges and stone circles, evidence of economic wealth and stability as well as considerable organisation and leadership. This suggests that there would have been good communication systems and well-defined routes at that time.

The most obvious overland routes were the relatively treeless ridgeways, running above valleys that were said to be impenetrable and home to fierce creatures. The word 'ridgeway' is taken from the Anglo-Saxon *hrycweg*, and by that time a complicated network of these green roads was evident. It seems to have been a

Uffington Castle

9

The Cobb, Lyme Regis

popular notion, even then, that these were prehistoric. The basis of the argument is that the ridgeways link places of prehistoric occupation – hillforts, burial mounds and henges. However, several archaeologists have argued that these are only the *obvious* bits of extant prehistory; most archaeological sites are actually in the valleys. But why should a migration or pilgrimage route pass through every area of occupation? While people may have *lived* on good farming land, they may well have preferred to *travel* across ground that was easy and safe. The ridgeways were routes over high chalk uplands where you could see where you were and where you were going, and where the ground was easier to cross. They would have been, quite literally, the highways of their day.

And the Greater Ridgeway, which combines the Icknield Way with the Wessex Ridgeways, is widely thought to be one of the oldest.

THE GREATER RIDGEWAY

The Greater Ridgeway (as we've called it) is a route along a chalk ridge that spans the entire width of southern England, running south-west to north-east from Lyme Bay to the coast of northern Norfolk. It's a route that some have called the oldest road. But what evidence is there that this route dates back to prehistory?

The axis of the route is Avebury, and if we start our investigations there things soon fall into place. From the Neolithic into the Iron Age (3000 BC to the Roman invasion of AD 43), Salisbury Plain was densely populated and the centre of cultural and economic life. There was considerable activity at Windmill Hill, near Avebury, long before the stone circle

Wessex Ridgeway out of Sydling St Nicholas

was ever built. Avebury was a site not only of spiritual significance but also, and maybe primarily, a place of political interaction or even power. As part of this (just like London today), it was the focal point of a series of prehistoric 'motorway' paths that stretched out to link the far-flung tribal groups around the country. One of those distant parts, and one that was also comparatively well populated, was Norfolk. In the Brecklands around Thetford was a similar centre of Neolithic activity – the ancient equivalent of the industrial north – based on flint mining and working. Connecting the two centres, presumably for purposes of trade and/or movement to religious festivals, was a track stretching for over 320km (nearly 200 miles), linking Wiltshire and Norfolk.

At least we think there was. Certainly there is evidence on the ground. We can positively trace an extant route, or series of routes, running from Avebury via Wanborough (near Swindon) to Streatley, and then to Wendover and Ivinghoe. It then follows a line along what is now the A505 to Great Chesterford and on into the Brecklands. This route follows the chalk scarp for a large part of its length and, given the odd deviation, is almost straight. It makes no particular sense in modern terms, but it joins a series of well-known archaeological sites.

But the historical record is less obvious. Antiquaries have been writing about the Icknield Way/Ridgeway for centuries, and yet their evidence is mostly anecdotal. When the poet Edward Thomas reviewed the documents just before World War I, he concluded that there was no definite evidence, only confusion, originating in part from the fact

Quaker's Walk, Devizes

that a number of routes have similar names. There was, for instance, an Icknield Street (or Way) that ran north to Worcestershire and Warwickshire. Geoffrey of Monmouth says that 'Hikenilde strere' ran from St David's in west Wales to Southampton. And then, of course, there was our route. The evidence for an Icknield Way running south-west to north-east along the course of the A505 is seen in the towns that developed where it crosses those other great roads: Dunstable (on Watling Street) and Royston (on Ermine Street). In Saxon times, this road was called *Icenhilde Weg* and it is generally assumed that it was to this route that William the Conqueror gave the privilege of the King's Peace, a form of special protection against highwayman and robbers. It was an 'honour' bestowed on just four roads (the others were Ermine Street, Fosse Way and Watling Street) as an indication of their importance to the king.

O.G.S. Crawford surveyed the route for the Ordnance Survey in 1912. He drew a line from King's Lynn to Dunstable, following what he thought was the most likely course of the Icknield Way (on OS maps his route is shown in Gothic lettering). Crawford thought that the Way was a herepath (a kind of warpath) along which armies were moved. In recorded history, at least, we can deduce that the invading Saxons and the Danes moved along the Way. We can suppose that the early Britons, defending against the Romans, would have done the same, as would the Romanised Britons against the early Saxons. And if the name does derive from the Iceni (the pre-Roman East Anglian tribe famed for being that of

Boudicca), Crawford supposed, then Icknield Way could be derived from *Icen-Hilde-Weg*, 'the war road of the Iceni'.

Others disagree strongly, and suggest that the name simply indicates a road, perhaps deriving from the British *yken*, or *ychen*, meaning oxen. The poet William Barnes said that it might come from a word meaning high or upper (*ychen* meaning 'upper') thus 'upland' way or, as Barnes suggests, the 'upper or eastern road'. Dr Henry Bradley stated categorically that the Icknield Way was named after a woman called Icenhild, but no such name or person is known in legend or record. Richard Willis in 1787 described a way he called the 'causeway', from Royston to Ogbourne St George. Despite all this, there appears to be general agreement that there is an ancient route from

Ridgeway path near Wayland's Smithy

Avebury to Newmarket. This central portion is that used (with allowances for rights of way and the avoidance of road walking) by the Ridgeway National Trail and the Icknield Way. It's only beyond these two extremes that the debate *really* begins.

At the southern end, various authors have suggested that the original course started at Axmouth. Others suggest Weymouth. I've even seen references to extensions to Cornwall or south Wales. Richard Willis said that the Icknield Way took its name from the River Itchen, and suggested that it began at Southampton and followed the river as far as Winchester. In fact, there are several mentions of an *Ikenildewey* or *Hykenyldewey* in Hampshire. Tom Stephenson's original suggestion for a long-distance footpath in 1956 ended in Seaton. I'm drawn to a route that bypasses Avebury slightly by going over Overton Hill and south to Alton Barnes where there are various ancient sites. From there, Stonehenge pulls the eager route searcher south. Patrick Crampton takes a flier by suggesting that travellers would have gone down the River Avon to the natural harbour at Christchurch. Certainly Hengistbury Head has evidence of extensive prehistoric activity, and Crampton argues that this would have been a good route for close cultural and trading links with the continent. On even more dangerous ground, he suggests that influences from the civilisations of the Mycenae, Crete and Egypt came this way leading 'to the conception of Stonehenge in its final form'. John Leland's *Itinerary* (1710) agrees with this general direction. His Ykenild Strete runs east–west from Salisbury to Bury St Edmunds via 'Dunstaple'. In devising a Wessex Ridgeway, the Ramblers Association were guided by good paths, good scenery and access (a particular issue on Salisbury Plain). Their route therefore starts at Lyme Regis and follows as many ridges as can be fitted in between the coast and Avebury. But it is unlikely that this is an ancient line.

At the northern end, there is no obvious route, and some suggest that it didn't reach the sea at all. As in the south, it's likely that there was more than one track. It could be that the route didn't head to Thetford until after the Roman invasion. However,

the name Icknield Way has drawn more than one author to suggest a link with the Iron Age tribe of the Iceni. One proposal has the line running via Hickling to the eastern Norfolk coast. Another went via Lincoln to Caistor. The poet Michael Drayton in 1616 had the Icknield Way running from Yarmouth to the Solent via the Chilterns. It was Rainbird Clark who stated positively that the Icknield Way started somewhere near or at Hunstanton. Anthony Bulfield in *The Icknield Way* in 1972 took a route from Newmarket through Elvedon, Ickburgh, West Acre, East Walton and Sedgesford to Holme-next-the-Sea. We will go roughly that way, but for reasons of ease of access will follow the Peddars Way, which is Roman in origin. Although it also finishes at Holme, its southern end is at

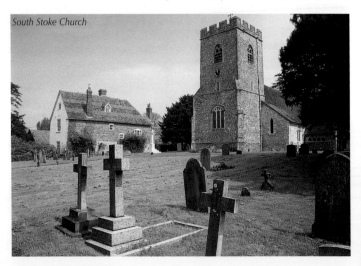

South Stoke Church

Westward View from Dunstable Downs

Chelmsford. That both routes head to the coast at Holme suggests that this was a significant 'port' for the journey across The Wash to Lincolnshire, and perhaps York.

To all this we can add 'cosmic stuff'. It may be coincidence, but the course of the Greater Ridgeway (or at least the Ridgeway and Icknield Way parts) corresponds, almost exactly, with something called the 'Michael/Mary Ley Line'. This runs from Land's End to Great Yarmouth, and is a twisting male and female line of activity that has been mapped by dowsers. Seemingly

it's quite unusual for ley lines to be so densely augmented, and there is speculation, some say certainty, that the Greater Ridgeway runs along this line with all its mystical significance. The Michael/Mary Ley Line is one of just two 'Global Serpents' or 'Driver Dragon Paths' worldwide. The lines apparently receive the energies from the entire Cosmos, and dispense this via ley lines. Avebury is thought to be the hub of the whole system. In addition it has long been noted that crop circles seem to occur most frequently along the Greater Ridgeway, making the whole area particularly powerful.

THE ROUTE OF THE GREATER RIDGEWAY

The Greater Ridgeway walk joins four already extant paths: the Wessex Ridge-way, the Ridgeway National Trail, the Icknield Way and the Peddars Way. The total distance from Lyme Regis to Hunstanton is approximately 584km (363 miles).

The Wessex Ridgeway, of which we walk 197km (123 miles), was devised by the Ramblers Association and first known as such in the 1980s. Dorset County Council picked up the idea and waymarked the route with a green wyvern-emblazoned disc – a wyvern is a two-legged dragon – and then officially declared it open in August 1994. The route starts on the Cobb at Lyme Regis and passes via Beaminster to Heytesbury and around Salisbury Plain to Devizes and thence Avebury.

The 137km (85-mile) Ridgeway National Trail (waymarked with acorn symbols), from Overton Hill over the Wessex Downs and Chilterns via Goring-on-Thames to Ivinghoe, was first suggested in the Hobhouse Committee report of 1947. In 1956 Tom Stephenson proposed a route from Cambridge to Seaton. In 1962 the National Parks Commission proposed what is basically the present route, and this was accepted by the Secretary of State for the Environment in July 1972. The National Trail was declared open in September 1973.

The 170km (105.5-mile) Icknield Way was devised by the Icknield Way Association. Finding a way round the fact that most of the original line is covered in tarmac or built over was always going to be hard, but the IWA devised a route that minimises road walking and yet stays as close as possible to the ancient line

from Ivinghoe to Thetford via Luton, Royston and Great Chesterford. The Countryside Commission designated the Icknield Way as a Regional Route in 1992. The Icknield Way is waymarked with the IWA's stone axe symbol.

The 74km (46.5-mile) Peddars Way (again waymarked with acorn blazes) runs from Knettishall to Holme-next-the-Sea via Little Cressingham and Castle Acre. A route was first discussed in the 1960s. In 1982, the Countryside Commission report was published which followed a line that was to become the National Trail route. The path was declared open in July 1986.

Caste Acre Castle

ORGANISING YOUR WALK

It doesn't matter where you begin, or where you end, but this book is organised from south-west to north-east: Lyme Regis to Hunstanton. You don't have to do the entire walk in one go; indeed, this would be impossible for most people. Fortunately this is a long-distance route that can easily be done in short-distance single-day steps. The book is divided into 25 sections with advice on how to use public transport to return to cars or accommodation left at the starting point. These sections can be loosely viewed as suitable for one day's walking. But don't stick rigidly to the sections, use them simply as a guide to suit your own needs.

Walkers should generally plan for 3–4 kmph (2–2.5 mph) so that stops can be made for sightseeing and refreshment. Head-down you can go faster on many of the ridgeway sections on good to firm going, even with the occasional stop, aided by that fact that there are no gates or stiles, and little need to check routes. On some of the steep, muddy, stile-ridden and confusing Wessex sections, I was much slower; and, as anyone who walks with them will know, photographers and bird-watchers can cause enormous delays.

However you plan to do it, the whole route makes relatively easy walking. The Wessex Ridgeway is undoubtedly the hardest because it is primarily the hilliest. The biggest hazard is the weather, be it wet or dry. Some parts of the walk can be *extremely* muddy, especially in winter, and possibly impassable; the clay

Ewelme Park

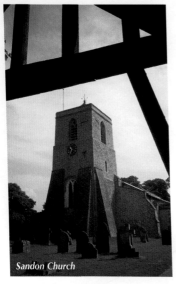

Sandon Church

layer, which overlies the chalk, holds water like a canal. This is a situation not helped by the 4x4 off-roader fraternity who equate the word 'ridgeway' with the word 'road'. (Arguably they are rapidly destroying the most glorious section of the route, from Fox Hill to Streatley.) In summer, the weather can be a problem because the route is so exposed. It is then that walkers should be suitably prepared to avoid both dehydration and sunburn.

Villages are avoided for most of the route, and thus pubs and village stores may be few and far between. This situation is exacerbated by the demise of both over the last ten years. But it can be possible to organise a convenient stop, and I have attempted to indicate this where possible. Walkers are, however, advised always to carry something to eat and drink, together with waterproofs and a small first aid kit.

Route directions are printed in normal type; miscellaneous personal observations and information on things to be seen along the way are printed in *italic*. So if you find yourself in pouring rain you can skip the mind-expanding minutiae to get straight to the directions or, alternatively, whilst shivering in the downmarket hostelry later, you can skip the plodding stuff to get to the meaty bits. In order to shorten the route instructions a smidgen, R means right and L means left. There are maps of the relevant sections of the walk. These are designed to aid route finding and are not definitive. You may wish therefore to purchase or borrow the relevant OS Landranger 1:50 000 maps, numbers 193, 194, 195, 184, 183, 173, 174, 175, 165, 166, 153, 154, 155, 144 and 132.

PART 1:
THE WESSEX RIDGEWAY

Stage 1: Lyme Regis to Beaminster

Start:	Lyme Regis
Finish:	Beaminster
Distance:	31.7km (19.7 miles)
OS:	Landranger 193 Taunton & Lyme Regis
Route Features:	Hilly and long
Information:	Tourist Information Centres: Lyme Regis (01297 442138; email: email@lymeregis-tourism.co.uk); Dorchester (01305 267992; email: dorchester.tic@west-dorset-dc.gov.uk); local tourist information point at Beaminster post office

Lyme Regis was a medieval port, and earned its royal title when Edward I used it during his French 'expeditions'. Lyme was useful because its anchorage was sheltered from the gales by a breakwater known as the Cobb. In Edward's time this was just a small timber-and-stone pier, but it enabled Lyme to become a significant port and shipbuilding centre. From 1500 to 1700 the Cobb saw trade in wool and wine, but by around 1780 ships were too large for Lyme's harbour. The Cobb was rebuilt in Portland stone in 1820. It makes for a fine stroll, exciting on a windy day, affording great views along the bay, dominated by the pyramidal Golden Cap (188m/617ft), the highest cliff on the south coast.

One of the most celebrated arrivals at Lyme's Cobb was the Duke of Monmouth, who landed here in 1685 to lead his rebellion against the king. James II (James VII

Lyme is a fine place to start a walk and is a good base for the first sections, with bus links to/from Beaminster, Maiden Newton, Cerne Abbas and even Shillingstone. The first stretch, however, is a tough one, primarily because there are no villages en route with facilities of any kind. The nearest we get to a pub is just after Lambert's Castle (the Bottle Inn at Marshwood). It's best to do the entire first section in a day, taking lunch and plenty of liquids with you. If you can't manage that, the village of Thorncombe is about half way and just 600m (0.3 mile) off the route.

The Cobb, Lyme Regis

of Scotland and brother of Charles II) was a Catholic, and although there was some widespread antagonism to his succession, the population as a whole didn't want a civil war. But Monmouth, who was one of Charles II's illegitimate sons, did; he set off for London, only to be soundly beaten at the Battle of Sedgemoor in July 1685 (the last land battle fought in England). Monmouth was duly marched to the Tower and beheaded. Judge Jeffreys and the Bloody Assizes rounded up his supporters and, somewhat notoriously, executed 300 and deported the rest.

Lyme went on to become a smugglers' town until the fashion for sea-bathing regained it some respectability and fortune in the eighteenth century, reflected today in its Georgian architecture and narrow streets. Notable visitors included Jane Austen, who spent time in Charmouth and Lyme Regis in the early 1800s, and used both locations in her novels *Persuasion* and *Northanger Abbey*. In the 1970s Lyme became famous for its own local author, John Fowles, whose *French Lieutenant's Woman* was set here, and made into a successful film. Fowles' house (Belmont House) is at the top of Pound Street, surrounded by walled gardens and with glorious views over the bay.

Lyme Regis is also famous for its fossils, with several museums, shops and attractions. Walk along the coast eastwards and you may pick up some for yourself after stormy weather. The most celebrated collector was a local girl, Mary Anning, who found an ichthyosaur here in 1811, then a plesiosaur, and then her greatest find, a pterodactyl, for which she was paid £23. The fossil can be seen in the Natural History Museum in London. The oldest fossils found here date back 200 million years, and the most common are ammonites, whose spiral shells can measure up to 2m (6.5ft) in diameter. The fossils can be unearthed when the rocks in which they are embedded crash into the sea. The most spectacular of these landslides occurred to the west of the town on Christmas Day in 1839, when several miles of cliff collapsed. Known as the Undercliff, it's now covered with dense woodland and plays host to the Lyme Regis-to-Axmouth section of the South West Coast Path, that runs for 987km (613 miles) from Minehead to Poole.

The walk starts at the end of the Cobb. Turn back inland and R along Marine Parade. After passing various seaside shops, the parade bends L to Bridge St. Turn R to pass the Pilot Boat inn and then go first L along Coombe St. Follow this round to pass Dinosaurland. At the end bear R along Mill Green. At the end, go on along a path with the River Lim to R, on to Windsor Terrace. The metalled path bends L and R past Higher Mill Flats and continues

Lyme Bay

with river L. Continue over Colway Lane and carry on along the metalled path, and straight on along a gravel path (the Liberty Trail) when a road forks to R.

The green Wessex Ridgeway waymark discs show a creature called a wyvern, a kind of two-legged dragon. The wyvern was a Roman emblem, and was subsequently adopted by others as a symbol of warrior machismo. There's one on King Harold's banner in the Bayeux Tapestry, and some say that the four-legged Welsh dragon derives from the Roman wyvern. The wyvern has also been long associated with the kingdom of Wessex.

The path crosses the river and reaches a kissing gate. Head over the field, straight on to the next gate with a thatched cottage L. Turn R over a bridge into woods. The path rises to go through two gates. Bear slightly R over the centre of the next field along a worn grass path, and through a gap between woods. Head straight up the next field to a gate and a gravel road. Turn L, and follow the drive as it bends R. After some cottages R, the route passes between buildings (at Rhode Barton) and then bears L and immediately R into woodland and along a rocky track. The path fords a stream, goes through a gate and continues along a windy but clear route through woods (on Hole Common) for over 1km. Pass some old sheds and a pair of gates L. Walk on with hedge L into the corner of the field. Ignore the footbridge L, but go through a gate into woods. The path again winds through trees, bending L after a waymark post to cross a boggy section. Go through a gate and bear R up to the field corner. Don't cross the stile, but go through a farm gate and up to the main road (A35).

Turn L. Cross the main road and then walk down the small road opposite. Turn R just before the cottage and along a drive. Just before the next farm, go R through double farm gates and over a stile. Bear L with a fence/hedge L to the next stile, and straight down the middle of the field to a gate near an oak tree. Cross to a gate and waymark post, and turn R with hedge R. Now head towards some sheds with corrugated iron roofs, and go through a gate that's hidden until you reach it. Just after the sheds, turn L and bear R across the corner of the field to a gate. The path descends past a pond R to a gate, and on to R of a barn, beyond which you can see a gate. Before this gate, turn R to go through another gate and across a long, narrow field. In the next field, the river joins L. Cross a concrete bridge L and then turn R. The path now goes through woods to a gravel drive. Turn R past some old farm buildings. This takes us to a small concrete bridge (more a step) and then up a narrow path away from the river into woods. Two stiles lead to a field. Go straight on through a hedge gap, walking on with hedge L. Then into the next field with hedge R. After 40m, go through a gate R. Head straight over the field to a hedge gap. In the next field, bear L to a second hedge gap. Go to R of a wooden barn to the field corner. After crossing a small footbridge and a stile, go on with hedge L to a gate and along a drive towards a farmhouse at Meerhay Farm. Just after entering the farmyard go L along a drive to reach Meerhay Lane on the outskirts of Wootton Fitzpaine. Turn R.

Wessex is the kingdom of the West Saxons, and the realm of the ever-present Thomas Hardy. Historically,

Wessex had no precise boundaries because they varied according to the fortunes of the king. Sometimes it stretched north of the River Thames; at others it even took in Devon and Cornwall; but its usual limits covered the modern counties of Hampshire, Dorset, Wiltshire, Somerset and southern Avon. This kingdom grew from two Saxon settlements, the first founded by the Gewisse led by Cerdic and his son (or grandson) Cynric, who landed in Hampshire in AD 494. The second influx probably came from the north-east and was led by Cæwlin. We'll follow their exploits when we reach Barbury Castle another 198km (123 miles) along the route.

The British, under Ambrosius, put up a stern defence against these Saxon incursions. He is thought to have been responsible for the 80km (50-mile) long linear earthwork, the Wansdyke. The dates are imprecise but, by the end of the sixth century, the first kingdom of Wessex had been established on the coast and soon extended into what is now Wiltshire. By the eighth century, after the death of the Mercian ruler, King Offa, Wessex had risen to dominance under King Egbert. Even distant Northumbria accepted his supremacy. But in AD 865 the Danes landed in East Anglia and advanced westward. At first, Wessex stood firm. Under Aethelred and Alfred they beat the Danes in a battle on the Berkshire Downs, but success was short-lived: Aethelred died and his brother Alfred was driven into Somerset. But there he regathered his forces, drove the Danes out of Wessex and earned himself the title, Alfred the Great.

With Wessex at peace, Alfred established burhs or fortified towns throughout the land, as well as a number of minsters, evident in place names such as Beaminster and Iwerne Minster. Even today a comparatively small place like Beaminster controls a large parish. Wessex's supremacy continued into the tenth century, when new Viking invaders threatened the peace. Wessex's King was Aethelred the Unready, a name relating to the Saxon Unraed or 'no counsel'. He did, however, prove himself unready to cope with the Vikings and fled to Normandy. It marked the end of an independent Wessex that under Cnut became part of the greater kingdom of England.

Walk along the road for about 400m. After crossing a stream, go L over a stile and straight up the centre of the field to a gate in the top corner. Go through this and turn R, with hedge R, and through two farm gates. Now turn L and walk on to the second gate on the L. In the next field, turn half-R and head over the centre of the field towards the wooded hill (Coney's Castle) in the distance. Cross a stile and bear half-R to a wooden farm gate. Cross this to a road and turn L. Walk on for just over 1.5km, passing Coney's Castle L and a National Trust car park R. At a pair of close road junctions, continue straight on along a footpath onto Lambert's Castle Hill. Keep on the L-hand of two tracks that cross the top, with fine views to R. At a major cross-track, bear R slightly and walk to the very end of the open grassy area to a fence and a gate bearing the Wessex Ridgeway waymark. This path bends R to reach a lane. Turn L to a road. (Turn R for the sixteenth-century thatched Bottle Inn at Marshwood in 650m). To continue the route, go straight across along a path that's signposted as an unmetalled road (Hawkmoor Hill).

Coney's Castle (National Trust) is a univallate Iron Age hillfort, thought to have been the camp of the Saxon King Egbert when he fought the Danes in the ninth century. The word 'coney' derives from an old English name for rabbit. Lambert's Castle is also National Trust, and the SSSI has some fine meadows that are home to hundreds of species of wild flowers as well as important populations of butterflies, most notably the pearl-bordered fritillary and the marsh fritillary. The hill, said to be named after King Lambert (King Cnut), is quite high (256m/840ft) and its slopes are wooded, leaving the summit bare. In the past this grassy area has been used as a racecourse, and may have been home to one of the Armada beacons. There are great views – most notably over Marshwood Vale and Lyme Bay – and it's a popular spot for picnics, walking the dog or just mooching about. Lambert's Castle hillfort is, like Coney's, a bit of an unknown quantity, and thought to be the most west-erly of all those controlled by the Durotriges tribe at the time of the Roman invasion. The defences aren't terribly impressive, but the area they surround is large considering there was only a single rampart. The fort had a strategic position next to the main track leading from Salisbury to the south-west, so could it have been the pre-Roman equivalent of a coaching stop? Along the stretch immediately after the hill, we pass briefly into Devon, then back into Dorset.

If you peruse the OS maps (Landrangers 193 and 194), you get a strong feeling that an original Ridgeway route would not take the line of the current Wessex Ridgeway (past Thorncombe, along Blackdown and through Beaminster), but would go through Birdsmoorgate, past Pilsdon Pen, through Broadwindsor and then on along a minor road to Horn Hill and over Beaminster Down towards Toller Down Gate. Going south it's also evident that the natural line goes to Seaton and Sidmouth rather than Lyme Regis.

Hawkmoor Hill becomes a metalled drive and reaches a road. Bear L to a road junction. Carry straight on (towards Thorncombe). After 200m or so, go R through a gap and over a stile. In the field, walk on with hedge R to a stile by a farm gate. Keep to the R-hand side to another gate and stile. Again keep to the R side of the field, and when you reach a gate and stile don't cross,

Blackdown from Blackdown Hill

but turn L to walk into the next corner with hedge R. Go through the gate and on with hedge R to a gate and footbridge. Bear R towards the farmhouse at Gashay Farm. Go through a gate to a lane. Turn R, and bear L out of the farmyard into a field with hedge and then woods to L. The path bends L over a ditch and through gates to a gravel drive. Turn L. At a fork bear R, and then before a pair of farm gates, go L in front of the fine thatched house at Grighay Farm.

This path leads out along a farm drive. Just before the driveway turns L and where there's a farm gate on each side of the drive, go R over a stile and then half-L uphill to the far field corner. Cross a stile to a road and turn L. (Turn R here for the Rose & Crown pub at Birdsmoorgate within 2km). After 50m, turn R and walk with woods L. This passes an old oil depot to L. Go through a gap in the hedge into the next field and continue, still with hedge L. Follow the hedge as it bends L. Go through a gate into the next field, and continue with hedge L, through which there is a view of Thorncombe church. Continue straight down, keeping hedge close L, to reach a farm drive. Walk on to go through a gate into the farmyard of Yew Tree Farm and out along a metalled drive. When you reach a road, turn R. (Turn L here for Thorncombe.)

Until 1842, Thorncombe was in Devon; now it's just on the border. Connoisseurs say that it still feels more like Devon than Dorset. Not a lot happens here, although in the nineteenth century the village had a vicar who fathered (in 1824 and 1827) two sons who grew up to be admirals: the Lords Hood and Bridport. Famous residents in the twentieth century were less celebrated: Mick Jagger's daughter Jade lived here for a while with her artist boyfriend Piers Jackson in 'rural idyll' in a nineteenth-century stone farmhouse.

About 3.2km (2 miles) north-west of Thorncombe is Forde Abbey, a splendid building set in the pretty Axe valley. The building of the Cistercian monastery started in the twelfth century, but wasn't finished until the sixteenth. Thomas Chard, who became abbot in 1521, built the great hall and a porch that forms a tower, and some commodious private quarters. The abbey only escaped destruction at the Dissolution by handing over all its property to the king. It was then used as a private house, and passed through several families before being bought by Edmund Prideaux in 1649. Prideaux was a Devon man and Cromwell's Attorney-General, and had Inigo Jones make various additions and changes to the building. Edmund Prideaux's son was one of those rounded up following the Monmouth rebellion, but he escaped execution and was fined £15,000 for his part in the skirmish. The house is open for visitors, and much of the early abbey can still be seen, including the refectory, dormitory and chapter house.

The abbey contains a fine collection of furniture, pictures and tapestries, and there are some 12ha (30 acres) of gardens, lakes and parkland, as well as 'pick-your-own' at the Forde Abbey Fruit Gardens.

Walk on for just over 1km to reach a T-junction by an old chapel. Go R, then L through a gate and up through two gates on the L-hand side of fields. At the top, go half-R to a stile at the top of the hill in the far R corner. Walk along the L side of the next field to a gate. Then continue with fence R to another gate. In the next field walk on slightly to the R of a pair of pine trees, and on along the ridge of Blackdown Hill with fine views. When the hedge R stops, go through the gate R and then slightly away from the fence L. Keep close to trees L to reach a gate and a road. Turn R and pass two road junctions. About 250m after the L-turning, go L up a grassy track to a gate, and then on with hedge close R. Go through a farm gate and turn L through another gate. Walk up the field with hedge L and a view L to Blackdown Hill. The path bends R to reach a gate and stile. Go straight on to a stile prominent on the brow of the hill. This leads us to a permissive path which continues straight over the Pilsdon Pen hill, with a fence R. After the next stile, cross the centre of the large field by going half-R into the unknown. We are aiming for a stile that is in the R-hand field border towards the far R corner of the field. After you've found it, cross and descend to a pair of gates. Go through the L one, and turn L to walk uphill with fence L. When you reach a barrier, bear L along a grassy path. This winds around the edge of Pilsdon Pen hillfort.

> Pilsdon Pen at 277m (909ft) was at one time thought to be Dorset's highest point, but Lewesdon Hill (reached before Beaminster) is actually higher. Sailors who saw the two together from Lyme

> Bay used to call them 'the Cow and Calf'. Some 14.5ha (36 acres) of Pilsdon Pen was bought by the National Trust in 1979. Much of their land is fields, but at the western end is an area of heather and scrub that surrounds an Iron Age hill-fort, occupied when the Romans arrived. It was captured by Vespasian's Second Augustan Legion in AD 43, and a Roman ballista (an engine used for hurling stones and other missiles) has been unearthed from it. Archaeologists have also discovered a number of late Iron Age huts, parts of a medieval rabbit warren, and a small goldsmith's workshop.

Just to the west of Pilsdon Pen (and only 1km/0.6 miles or so further along the road) is Racedown Farm, where William Wordsworth first started to write seriously. William and his sister Dorothy settled here for about two years at the end of the eighteenth century. Here they first met Coleridge, who apparently 'leaped over a gate and bounded across a pathless field to greet the waiting Wordsworths', a feat that impressed them enormously! The hill of Pilsdon Pen is said to have consoled Dorothy, who was pining for her Lakeland mountains.

Eventually the path comes to a more open area and a cross-track. Turn L to walk on, with fence L, to a gate. Turn R and walk to the end of a fence L. Turn half-L to go downhill to a gate. Walk on between two fields, and at the end cross the road and walk on along the drive for Lower Newnham Farm. On reaching the first building, go R and follow the path L past some cattle sheds. The route then leads out of the farmyard along a dirt drive. After bending, the drive turns R through a gap in the hedge R, and on with a conifer hedge L. The track now bends L and just before reaching a field, we go R over a stile to walk on with hedge L. Go over a double stile and on to the far L corner of the field. Go through a gate, and turn R along a green lane. Even in midsummer, this is very boggy and is appropriately named Sheepwash Lane. Eventually it reaches a concrete lane near Courtwood Farm. Go straight on to a road. Turn L. By a corrugated iron-roofed garage, turn R (for Wall Farm) and immediately L along a footpath (Lewesdon Hill Lane). Stay close to the L edge of the dense woodland of Lewesdon Hill. Just over 2km after the garage, the path reaches a road at Stoke Knapp. Go straight across into a farm and out via a gate up a clear farm drive into a field. This track bends R and goes through a gate to continue with fence L. The path goes on, over Waddon Hill, through a series of gates or gaps.

Waddon Hill bears the remains of a Roman fort, perhaps occupied by detachments of Legio II Augusta when that

legion was at Exeter. The fort, which remained operative
until about AD 79, would have been part of a chain of
signal posts that ran across the south-western peninsula
from here to Wiveliscombe in Somerset, and to a signal
station on the north Devon coast. One of the siginificant
archaeological finds at Waddon was a large quantity of
hare bones. The Celts thought the hare a sacred animal
and allowed it to proliferate; the Romans, on the other
hand, were only too happy to kill them for sport, and to
eat them. One of the many treasures found at Waddon
was a gemstone on which is depicted a scene from the
Trojan war, that of Ajax lifting the body of Achilles.

Towards the end, and just before a house, take the lower
of two paths to a metal gate. Go into the field L and
follow the track uphill. Just before reaching the top of
the hill, go R over a stile and then on with fence L
through two gates to the beech-tree-clad top of Gerrard's
Hill. Continue on along a worn grass track that goes
downhill to the far L-hand corner of the field. In the next
field, go downhill over the centre, passing a waymark
post, and down a very steep slope to a stile. Go half-R
through a new tree plantation, up over a stile and on to
a double stile. Continue straight on to turn R just after
the corrugated-iron-roofed barn. Go through a pinch
stile, and half-L to the far corner. Another pinch stile
leads to a road. Go R to a T-junction, and then L. Just
before a more major road, go R into a long thin field.
Walk the length of it and on along a gravel path through
a tunnel of foliage. This leads to a metalled lane between
houses. Keep roughly straight on to reach the church R,
and follow Church St as it bends L to reach the square
at Beaminster.

Beaminster is actually pronounced 'Bem-inster' with a
short 'e', as in 'egg'. Thomas Hardy renamed the town
'Emminster' in *Tess of the D'Urbervilles*, which perhaps
is closer. Emminster Vicarage was where Tess came to
find Angel Clare's parents after, appropriately enough, a
long and gruelling walk. Beaminster is a smart little
town, rich in snug eighteenth-century houses made of

the local golden Ham Hill stone. Despite being destroyed by fire three times (1644 during the Civil War, 1684, and 1781), the town's centre is a Conservation Area with over 200 listed buildings. Beaminster owes this rich heritage to the fact that it once made a good living from wool cloth, sailcloth and sackcloth; it is also home to Blue Vinney cheese. Some authors have described Beaminster as dull, but for those who have walked all the way from Lyme, the presence of three pubs, a supermarket, some other shops and a bus stop (routes to Bridport and Yeovil) will seem nothing short of miraculous!

I'm told that the church bells play the hymn tune 'Hanover' every three hours, but I missed it. The church itself is mostly fifteenth-century (with a Norman font) and gloriously large. One of Beaminster's sons was Thomas Hine, who gave his name to Cognac Hine. Hine was born here in 1775, and left to seek French fortune when he was 17. He soon found work in a brandy busi-

*Market Place,
Beaminster*

ness in Jarnac. He married the boss's daughter, became a partner and went on to own the business. After the Napoleonic Wars, he started to put his own name on the bottles: and it's still there.

Just south of Beaminster, on the road to Bridport, is Parnham House. The first house was built in 1400 by the Gerard family, and passed into the hands of the Strode family, who were good at marrying money: Sir Robert Strode, for example, married the daughter of Sir John Hody, Henry VIII's Lord Chief Baron of the Exchequer, in 1522. Her money was used to rebuild the house. In 1810, Parnham was again restored and enlarged, this time by the eminent John Nash. It was Vincent Robinson who, having purchased the house in 1896, filled it with Renaissance furniture and art. The early twentieth century saw a succession of owners, including William Rhodes-Moorhouse, the first pilot to win a posthumous VC in World War I. He's buried in a private grave here along with his son, another flying ace, who was shot down in the Battle of Britain. In the 1920s the house was a country club often frequented by the Prince of Wales (Edward VIII). During World War II Parnham was an army hospital, and later a base for the Americans planning the Normandy landings. In 1976 Parnham was bought by John Makepeace for his cabinet-making business. Since then, it's been a non-profit-making educational trust that provides funds for 'The School of Craftsmen in Wood'. There's a furniture-making workshop and exhibitions by designers and craftsmen. The house, grounds and school are open to the public in the summer (enquiries tel: 01308 862204).

Mapperton House and gardens are also nearby. The house is Elizabethan in origin, but Mapperton is primarily known for its gardens. There's an Italianate garden and fountain court; fishponds, an orangery and summerhouses; a wild garden with specimen shrubs and trees. The manor house, with its church, stable block, coach house, dovecote and courtyard, has been described as 'a glorious harmony of golden sandstone'. The garden, but not the house, is open throughout the summer (enquiries tel: 01308 862645).

Stage 2: Beaminster to Cerne Abbas

Start:	Beaminster
Finish:	Sydling (for Cerne Abbas)
Distance:	22.5km (14 miles)
OS:	Landrangers 193 Taunton & Lyme Regis, 194 Dorchester & Weymouth
Route Features:	Hilly
Information:	Tourist Information Centre: Dorchester (01305 267992; email: dorchester.tic@west-dorset-dc.gov.uk); local tourist information point at Cerne Abbas village stores

Cerne Abbas is not actually on the route, but 1.8km (just over 1 mile) from Higher City Farm, making it 26km (16.25 miles) from Beaminster to Cerne. Although we pass through a couple of villages on the way, it's not until Maiden Newton (18.4km/11.5 miles) that we find a pub and shop. Maiden Newton also has buses and a railway station for links via Dorchester. Sydling has a pub. Cerne has pub, shop and accommodation, and bus links to Sherborne and Dorchester.

From Beaminster square, bear L along Fleet St. Then bear L into Newton, and on along the road past Beaminster School L. Just after this, fork R into Hurst and then into Bowgrove Road. After Meerhay Manor R, the metalled lane becomes a green lane. Bear R along a gravel drive uphill to a road. Turn R. After 500m, walk past a path R (to Higher Meerhay Farm) and, 20m on, go R through a farm gate and walk on with hedge R. Keep straight on to reach a road. Bear slightly L to continue along a gravel drive. Ignore a tempting footpath gate to L, and keep on a main farm drive that eventually reaches a bend in a metalled lane. Go straight on to the road and turn L. Just after the entrance to Pipsford Farm, go R through a farm gate and on along a grassy path to a gate. Walk on along the drive with a church L. This is Toller Whelme.

> Toller Whelme, literally the source of the River Toller (now called the River Hooke), is a wonderfully serene place with its sixteenth-century manor house and church. It was once all the property of Forde Abbey, and this may explain the extensive fishponds hereabouts.

The metalled lane becomes a gravel drive and passes a pond L, and then a small lake (R). At the next road turn L, and then just before the road bends L, go L through a gate and turn immediately R to walk with hedge R to a stile. Cross and turn L to walk on with woods L towards some masts. Cross the next stile which is in the corner of the field. In the next field, head slightly L to a gate and a waymark post. At the road, turn L. The road soon bends R into Hooke and passes Hooke Court.

> Hooke is a village of two halves. The northern bit is clustered around a large pond with Hooke Court, a seventeenth-century manor house. The rest of the village lies 300m to the south, with its part medieval, part Victorian church near a small crossroads. We're well into Thomas Hardy country now. Hooke Mill appears as 'Tewnell Mill' in *Far from the Madding Crowd*, and the surrounding downs are said to be where Gabriel Oak had his sheep farm before he entered into Bathsheba's employ.

Hooke Court

As the road bends R (after pond L), bear L towards a house. Just before the house bear R (with house L) to go along a narrow path which doubles as a stream. This reaches a road. Cross straight over to go through a gate and along a green lane with the masts on Rampisham Down L. Go through a gate and on with hedge R. When this bends away, stay with it to reach a farm gate. Now aim towards the second of two jutting corners where there is a gate into the next field. Walk on with hedge close L to reach a gate that gives access to a green lane. The next gate leads to a road. Turn R, downhill, and then L through a gate. In the next field, stay in the valley to reach a footpath gate. This path runs along the edge of

Kingcombe Coppice. At a path T-junction, go R to reach a gate. The path now goes on along a similar line to another gate and, in summer at least, a very dark green lane. At the bottom, the path becomes a stream. We soon reach a road; turn L and go into Lower Kingcombe.

Rampisham is pronounced 'Ransom', and the masts belong to the BBC. There's a village of Rampisham just over on the northern side of the hill, set in a narrow, lonely chalk valley with a stream and a pub called the Tiger's Head. The village is overlooked by the church and manor house. The church of St Michael and All Saints is particularly rich in gargoyles, and has a carved cross, dated 1516, in the churchyard.

Higher and Lower Kingcombe are hamlets on the River Hooke between Toller Porcorum and Hooke. Lower Kingcombe has a famous nature reserve and conservation centre. John Wallbridge bought the 180ha (446-acre) farm in 1918, when it was described as 'a famous dairy farm noted for its Dorset Blue Cheese and Butter'. The key to its later fame is that, unlike virtually everything surrounding it, the farm, including the hedgerows and hay meadows, has remained unsullied by modern agribusiness, never sprayed or treated with artificial fertilisers. When Arthur Wallbridge died in 1985, the Dorset Trust for Nature Conservation launched a worldwide appeal and raised £320,000 to buy 132ha (327 acres) of it. The Kingcombe Trust established an information centre and residential visitor centre in the old buildings, and runs courses in natural history and conservation.

As the road bends R, go straight on along a gravel drive. At a fork, go L then almost immediately R to pass some farm buildings. Go through a gate and walk roughly straight ahead and just to L of an oak tree in the middle of the field. This leads to a gate. In the next field, go half-R, not to a gate but to L

continued on page 38

37

of a line of beech trees, and diagonally uphill to a
partially hidden gate in the hedge. In the next field, go
straight over to farm gate and
bear half-L to a gate and
road. Turn L.

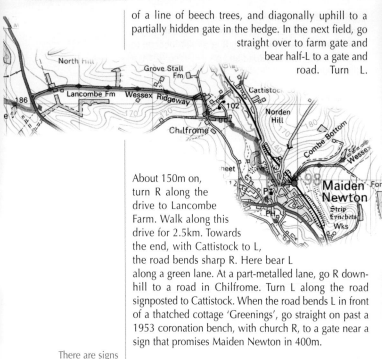

About 150m on,
turn R along the
drive to Lancombe
Farm. Walk along this
drive for 2.5km. Towards
the end, with Cattistock to L,
the road bends sharp R. Here bear L
along a green lane. At a part-metalled lane, go R downhill to a road in Chilfrome. Turn L along the road
signposted to Cattistock. When the road bends L in front
of a thatched cottage 'Greenings', go straight on past a
1953 coronation bench, with church R, to a gate near a
sign that promises Maiden Newton in 400m.

Tiny Chilfrome sits amid the water-meadows between
Maiden Newton and Cattistock. The Holy Trinity church
was originally thirteenth century, but was heavily
restored during Victorian times.

There are signs
hereabouts for the
Macmillan Way, a trail
running for 378km
(235 miles) from
Oakham in Rutland to
the coast just south of
Abbotsbury in Dorset.
It's named after
Douglas Macmillan
who was born and
grew up in Castle
Cary, Somerset, and
who founded the
Macmillan Cancer
Relief Fund.

Keep fence close R to reach a stile. In the next field bear
slightly L to a stile. In the next field, turn L and walk
with hedge L. This bends R to another stile. Cross and
go straight on over a small footbridge. The path crosses
to the far side of the field and turns R with a stream, the
River Frome, to L. The path now winds round to go
through a railway arch. Bear R (don't cross the bridge
near sluice gates here) but carry on with river L. Then
go L over a footbridge waymarked as the Maiden
Newton Village Trail. This path goes L and up away from

the river to the church. At the church wall, go L to a stile and then R along Church Road to the war memorial. Turn L along Station Road. Turn R at a road junction to continue along Church Road and past Maiden Newton railway station.

Maiden Newton has a pub (The Chalk & Cheese), a shop and a railway station, with trains to Dorchester, from where bus links run to Beaminster, Cerne Abbas and Shillingstone. Trains are comparatively infrequent, and good planning and plenty of time are needed. The village developed where the River Hooke joined the River Frome, and the area has been occupied since Roman times. In the nineteenth century a Roman villa complete with some Roman pavement (depicting Neptune fighting a sea monster) was unearthed here, but curiously their precise whereabouts now is unknown. St Mary's church is renowned for a door in the north entrance, dating to 1450 and said to be one of the oldest in England. It apparently hangs on the original hinges, and bears the scars of Oliver Cromwell's guns! During the Civil War, Charles I stayed at the Rectory, and in 1952 Queen Elizabeth II spent the night in the Royal Train, parked near the station. The author

Wessex Ridgeway out of Maiden Newton

and poet Sylvia Townsend Warner lived and died in Maiden Newton.

The way continues under the railway bridge and up the rising green lane beyond. The route bends slightly R and then comes to a fork. Bear L to go through a gate and out into open farmland. Continue through a farm gate, passing some barns (New Barn) before walking along a farm drive to reach a road (A37) on Break Heart Hill. Cross the road and continue through the pedestrian gate opposite. Immediately bear L, through a farm gate, to walk on with a fence and hedge R. After the next farm gate stay close to the hedge R. The route descends to the field corner where the way passes through a gate and along a path through a copse. The path soon becomes an open green lane. The lane bends R then L,

and re-enters a copse. As the path bends R to reach the outskirts of Sydling, ignore the tempting stile L and continue to a drive (turn R here for the church, Court House and tithe barn). Turn L to reach the stump of the old market cross and the Dorchester Road in central Sydling St Nicholas.

Sydling St Nicholas is a delightful place, straddling the quiet Dorchester Road and gently infiltrated by three

continued on
page 42

tributaries of the Sydling Water; there are little bridges
everywhere. The Saxons were the first to settle here, but
in AD 933 the land was given to the Benedictine monks
of Milton Abbey. There are some delightful sixteenth- to
eighteenth-century houses, including the fine Tudor 'Old
Vicarage' just at the crossroads. The house next to the
Old Vicarage, dated 1733, was the bakery, and has fine
mullioned windows. Further on along the High St, en
route for the Greyhound pub, is East House, a red-brick
Georgian house with a Venetian window.

Go back up Church St and through the gate at the
end to reach the fifteenth-century church of St Nicholas.
It has a fireplace inside the porch, to keep the villagers
warm during parish meetings, and a font thought to be
over 1000 years old, carved from a Roman pillar capital.
The clock dates from 1593, and is hence one of the
oldest in the land. Although it has no face, it strikes the
hours. The tithe barn to the left of the church has flint
walls with stone buttresses, and the roof is supported by
great oaken beams and pillars. Within this little complex
is also the manor house, Court House, formerly a
meeting place for the court leet which dealt out punishment to local delinquents. Notable among its later
tenants was the Elizabethan 'soldier-poet' Sir Philip
Sydney, and his mother-in-law, Lady Ursula
Walsingham. She was the second wife of Queen
Elizabeth I's Principal Secretary, Sir Francis Walsingham.

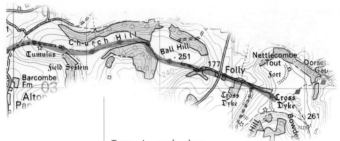

Turn L and then immediately R along East St. After crossing a stream, turn R at a T-junction. At the end continue straight on along a concrete drive. After passing a stile R, turn L along a green lane that goes uphill. When the lane bends R, go straight on through a gate and on with an embankment R. Continue through a farm gate and uphill, now going through a gate set at a slightly oblique angle to L of the path. After this, walk diagonally over the next field to a stile. Don't cross this but bear L to walk on with a fence R and under power lines. At the fence corner, turn R to walk on with fence R. In the corner of the field, go through the gate R. About 10m on, turn L through a hedge gap. Continue along a farm drive with hedge R to reach some large barns at Higher City Farm. Turn L to a road. If completing this section at Cerne Abbas, turn R along the road for approximately 1.8km.

Cerne Abbas is strangely redolent of a Cotswold village, with a choice of pubs, some accommodation and a shop, and some bus route contact with Dorchester. There are also some fine medieval buildings amidst the old streets, and the abbey ruins are visible (tel: 01300 341284). Cerne Abbey was founded by Ethelmaer, Earl of Cornwall, in the ninth century, and became a Benedictine establishment in about AD 987. The last Abbot before Henry VIII's Dissolution was Thomas Corton, said to be a hot-blooded fellow who could be relied on for a good wine, women, song and gambling party. Cerne also has a fourteenth-century tithe barn (at the southern end of the village), an early Christian wishing-well in the graveyard, and, of course, the famous Giant.

The Cerne Abbas Giant is a chalk carving of a naked, club-wielding man, 55m (180ft) tall, with a phallus of just over 9m (30ft) long; impressive by any standard. One school says that he's Romano-British (c. AD 191) and that he represents Hercules, based on the fact that the Emperor Commodus (AD 180–93) fancied himself as Hercules reincarnated and promoted a Herculean cult. Imagery from that time reveals Hercules portrayed naked, with a club in his right hand and a skin draped over his left; excavation has shown that the Giant was originally carrying an animal skin. Another expert states that the Romans simply adorned an already cut figure by adding the club; yet another associates the Giant with St Augustine's visit in the sixth century. Recent theories suggest that the Giant was carved 350 years ago as protest against Oliver Cromwell, or that the figure provides evidence of the existence of giants in Medieval England.

Whatever his origins, the Cerne Giant's status as a fertility symbol is reasonably self-evident. Since Victorian times (at least), it has been widely rumoured that an infertile woman could be rendered otherwise by simply sitting on the fellow. Others have taken things even further: in 1998, in response to some vigorous nocturnal activity at the site, the National Trust had to appeal to couples not to make love on the Giant, and he is now fenced off. The best view of the big man is from the lay-by on the A352 just north of the village.

Throughout the centuries, and particularly in Victorian times, many people have suggested that the big man should have his virility covered or somehow removed. The Cerne Giant, however, was stoutly defended by General Pitt-Rivers (of whom more anon) who acquired the site and steadfastly defended our hero's manhood. The Pitt-Rivers estate presented the Giant to the National Trust in 1921.

Stage 3: Cerne Abbas to Shillingstone

Start:	Cerne Abbas
Finish:	Shillingstone
Distance:	29.8km (18.5 miles)
OS:	Landranger 194 Dorchester & Weymouth
Route Features:	Hilly and long
Information:	Tourist Information Centre: Blandford Forum (01258 454770/451989)

This is the last of the great village-less stretches over the Dorset downs, and arguably the toughest. Take refreshment with you, and unless you're really organised, you'll have to do all 27.7km (17.25 miles) in one go (don't forget to add 1.8km/just over a mile if starting from Cerne). If you want to be picked up/dropped off en route, the area around Bulbarrow Hill/Woolland Hill makes a useful break point with plenty of car parking. There's not a sniff of pub, shop or transport until Shillingstone. The Crown Inn at Ibberton is a possibility, but adds 2.4km (1.5 miles) to the walk. At Shillingstone there are two pubs, and buses to Sturminster Newton or Blandford Forum. Treat the remoteness as a bonus!

If starting at Cerne Abbas, return to the route by taking the lane from Cerne signposted for Sydling St Nicholas. This reaches Higher City Farm after 1.8km; here turn R along the clear waymarked track. If continuing from Higher City Farm, simply cross the road to take the track. Walk on for over 3km. The track is joined by a farm drive from the L and then one from the R. About 200m after this second track, turn R near a prominent waymark post.

Follow an unclear path through a gap in the hedge. Cross the next field by heading towards the L-hand edge of a clump of trees. When you reach the trees continue along a dirt drive with trees R. This path crosses the ridge-like Wether Hill, bends L and descends to a dirt drive T-junction. Turn R to walk along a country lane with fine views ahead to Up Cerne manor.

> Up Cerne is said to lie 'among the downs smiling to itself like a child in hiding'. The rather fine gabled manor house is primarily sixteenth century, although it was built as an extension of a medieval hall. The church, just beyond, is built of banded flint and stone rubble, with stone dressings. Although the chancel dates back to the sixteenth century, most of the church was built in 1870.

At the T-junction, turn L to the main road (A352). Turn L and then first R along a road signposted 'Minterne Parva only'. This road winds round to reach Minterne Parva.

> The round building on the right as you walk into the hamlet of Minterne Parva is thought to be an eighteenth-century cockfighting ring. The remains of the old village cross are just in front of it. To the north of here are Minterne Magna and the Victorian Minterne House, renamed by Thomas Hardy in *The Woodlanders* as Great Hintock House. The current house is Edwardian, and surrounded by some impressive gardens which are open to the public from early spring to late autumn (tel: 01300 341370). The original Minterne House had been a seat of the Churchill family, and their connection with the house continued into the twentieth century via Pamela

If you go straight on at the waymark post, you reach a minor road at Gore Hill, where there's a prehistoric stone monolith called the 'Cross and Hand' or 'Crossy Hand'. It once represented a hand, but the palm and fingers have worn away. It may have been a boundary stone, but some say it's the site of either a grisly murder, or a miracle, or both. Thomas Hardy wrote a poem about it, and it's mentioned in *Tess of the D'Urbevilles*, where a passing shepherd pointed out to Tess that it was, 'a thing of ill-omen miss. It was put up in wuld times by the relations of a malefactor who was tortured there by nailing his hand to a post, and afterwards hung. The bones lie underneath. They say he sold his soul to the devil.'

Manor House ponds, Up Cerne

Harriman, born Pamela Digby here in 1920, daughter of Lord Digby and granddaughter of Lord Aberdare. By marrying Randolph Churchill she became Winston Churchill's daughter-in-law, and then the paramour of the some of the world's richest men. She took the names of all her husbands, eventually becoming the Honourable Pamela Digby Churchill Hayward Harriman. At the time of her death in 1996, she was the American Ambassador in Paris. Her second husband, Leyland Hayward, described her as 'the greatest courtesan of the century'.

After the Dower House, the road bends R. When the tarmac ends, go R. This track soon bends sharp L and gently R. It then descends slightly before climbing the hill with hedge and fence close R. The path then bends L and crosses the middle of the next field to a gate. After this the path swings R. The land here is grassy and the paths confusing. Go over a cross-path and continue uphill, bending back L slightly. The route soon bends R again and passes between gorse and bramble bushes to enter a scrubby area beyond with a fence and field ahead. Bear R here to walk on with the fence to L. After 100m, go through a gate in the fence L. In the field, bear half-R to a gate. (Turn R here for Cerne Abbas, roughly 2km downhill). In the next (very flinty) field, go straight on (and across) to a field gate and the road at Giant's Head.

Cross directly into the entrance of the camping and caravanning park opposite. Go past the office and straight on, passing to the R of a clump of conifer trees.

Cerne Giant from Giant's View

Walk on to go through the R-hand of two farm gates, and then on to the next gate. Continue to go through a further gate in the L-hand corner of the field. (Note this route through the campsite may be diverted to go R just after the entrance and then round L to the gate in the corner of the field.) On rejoining farmland, walk on close to the hedge L to reach a gate L in the far L-hand corner of the field. Continue with hedge R to go through a gate and on, passing through another gate to reach a point where there are barns (Black Barn) to R. Walk on with hedge close R. The clear track soon bears L to run between fields. It gradually becomes more enclosed and passes some farm buildings. At a farm road bear R to reach a road. Turn L.

After 50m turn R through a farm gate. Walk straight on along an enclosed path to reach a field. Continue with hedge close L to reach a gate L in the corner of the field. Don't go through this, but turn R to continue with hedge L. Go through the gate in the next field corner to continue with hedge L. The route now passes a field barn, and goes through a gate to continue with a fence L. After another gate the route passes along a fine ridge on Church Hill. Go past an ancient enclosure R and on through a gate into thin woodland. Continue out along a clear driveway to leave the wood by a stile next to a gate. Walk on with fence and hedge L over Ball Hill to the far L-hand corner through a gate. The muddy path now goes downhill. After a further gate the trackway becomes a green lane which goes steeply down hill. Cross the road at Folly.

The old Folly Inn

This whole area is criss-crossed with deeply scoured, and comparatively narrow, ravines. This is the Dorsetshire Gap, an important early road route right into the nineteenth century. Theories suggest that travellers originally took advantage of the slight dips in the hill-side to make their crossing (principally north-west to south-east), and that over the centuries these became worn into deep gullies. In the early 1970s, a writer known as 'Valesman' left a sandwich tin here containing a notebook. It was his hope to conserve the Gap. There is still a tin here, containing a number of notebooks and, if you're lucky, a pen. Use both to record your visit to the Dorsetshire Gap.

One of the two houses that now make up Folly was once the Fox Inn, and is known now as 'The Old Fox'. It was popular with drovers who worked the network of routes hereabouts.

The track continues straight on. At a fork bear L following the waymark post. About 100m further on, turn L off the more obvious route, up a steep muddy path. This eventually reaches a farm gate and continues on. When the hedge to L stops and there is a gap in the hedge R, turn L in the direction of the masts on Bulbarrow Hill in the distance. This path goes under power lines and passes an oil tank to reach a pedestrian gate. Walk straight on for about 10m and bear R to continue along a gully to reach a farm gate into woods. About 40m after the gate (and 10m after the waymark post), bear L up a narrow footpath. This leads to a deeply sunken cross-path. Turn R. There is now a confluence of paths that marks the crossing of the Dorsetshire Gap.

Turn R to go uphill slightly, through a farm gate and continue on along a hollowed path. This passes along a ridge with views to both sides to a pedestrian gate. Bear L over the next field to the far L corner. Go through the farm gate and walk down through the farmyard of Melcombe Park Farm and then along the farm drive. When the drive turns sharp R, go straight on into wood-land. A short distance in, bear L to stay close to the L edge of the woods. This leads to a field. Walk on with hedge close L. After 250m, near a waymark post L, turn R to cross the field and go through a gate in the opposite hedge. In the next field, cross diago-

nally to go through a farm gate. Turn R to enter the next field and walk over it diagonally towards a barn. Go through two gates to walk on along a concrete driveway and another farm gate. The route now goes through the farmyard at Crockers Farm.

Cross the road and continue along a green road. At a fork bear L to reach a stream. Cross this and turn R along what should be a path but which can be a stream. In the next field carry straight on with hedge close R. This rises to a farm gate, and crosses the next field roughly to L of centre taking a clear worn grassy line. After a farm gate, go half-R again along a worn grassy path towards another farm gate. Go straight on passing to R of some clumps of gorse. Go round the outer ramparts of the Iron

continued on page 50

Age Rawlsbury Camp (to L). After a gate, stay on this outer edge to reach a cross-path. Turn R to reach a road. Here turn R with views over Blackmoor Vale L. Go straight on at the first road junction, bear L at the next, and at the next bear L, and L again to pass a parking area R with a topograph.

This is Bulbarrow Hill, 275m (902ft) above sea level and the second highest point in Dorset. It offers one of the best views around over Blackmoor Vale. Thomas Hardy apparently loved the view of and described it in detail in Tess and in the poem 'Wessex Heights', where he wrote of the spot, 'Ghosts then keep their distance; and I know some liberty'. He would find little different today, although the large parking area suggests that it's a popular spot on a summer Sunday. The topograph will help identify places in the view: Shaftesbury, Stourhead, Glastonbury Tor and, even, the Quantocks. It doesn't mention Ibberton, the small village at the bottom of the hill, where Eadbeorht the Saxon and his people set up home. There are a number of thatched cottages built on various levels, and a manor house dating from the mid-seventeenth century.

Continue walking along the road for roughly 2.4km until you pass a road junc-

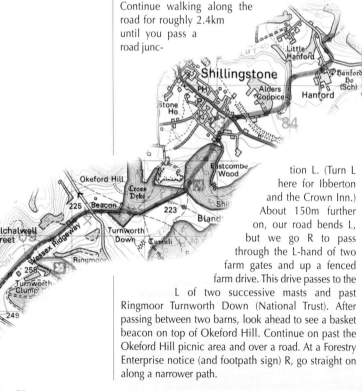

tion L. (Turn L here for Ibberton and the Crown Inn.) About 150m further on, our road bends L, but we go R to pass through the L-hand of two farm gates and up a fenced farm drive. This drive passes to the L of two successive masts and past Ringmoor Turnworth Down (National Trust). After passing between two barns, look ahead to see a basket beacon on top of Okeford Hill. Continue on past the Okeford Hill picnic area and over a road. At a Forestry Enterprise notice (and footpath sign) R, go straight on along a narrower path.

The path now goes through some woodland to emerge at a five-path cross-track. Go straight on with woods L and gorse (later a field) R. Just before the field ends, the Wessex Ridgeway takes a pointless detour R to pass a trig point. It then goes on to a spot where a path comes in from the R. Here go 90° L over the field. There's no clear path, so bear generally L towards a gap in the shrubbery in the corner of the field. When you find it, the path descends to an open flattened area. Go straight on and down into the woods. The path becomes narrow, steep, bends R, then L, and reaches a lane. Turn L to walk into the outskirts of Shillingstone. At a road junction, bear L and walk on for 200m. Just after 'Greenhills', go R along a fenced path with a newish housing estate to L. Straight ahead is Hambledon hill-fort (of which more anon) and half-R is Hod Hill. This path soon reaches a main road. Turn L for central Shillingstone. Turn R to continue the route.

Originally called 'Shilling Ockford' (Child Okeford and Okeford Fitzpaine are both nearby) Shillingstone grew up around the ford over the River Stour. The village once boasted a busy lime industry (the quarry is cut into Shillingstone Hill), but has since diminished. Thirsty folk can quench their thirst at the pub, and there are sporadic buses to Blandford and Sturminster Newton.

Hod Hill is home to a multivallate fort covering a rectangular area of over 22ha (55 acres), making it the largest hillfort in Dorset. It was defended on three sides by two ramparts, while the fourth falls steeply down to the River Stour. Hod Hill was first fortified in the early Iron Age (third century BC), and further strengthened before the Romans arrived. Much of the building material came from quarries on the inside. In practice, the fort would have been more like a town than a castle, and contained hundreds of circular huts, detectable as depressions. The Romans' ballistae fire was seemingly so devastating that archaeologists believe the fort surrendered before too much damage was done. The Romans then used the fort to house some 700 soldiers, before abandoning it around AD 50.

Harvested field above Shillingstone

Stage 4: Shillingstone to Ludwell

Start:	Shillingstone
Finish:	Ludwell
Distance:	23.3km (14.5 miles)
OS:	Landrangers 194 Dorchester & Weymouth, 195 Bournemouth & Purbeck, 184 Salisbury & The Plain
Route Features:	Easy country
Information:	Tourist Information Centre: Shaftesbury (01747 53514)

Both Shillingstone and Ludwell are on main roads with bus routes, but if you wish to go from one to the other, you have to visit Shaftesbury (about 5km/3 miles from Ludwell) and Blandford (about 8km/5 miles from Shillingstone). So it can be done, but needs planning and time. Both towns can be useful for accommodation. There are pubs at Shroton, Tollard Royal and Ludwell.

Just after the Willows tearooms, go L along Holloway Lane. This goes under an old railway bridge and past Holloway Farm to R. When the drive turns sharp L into woods, go straight on through a gate. Cross the field to another gate that leads to a footbridge over the River Stour. At the end, turn L and walk with river L to a gap in the hedge ahead. Just inside this gap, go L through a gate. This path winds to and fro to eventually reach a gate R. Go through this and walk on with fence close L. In the far corner, go through two successive gates and on with the buildings of Hanford Farm and school to R.

Carry on through another two gates, and then over the end of a field to another gate. Go through this and turn L along the drive. This bends R to a road. Here turn L. The road soon bends R to reach a gate R. Go through this and take the R-hand track. This rises steeply to go through another gate. Walk up the field, staying close to the fence L. This steep haul takes us to a pair of gates L, the sign for the Hambledon Hill National Nature Reserve, and a view to Hambledon hillfort. Go through the second of the two gates and walk on along a worn grass path that goes to the R of a fenced-off area and on towards a farm gate in the far fence. Don't go through this, but turn R, with fence close L, to a pedestrian gate. Go through this and on along a fenced path to reach a trig point from which there is a splendid panorama. Go straight on here to visit Hambledon hillfort, or turn R to continue the walk.

Hambledon camp looks impressive, but at just 12ha (30 acres) it's smaller than some. This multivallate fort was built in three phases, the first in the third century BC and the last immediately before the Roman invasion. Several hundred depressions within the fort suggest the sites of huts. The general assumption is that Hambledon Hill, like Hod Hill, fell to Vespasian's forces by surrender. Curiously there's an earlier Neolithic long barrow inside the fort on the highest point of the hill, associated with what is thought to be a Neolithic causewayed camp just outside the south-east entrance to the hillfort. This was clearly a place of some significance for a substantial period. There's a fantastic view all round, and it's splendidly isolated; it's said that even Hardy once got lost here in a fog.

The old railway bridge once bore the weight of the Somerset & Dorset Joint Railway, opened from Bath to Bournemouth in 1863, but sadly closed in 1966. It has been suggested that the footbridge over the Stour was once the site of a Roman ford, and that this could have been the spot where the original Ridgeway crossed the river. Hanford House School is based in a seventeenth-century house, and has one notable feature: a ghost of 'a sweet little old lady dressed in brown'.

Our path now descends steadily with views down to Iwerne Courtney – more popularly Shroton – including the fine fluted Corinthian pilasters of its manor house, Ranston, to eventually reach a wall. Turn L and walk down to a stile in a field near a cricket pavilion. Cross this and turn L along the road. When the road goes sharp L, bear R along a path with houses R and fields L. This comes out at Frog Lane. For the centre of Shroton, the Cricketers pub and bus stops for Blandford or Shaftesbury, turn R along Main St.

Until World War I there was a great annual fair at Shroton, said to be one of the events of the year in the whole of Dorset. There were games and amusements, as well as horse and pony sales. They were also great feasts and excuses for a good deal of imbibing. Both Thomas Hardy and the Dorset poet William Barnes came to a Shroton fair or two. Today you just have to make do with the Cricketers pub if you're seeking refreshment.

Shroton is a pleasant little village, thankfully situated off the main Shaftesbury to Blandford road. The two names can cause confusion: the Domesday 'Werne' became 'Yuern Curtenay' in 1244 when it was owned by the Courtenays, Earls of Devon. The name Shroton probably comes from the fourteenth century when the place was called Schyreueton or 'sheriff's estate', from the Old English scir-refa and tun. This related to the fact that the manor belonged to Baldwin of Exeter, sheriff of Devon.

The Romans were here, too; Iwerne villa, just to the west of the current village, was excavated in the 1890s, and extensive areas of wall painting found. But the village came to more national prominence at the time of the Civil War, when a group of about 300 local folk grew tired of being fought over by both Cavaliers and Roundheads. Armed with pitchforks, clubs and scythes, and wearing white cockades, 'The Clubmen' were led by the Rev Bravel of Compton Abbas. They took a thorough beating when they defended their land, so retreated up Hambledon Hill and became entrenched. In 1645, Oliver Cromwell sent in 50 dragoons, who locked The Clubmen in Shroton church before Cromwell

decided that they were mostly harmless, and had them
sent home under strict orders to behave themselves.

To continue the walk, bear R along Frog Lane. Walk on
to cross the main Shaftesbury to Blandford road and the
stile opposite. Walk up the L side of three consecutive
fields to reach a farm drive. Go straight on along this
windy track, ignoring a L and then a R turn, to finally
reach a gate and a road. Go L and then R through a gate
and along the L-hand side of the field. This continues
into a corner of the field where the woods L bend R.
Here go through a gap L into the woods. Follow the
woodland path to a road and turn R. After about 800m,
go L through some wooden gates and walk on with
woods L. This winds L to go through a gap between
woods, after which keep to the L side with woods L. In
a field corner, enter the wood and go down a muddy
slope. This reaches a path T-junction. Go R. In a short
distance, just before a barbed-wire fence, go L with
fence close R. This continues just inside the R-hand edge
of the woods for just over 1km to a point where a view
opens R through some birch trees. Here there is a
waymark post, and we turn L along a clear woodland
track. A farm track joins from the R. Go straight on and
follow this farm drive to a road in Ashmore (2.4km from
the turn). Turn R to reach the pond.

'There is a freedom in
this vastness, these
open downs, which
far surpasses the most
picturesque of land-
scape where the
traveller cannot quit
the beaten path.' So
wrote Richard Jefferies
in *The Wiltshire
Downs.* But 'This
Wiltshire is a horrible
county,' wrote the
inestimable William
Cobbett in *Rural Rides*
in 1830. And he
wasn't alone in his
impressions. The
seventeenth-century
antiquarian and writer
John Aubrey described
the people of
Wiltshire thus: 'The
"indigenae" or aborig-
ines speake drawlinge;
they are phleg-
metique, skins pale
and livid, slow and
dull, heavy of spirit...
they feed chiefly on
milke meats, which
cools their braines too
much and hurts their
intentions. These
circumstances make
them melancholy,
contemplative and
malicious...'

Ashmore War Memorial

Tollard Royal

Ashmore is the highest village in Dorset, 213m (700ft) above sea level. The name is Saxon – ash-mere, or 'the pond of the ash tree' – but people have probably lived here since Romano-British times. Embanked ponds like this are said to date back to the beginning of the Christian era, or even earlier. The pond would have been the nucleus of the village, also providing a vital water supply during dry summers. As Richard Jefferies pointed out in *The Wiltshire Downs* in 1877, 'Water is as precious here as in the veritable deserts of the East'. Ashmore pond is reputed never to dry up, and at an annual midsummer festival the locals celebrate their pond in 'Filly Loo' (said to be a celebration of magic and water – l'eau). There haven't been any pubs here since the early 1800s, when one Luke Howard, a Quaker incomer from London, ordered their closure.

Turn R just after the pond, and continue up a lane for a short way to turn L along a path signposted to 'Bealesmead'. Go through a farm gate and along a fenced path to a stile in the far R corner. Cross and go straight on (not R) over a stile and then over the centre of the field ahead. Here we leave Dorset and enter Wiltshire.

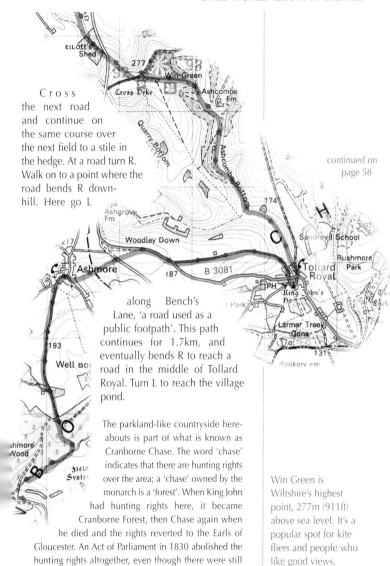

C r o s s the next road and continue on the same course over the next field to a stile in the hedge. At a road turn R. Walk on to a point where the road bends R downhill. Here go L

continued on page 58

along Bench's Lane, 'a road used as a public footpath'. This path continues for 1.7km, and eventually bends R to reach a road in the middle of Tollard Royal. Turn L to reach the village pond.

The parkland-like countryside hereabouts is part of what is known as Cranborne Chase. The word 'chase' indicates that there are hunting rights over the area; a 'chase' owned by the monarch is a 'forest'. When King John had hunting rights here, it became Cranborne Forest, then Chase again when he died and the rights reverted to the Earls of Gloucester. An Act of Parliament in 1830 abolished the hunting rights altogether, even though there were still

Win Green is Wiltshire's highest point, 277m (911ft) above sea level. It's a popular spot for kite fliers and people who like good views.

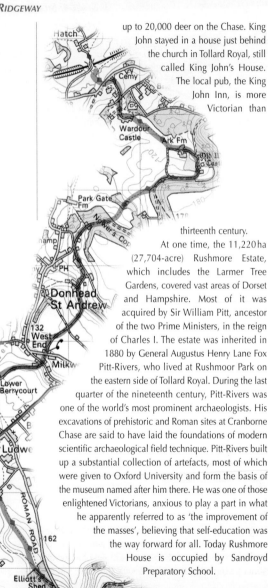

up to 20,000 deer on the Chase. King John stayed in a house just behind the church in Tollard Royal, still called King John's House. The local pub, the King John Inn, is more Victorian than thirteenth century.

At one time, the 11,220ha (27,704-acre) Rushmore Estate, which includes the Larmer Tree Gardens, covered vast areas of Dorset and Hampshire. Most of it was acquired by Sir William Pitt, ancestor of the two Prime Ministers, in the reign of Charles I. The estate was inherited in 1880 by General Augustus Henry Lane Fox Pitt-Rivers, who lived at Rushmoor Park on the eastern side of Tollard Royal. During the last quarter of the nineteenth century, Pitt-Rivers was one of the world's most prominent archaeologists. His excavations of prehistoric and Roman sites at Cranborne Chase are said to have laid the foundations of modern scientific archaeological field technique. Pitt-Rivers built up a substantial collection of artefacts, most of which were given to Oxford University and form the basis of the museum named after him there. He was one of those enlightened Victorians, anxious to play a part in what he apparently referred to as 'the improvement of the masses', believing that self-education was the way forward for all. Today Rushmore House is occupied by Sandroyd Preparatory School.

Just before the pond, turn L. Don't take the clearly sign-posted path over a footbridge, but go on along a gravel drive and then fork L along the lower of two tracks through a farm gate. (Incidentally, the Hardy Way, waymarked just here, is a 322km/200-mile amble around places where the writer set his novels.) This pleasant path winds along the bottom of a steep slope R. Go through a farm gate at the end and then take two stiles to R. After the second, turn R to walk along an indistinct grassy path in the bottom of a valley. This bends L to meet a chalk drive and then continues along the valley bottom. When this bends R through a farm gate, bear L slightly to cross a stile into an overgrown area. A much-obstructed path eventually reaches a well-tended lawn! Walk along the R-hand side and then pass to the R of a house. Keep straight on with a fence close R and then straight on along a drive. This bends sharp L with Ashcombe Farm on the hillside R.

When the drive forks, go L up a flinty track. Where this becomes indistinct, bear R down into a dip and then rejoin the flinty track. This section is very steep. Just as it levels out again, look for a L turn into the woods (there's a waymark post R). The next section through the woods can be very indistinct, with numerous paths going nowhere. We need to go straight up. One easy route is to bear R where the paths appear to fork. Follow this route round to a point where it starts to descend. Here there is a clear path that goes up L, leading to a wooden kissing gate. Go through it and up to the top of the hill to a gate with fine views opening up all the time. Go though the gate to reach a driveway. Turn R and follow the drive to a car park for Win Green.

Continue past the car park entrance for 50m, and then cross a stile R. Go downhill with fence to R. More than half way down, the fence bends R slightly. Our path goes straight on along the remains of Cross Dyke to reach a path on the far side. When you reach this, turn R and go downhill to a stile. At the road go R for a short distance and then L through a gate into woodland. At the end of the wood, fork R into a field. Now follow an indistinct path (depends on the state of the crop) taking

Tollard is also famous for the Larmer Tree, a wych elm that grew on the boundary between two counties and three parishes. It marks the spot where the Chase Courts were held, where the king could hear grievances and decide on matters forestry. The original Larmer Tree died long ago, and the spot was marked for a while by a nineteenth-century oak, though in January 2000 a wych elm was again planted there. The Larmer Tree Gardens became a popular destination for the affluent Victorian classes, with an estimated half-million visitors by 1900. Although there was a period of decline, the gardens (which can be found just behind the house which is just behind the church) are now open most of the summer (tel: 01725 516228).

Old Watercress Beds, Ludwell

a course towards the R-hand tree of a line of partially hidden trees ahead. Here is a stile. Cross it and go down ill with fence close R, over a stile and on to reach a farm gate between a bungalow L and a farmyard R. At the road, turn L for 20m, and then go R along a narrow path with hedge L and fence R. Some way on, cross a stile into a field and continue with an old watercress farm to L. The path eventually leads to a stile and a driveway. Follow the drive between houses to reach the road at Ludwell. The Grove Arms (pub and B&B) and bus stop for Shaftesbury are to R. Shaftesbury itself is about 5km along the road to L.

Stage 5: Ludwell to Heytesbury

Start:	Ludwell
Finish:	Heytesbury
Distance:	27.3km (17 miles)
OS:	Landranger 184 Salisbury & The Plain
Route Features:	Easy but long
Information:	Tourist Information Centres: Shaftesbury (01747 53514); Warminster (01985 218548)

Ludwell is on the main Shaftesbury-to-Salisbury road. Getting from Shaftesbury is easy (failing a bus, try Tourist Information for a taxi company), but getting from Heytesbury to Shaftesbury is hard. There is no public transport between Warminster and Shaftesbury. The only way to join the two ends of this walk is to use the railway station at Tisbury, travelling to or from Warminster via Salisbury. It's best to continue walking, and to make use of the relative abundance of accommodation within a short distance of each end. Luckily, this stretch has some very conveniently sited inns at Hindon (roughly half way).

Turn L for a short distance and then R through a gate and uphill. Follow this path over a field to a green lane and turn R. The lane passes a radio mast L and goes through some woods to a road. Turn R, and then L along a no through road. Just before Lower Berrycourt Farm, bear R and continue along a green lane. Shortly after, take a L fork, and then a second L fork which descends along an overgrown high-hedged path to a gate. Walk over the next field with hedge L to pass a house and then go through a gate. Go straight on to pass a thatched house L. At a T-junction, go straight on up a path between cottages. This steep ascent ends at a road. Turn R, then L to pass a phone box. The green lane continues and bears L to go through a farm gate. It then descends and bears L along a concrete section of farm track. Just before Dengrove Farm, turn R though a farm gate and over a stream. (We're now on the outskirts of Donhead St Andrew.) Follow the lane uphill to a road and turn L. At a road junction, turn R along a no through road. This passes some houses and then goes by a gate into Wardour Wood (by a Forestry Commission notice). About 200m after the notice, the conifer plantation L ends and the main track swings R with some broadleaved woodland to L. Here go L along a narrower path that forks R and descends to a stile. Head straight across the field ahead to a stile that takes the path on with a lake R. Pass a hermit's hut L to reach a stile. Now continue up the L-hand side of a field with views over to New Wardour Castle. Walk on with woods to R and a view of Old Wardour Castle ahead. The path eventually bends L to continue past a Gothic pavilion on the outer bailey wall and on with castle R and lake L to reach the car park and castle entrance.

> The building of Old Wardour Castle – more a fortified 'tower house' – was started in 1393 by John, Lord Lovell. A veteran of the Hundred Years War, Lovell was given a licence to crenellate his home. The hexagonal design is said to be unique in England, and closest in style to the Château de Concressault in France. During the Civil War Lady Blanche Lovell, then about 60, defended the castle for the king; with just a handful of men she held out against Sir Edward Hungerford and an army of more than

Old Waldour Castle

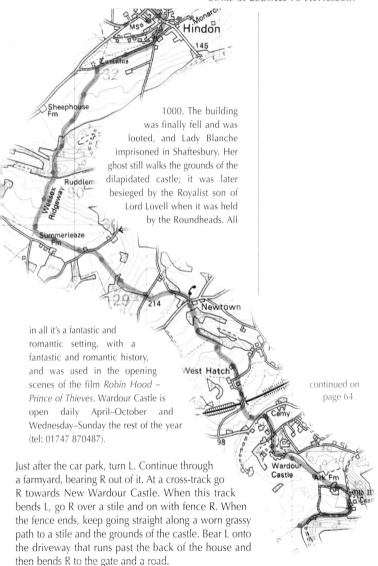

1000. The building
was finally fell and was
looted, and Lady Blanche
imprisoned in Shaftesbury. Her
ghost still walks the grounds of the
dilapidated castle; it was later
besieged by the Royalist son of
Lord Lovell when it was held
by the Roundheads. All

in all it's a fantastic and
romantic setting, with a
fantastic and romantic history,
and was used in the opening
scenes of the film *Robin Hood –
Prince of Thieves*. Wardour Castle is
open daily April–October and
Wednesday–Sunday the rest of the year
(tel: 01747 870487).

continued on
page 64

Just after the car park, turn L. Continue through
a farmyard, bearing R out of it. At a cross-track go
R towards New Wardour Castle. When this track
bends L, go R over a stile and on with fence R. When
the fence ends, keep going straight along a worn grassy
path to a stile and the grounds of the castle. Bear L onto
the driveway that runs past the back of the house and
then bends R to the gate and a road.

The Palladian New Wardour Castle isn't quite as romantic, but is still impressive. It dates from the middle of the eighteenth century and was originally built for the Earl of Arundel. It was once famed for its fine collection of paintings, and Thomas Hardy aficionados tell us that Jude took Sue for an excursion here from Salisbury. After the death of the last earl in 1944, the place fell into disrepair and the pictures were dispersed. The family finally sold the old house to a religious order that planned to pull the place down. It was rescued and, since the 1960s, has been home to the Cranborne Chase School for Girls.

Continue down the road to a T-junction. Turn L and walk on to a footpath sign R, directly opposite Wardour Primary School. Go straight over the field to cross a footbridge and then up the next field to a stile. At a road, turn R to go over a railway bridge. About 100m further on, take a signposted path R. Don't go through the low gate, but continue up the field with hedge L to a stile in the far L corner to reach a road. Our route now goes straight up a tunnel-like path ahead. After passing a collapsed stone barn, go straight on across a field and under power lines to a fence. Turn R to the wood and then L to walk uphill with the wood close R. A little way up, the edge of the wood bends R. Go through a farm gate here to reach a footpath gate shortly after. Keep the fence close L to reach a stile and path that winds through the woods. This reaches a stile and a field. Keep hedge close L and go straight to a stile and a road. Turn R then L. This is Newtown.

The Lamb, Hindon

Walk past some houses. The road bends L, and just as it bends R again, go L through a gap in the hedge. Continue half-R over a field just L of a solitary oak. Then go to L of some old farm buildings to a road. Go straight into the next field and bear L to walk on with woods close L. This curves R downhill to a gate into the woods L. Go through this, and on to a gate and a field. Walk along the R-hand side of the field with fence R to a farm gate and a road. Turn L. Just after a house, go R through a farm gate and then immediately L through another. Now turn R to walk with fence close R to a footpath gate in the field corner. Cross a stream and then go through another gate L. Turn R again to continue with a fence R to another gate. This leads to a tunnel gap in the tall hedge ahead. Carry on with hedge R, past a gate R. After going through the next gate, the path becomes confined and we are tunnelled to a footpath gate. This leads to a prominent cross-track in front of a fence. Turn R and walk up the R-hand side of the next field to a fenced path. This goes uphill into woods. Keep on the broad dirt track all the way through. It eventually leaves the woods and continues along a fenced and hedged path between fields. This path now continues for about 1.2km to a prominent cross-track. Go R here to a lane and turn L. The lane then reaches the centre of Hindon. Turn L along a street with pollarded limes to reach The Lamb.

The Lamb was listed as one of the inns supplying post horses for coaches, and it kept up to 300 for this purpose. But when Prime Minister William Pitt stopped here in

W.H. Hudson, who stayed at The Lamb in 1909, described Hindon as 'a delightful little village, so rustic and pretty amidst the green swelling downs'. It still is. At one time the village was on the main route between London and the West Country, and two posting inns still remain: The Grosvenor Arms and The Lamb.

1786, he was upset to discover that there weren't any fresh ones available. The Lamb also links us to the Wiltshire moonrakers' story that will be related in Walk 7, Coulston Hill to Devizes. Silas White, a notorious smuggler and leader of the Wiltshire moonrakers, once used The Lamb as his headquarters. It's said that there are passages underneath the inn that were used as contraband storerooms. Hindon does have some bus services and although sporadic, it is possible to get to Tisbury railway station from here.

Continue up the street past the shop and church. As the road bends gently R out of town, go R along a fenced path between bungalows to a stile. Continue straight over the field to a road. Turn L uphill. The road bends R and then L. As it does so, go straight along a hedged path to a gate, and then roughly straight on over a field. This path descends to the corner of the field; bear R to join a green lane, and then bear R again to the main road (A303). Go straight over and through a gate. Continue uphill along a green lane. This joins a track coming from R and continues uphill to a wood. Near the top, and before the woods, the track bends L. Just after this, go R through a gap between woods along a grassy path. Walk on with field L and woods R to the field corner where the path plunges straight into the wood. The path bends R to a cross-path near a wooden lookout tower. Go L to reach a gravel drive that runs along a clearing in the wood. Turn R along the drive.

Wessex Ridgeway entering Heytesbury

About 1km further on one part of this drive goes R, but we go straight on. The drive then bends L and passes a clear turning R. Continue straight on along a broad track with views L over Corton Down. Continuing on the same line, the route passes a gate into a narrower fenced path. We pass a corrugated iron barn L and raised water tank R, all the time with views L towards Warminster. At a metalled lane, turn L. The lane comes to a crossroad. Turn R along a drive signposted Boyton Farms and then just before the sign, bear L to go along an enclosed path to a road at Corton.

Cross this and go down some steps to the next road with a thatched wall ahead. Turn R. The road bends L past The Dairy Cottage and bends L to pass Corton House. The road bends L again at Sundial House. Just after The Lodge R, turn R along a no through road. Go under a railway bridge and straight along a dirt road. Shortly this turns R and we go straight on along a hedged path. After going over a cross-track, the path swings R to a bridge and stile. In the next field go half-L across the centre to a footbridge with Knook Manor slightly to R ahead. Continue along the same line to another footbridge and then just before a further more substantial bridge over a small river, cross the stile L and walk on with river R. After 100m, the river bends R and the path goes L to a farm drive. Cross straight over and walk on at roughly 90° to the river (and about 10–20° to the L of a house in front of a hill) and over the field. On reaching the hedge, go R with hedge L to a gap in the fence. This leads immediately to a path with a footbridge to L. Don't cross this but turn R. This joins another path and goes on over a footbridge to a road. Turn R over a bridge and immediately L through a gate, and walk on with river to L to a kissing gate. Walk on over the field bearing slightly L so that the fence is close L. This heads to a fenced path with river L and thatched cottage R. The route joins a

continued on
page 68

metalled drive. At a T-junction, go R to a crossroad and turn L along Heytesbury High St with The Angel L.

'This place, which is one of the rotten boroughs of Wiltshire, and which was formerly a considerable town, is now but a very miserable affair.' So reported William Cobbett in *Rural Rides*. Not so much a miserable affair nowadays, but gloriously quiet since the building of bypass in 1986, which runs near Heytesbury House on the north-eastern side of the village. Siegfried Sassoon, the war poet, bought this 52-room Georgian house in 1933, and lived here until his death in September 1967. Sassoon enlisted in World War I and was seriously wounded twice. At first they put his antiwar sentiments down to shell shock, but his views were sustained even though he remained in the army and won the Military Cross. Sassoon's poetry about his experiences with the Royal Welch Fusiliers in Flanders, together with his book *Memoirs of a Foxhunting Man*, won him huge literary acclaim. The family finally sold the house in 1994. The village used to be a coaching inn stop, and The Angel Inn is a seventeenth-century coaching inn that still opens for lunch and dinner. The Red Lion pub is a little further on the left.

Stage 6: Heytesbury to Coulston Hill

Start:	Heytesbury
Finish:	Coulston Hill
Distance:	21.6km (13.5 miles)
OS:	Landranger 184 Salisbury & The Plain
Route Features:	Easy country
Information:	Tourist Information Centres: Warminster (01985 218548); Westbury (01373 827158)

Heytesbury can be reached by frequent buses between Warminster and Salisbury. The village of Edington at the bottom of Coulston Hill has a less frequent service that runs between Devizes and Westbury. As this section stays mostly up on Salisbury Plain, lengthy diversions are needed if you wish to visit a pub. Central Warminster is about 1.5km (1 mile) off the route after the army camp, and Westbury is about the same from Beggar's Knoll, a point just off the Imber Range Path before the White Horse. Both towns offer shops, hostelries and transport galore. Edington, about 1km (0.6 miles) downhill, has a pub as well as buses. There is a small shop near the army camp in Warminster.

Continue along the High St to pass the church and then the Red Lion. Take the next R along Chapel Road. Turn R along Newtown and then go immediately L up a metalled drive. Go through a farmyard to a stile. Cross the A36 to a fence and narrow steps opposite. Bear L uphill through a gap in the trees to a field. Turn L to walk round the field edge and uphill to a major cross-path: the Imber Range Path. Turn L.

Salisbury Plain has probably altered very little since the 1600s when John Evelyn thought it a 'goodly plaine...

The closure of the Plain by the military, and the restriction of access to Imber, has had one major consequence for the Greater Ridgeway path. If it were open, then the Wessex Ridgeway would undoubtedly run from here (or Battlesbury) straight across the Plain, through Imber and on to Gores Cross on the A360 between Tilshead and West Lavington. These routes are marked on the OS map, although we won't join them until just after West Lavington.

and one of the most delightful prospects of nature'. It still is, if you can ignore the gunfire heralding from somewhere just over the horizon. There's a real sense of solitude and remoteness up here. The Plain is roughly 32km (20 miles) east–west and 19km (12 miles) north–south. It's not very high – on average just 137m (450ft) above sea level – but it feels both lofty and remote. The Imber Range Path is a 48km (30-mile) circular walk around the perimeter of the Imber Range Military Firing and Training Area. The range is named after Imber village; closed by the army in 1943 and now used for street-fighting practice. The village church is still intact and hosts one service a year on a September Sunday.

The path runs through the centre of a wood. Go straight across the field ahead, passing to R of the tumulus on Cotley Hill. There are fine views over the Plain R and the hills ahead including Scratchbury, Middle and the wooded Battlesbury. From the tumulus bear R towards a white post in the distance. At a fence, turn R and then L at the corner, keeping the fence close L. Go through a gate L and turn R to walk on with fence R. This path winds round to a stile. Cross and go slightly L and then R over the field towards a stile to the R of centre on the earthworks of Scratchbury Hill ahead. If you can't spot it, don't panic, the exact position of the stile becomes more apparent the closer you get. Cross the stile and turn R to walk round the hillfort with fence close R.

The village lock-up at Heytesbury

Copse near Scratchbury Hill

Scratchbury and Battlesbury hillforts have much in common: they're big; their defences are impressive; they are magnificently placed, overlooking the Wylye valley. Both were probably occupied in the Iron Age (100 BC to AD 60). The fact that they are so close together (only 1.5km/1 mile apart), and that there are two more only 6.4km (4 miles) away (at Bratton and Cley Hill), suggests that this was a pretty dangerous place to live. 'Scratch' is a West Country term for the devil, although how it relates to the hill is difficult to say.

When the fence turns R to go downhill to a farmhouse, keep L and follow the earthworks round L to a white post. Keep on along a grassy path towards the next white post, but just before it bear R down a clear track to the lower ramparts. Continue along the path which descends gradually to a fence and a stile R. Cross this and go downhill with fence L to a stile. Cross into the lane and turn L. Go straight up a clear path that heads to the R-hand edge of a wood. This path then winds round the contour of the hill bearing R and then L slightly down hill. When the fence L ends, continue straight on down to a wide concrete road. Turn R, then L up some steps and walk on with a low hedge to R. At a cross-path, go straight on uphill with fence L to a gate and stile. Walk on a little further and turn L to walk along

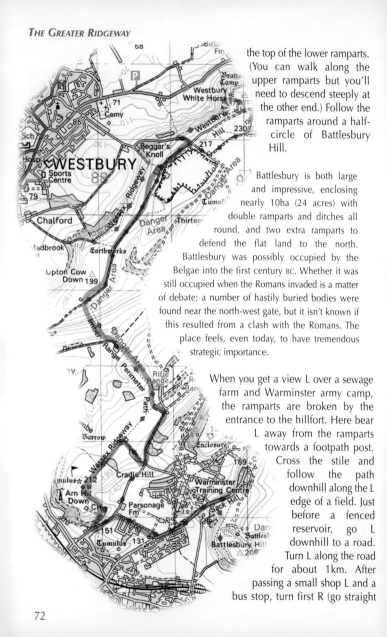

the top of the lower ramparts. (You can walk along the upper ramparts but you'll need to descend steeply at the other end.) Follow the ramparts around a half-circle of Battlesbury Hill.

Battlesbury is both large and impressive, enclosing nearly 10ha (24 acres) with double ramparts and ditches all round, and two extra ramparts to defend the flat land to the north. Battlesbury was possibly occupied by the Belgae into the first century BC. Whether it was still occupied when the Romans invaded is a matter of debate; a number of hastily buried bodies were found near the north-west gate, but it isn't known if this resulted from a clash with the Romans. The place feels, even today, to have tremendous strategic importance.

When you get a view L over a sewage farm and Warminster army camp, the ramparts are broken by the entrance to the hillfort. Here bear L away from the ramparts towards a footpath post. Cross the stile and follow the path downhill along the L edge of a field. Just before a fenced reservoir, go L downhill to a road. Turn L along the road for about 1km. After passing a small shop L and a bus stop, turn first R (go straight on for central Warminster) along a road that passes some army housing to a T-junction. Turn L for about 400 m and then go R up a private drive for the golf course.

> There was a thriving agricultural community here when the Romans came, although Warminster as such didn't exist. By the time of King Alfred it was a royal borough. One hundred years later coins were minted here, and this probably ensured the success of the town market. The royal manor went on to be held by Edward the Confessor and passed to William. In 1156 the Crown sold the manor to Robert Maudit, whose family sold it in the sixteenth century to the Thynne family of Longleat. The Marquis of Bath is still the lord of the manor today. In the Middle Ages the town had a significant wool and cloth trade as well as a prosperous corn market. The Old Bell Hotel is a fourteenth-century coaching inn, and there are others. The town's prosperity during the eighteenth century has left a rich heritage of houses and mullion-windowed cottages. Nowadays, however, the town is primarily famous for its army connections, most prominently with the Warminster Training Centre (formerly the School of Infantry) and ABRO (formerly the Reme Workshops).

Immediately after the sign for the West Wiltshire Golf Club, bear R along a narrow path that passes close to L of a garage. Follow this round to the edge of the golf course, keeping the fence and views down Kidnapper's Hole to R. The path turns R to join a dirt track on Arn Hill Down, site of great UFO activity in the early 1960s.

Westbury White Horse

For travellers (including those on passing trains), Westbury means only one thing: the White Horse cut into the hill just below Bratton Castle hillfort. It's thought to be the oldest in Wiltshire, and popular opinion has it that the original was made to celebrate King Alfred's victory over the Danes. The original faced right, and is said to have resembled an elongated dachshund with a saddle and a peculiar upturned tail. Some say it was Saxon, some that it was made in 1700. It was overcut by 'Mr Gee', steward to Lord Abingdon, who apparently thought the original rather primitive in style and put this, somewhat larger, one here instead. The present horse, made of concrete and not chalk, is nearly 55m (180ft) long and has an eye measuring 7.6m (25ft) round.

Go straight on to leave the golf course. Continue in the same direction towards a prominent clump of trees. Pass a barn and go straight on with a fine view of Battlesbury hillfort R. At the next stand of trees (with a mast), don't walk onto the firing range but go L with fence to R. This path passes some barns and goes on to a farm road. This bends L. After 100m, go R over a stile and immediately L downhill and then up (keep strictly to the L side of the field here). At the top field corner, turn R along a fenced drive.

This track bends L and then R to a bridleway sign pointing L. We go straight on. (If you wish to follow the exact course of the Ramblers Association's route, go L here, then R through some woods to a T-junction, and turn R to return to our route.) After passing a massive cement works chalk pit R, continue to a road. Here turn L (leaving the Imber path). Go downhill for about 150m and then R over a stile into a field (Continue down this road for Westbury in 1.5km.) Go directly down to the edge of the hill. Turn R to walk towards Westbury White Horse with fence close L, crossing two stiles before reaching some seats and a topograph on Westbury Hill.

Westbury is a small town, most notable nowadays for its transport links; many commute daily to London. In former times it was a small weaving and glove-making town, and before

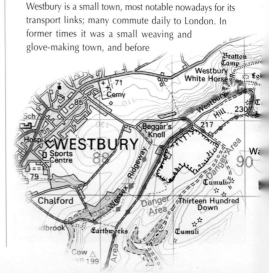

that a residence of the Kings of Wessex. From Westbury
Hill the Blue Circle Cement Works dominate the town.
Kimmeridge Clay from the quarry we passed earlier is
brought here as slurry by pipeline. This clay is quite rich
in fossils; the Westbury Pliosaur was unearthed here in
1980. This creature, some 150 million years old and
6–7m (19.7–23ft) long, has been described as a fear-
some beast with huge eyes and massive teeth: the
reptilian equivalent of today's toothed whales or sharks.
It now resides in Bristol Museum.

At Bratton Camp or Castle, Salisbury Plain reaches
its highest point at 230m (755ft). The hillfort, built some
time between 300 BC and AD 43, covers just over 10ha
(25 acres) within double banks and ditches on three
sides, and occupies a splendidly imperious position.
Following the Battle of Ashdown (see Walk 11,
Scutchamer Knob to Mongewell),
the Vikings left Wessex and
settled in the north and east.
But then they fought
back, and in January AD
878, Wessex was
overrun and King
Alfred's troops

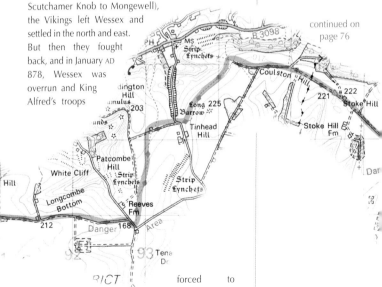

continued on
page 76

forced to
retreat to Athelney
in the Somerset fens, where he raised a new army. After
grouping at Iley Oak (Warminster) in May that year, he
fought the Vikings at the Battle of Ethandun. The Saxons

overwhelmed the Danes and chased them to Chippenham. After a two-week siege, the Vikings sued for peace. Their leader, King Guthrum, accepted Christianity and, at the close of 878, their army returned east to settle. The Battle of Ethandun therefore turned the tide for both Alfred and Wessex, and Alfred became the most powerful ruler in Britain. It is generally accepted that the site of the Battle of Ethandun is just up the hill from the village of Edington, either on the slopes of Bratton Castle or on neighbouring Edington Hill.

Bratton, some 4.8km north-east of Westbury, contains a number of sixteenth- and seventeenth-century houses, and a Baptist chapel of 1667. All the villages along this northern escarpment of Salisbury Plain have wells or springs; Bratton's Cat's Well is named after St Catherine, and is a rectangular 'dipping well', with steps leading down to standing water. The Well of the White Horse, or Bridewell springs, is between Westbury and Bratton just below the White Horse. The name may mean 'bride's spring'; perhaps drinking the waters stimulates some good old-fashioned fecundity. Local legend has it that when Bratton church clock strikes midnight, the White Horse goes down to Bridewell springs to drink. The problem is that Bratton church doesn't have a clock ...

Continue on to the edge of Bratton Camp. Go past two benches (don't go into the camp enclosure) and on in this general direction along any of the rather indistinct grassy paths to the drive for the site car park. Bear L along the drive to the road and site entrance sign. Here turn R along a gravel road to some old buildings at White Horse Farm. At a T-junction, turn L and walk on for 3km. At the next T-junction, turn R to reach the MOD hut, then go almost back on yourself to take a grassy path between the two gravel roads. This goes uphill and bends R to reach some barns. Just before the barns, turn R to a lane. (Turn L here for Edington.)

> The village of Edington is just over 1km down in the valley, and has a pub, as well as buses to Westbury or Devizes. It also has a fine priory church of St Mary, St Katherine and All Saints, founded in 1332 as a priest college by William of Edington, Lord Chancellor of England and Bishop of Winchester. It later became a monastery for the Augustinian Order of Bonhommes. In the fifteenth century, the Bishop of Salisbury, the Venerable William Ayscough, was a close advisor to the much-berated Henry VI. When a popular uprising against the king occurred in 1450 ('Jack Cade's rebellion'), Ayscough became a target; he was dragged from the church into the fields around Edington Hill and murdered.

Turn R, then shortly after, L to a fence before a field. Turn R, go through a gap and walk up the L-hand side of the field. This path bends L with a hedge to L and winds its way round to cross a stile. There are a series of cross-paths; head towards a prominent by-way sign and turn R to walk over Coulston Hill. (Turn L here for Edington.)

Stage 7: Coulston Hill to Devizes

Start:	Coulston Hill
Finish:	Devizes
Distance:	24km (15 miles)
OS:	Landrangers 184 Salisbury & The Plain, 173 Swindon & Devizes
Route Features:	Hilly, then country
Information:	Tourist Information Centre: Devizes Visitor Centre (01380 729408); Devizes Museum (01380 72769)

Edington has buses to Devizes and Westbury; Devizes is the local hub for buses that go in all directions, including to West Lavington, a village on the A360, so that could make a useful stop/start point. West Lavington has a very conveniently sited pub and there's a choice of pubs at Urchfont.

The path over Coulston Hill soon becomes a gravel drive and then arrives at a U-bend of a metalled road. Bear R and walk on for over 3km. (The road returns to being a gravel drive about half way along.)

Salisbury Plain is famous for its archaeology and wildlife. Of its 40,000ha (nearly 100,000 acres), about half is under SSSI protection. There are about 2300 archaeological sites, 550 of which are scheduled monuments. It may seem strange that, since the end of the nineteenth century, the MOD have been using 11,000ha (27,000 acres) for training. Most of us would imagine that wildlife and archaeology don't live happily with mortars and tanks – yet, strangely, they do. The key factor is that the area hasn't been grazed since the 1940s, and it's neither ploughed nor treated with herbicides. Some 40 per cent of the so-called 'unimproved' chalk grassland of Britain is on Salisbury Plain, rich in plant and animal species, with an impressive variety of butterflies and moths. Notable birds include stone curlew, hen harrier and merlin, and there's also a healthy population of roe and muntjac deer. Curiously, the deer are doing rather well in what would otherwise appear to be an alien environment for them.

The next section's a bit tricky and, at the time of writing, is almost totally devoid of waymarks or even obvious paths. The key to leaving the Imber path is a division of the road into two (the one straight on is restricted access) and an army camp to R amidst some trees (New Zealand Farm Camp). At this junction and almost directly opposite the entrance to the camp, we turn L to cross some grassland. There's no obvious path here. So with a fence about 100m away to L, head off (in hope) to soon go downhill. The view ahead opens up and there's a small copse about 150m away to L. Take a line towards another distinct plantation (which appears from here to be in a squashed figure of eight). Keep roughly straight down into the bottom of the valley. Our way passes close to the R-hand edge of this plantation and round it, along a broad grassy track, towards a more mature copse in the distance. This path has a grassy bank close R. It then joins a farm road and heads on, keeping the copse mostly to R. The chalky road goes uphill to a field. Turn

Wessex Ridgeway near West Lavington

L and walk along the L edge of this field for about 1km with views opening up ahead. Towards the end, a clear dirt drive leaves the field to L and goes past a corrugated iron barn in a hollow L. The drive goes downhill through a small area of woodland with a view of Dauntsey's School in West Lavington ahead. About 100m after leaving the wood, go R just after a pair of gates. Around 400m after this, take a path L which runs alongside a line of trees that separates two fields. This path continues with the fence close R and then becomes a fenced path with Dauntsey's playing fields L. At a T-junction, turn R and follow the path to a road. Turn R to walk along this road, past the graveyard and a road that goes to the church, to a point where the road bends L along Rickbarton. Go down here to the main road at West Lavington (turn L for The Bridge pub in 50m).

West (formerly Bishop's) Lavington is a long, straggly village that lies along the A360.

The church dates from the twelfth century and is noted for the Beckett chapel which commemorates a local family. The south chapel was built by the Dauntseys who started living in the village in the fifteenth century, and who founded the school in 1543.

Our route continues over the road, past The Dial House L, and up Rutts Lane

80

which bears slightly R. At a T-junction near a thatched cottage, turn R and almost immediately L up a dirt track to a broad cross-track in woodland. Turn R into a woodland gully. This leads back to the lane. Go straight on and then bend L with the lane onto a dirt track and up onto the downs. At a road turn L (this rejoins the Greater Ridgeway route that would have run from the Heytesbury via Imber had the Plain been open) and walk on for about 1.5km to the MOD hut (Lavington Hill vedette). Go straight on here along a gravel road and walk on for 3km to where the road splits. The MOD road goes R and we go L around New Plantation, a small copse with views to Urchfont (in the valley) and to Roundway Down half-L in the distance. The next turning can be tricky to spot as there's no waymark post. On the far side of the copse, continue for about 200m, watching for a partially hidden dew-pond to L, just before a series of posts with red-and-white bands painted on them. Go L here, with pond L, and go straight down an increasingly obvious path into Urchfont. At a road, turn R. When this road bends R, go L passing the Nags Head pub to reach Urchfont village pond.

Urchfont is one of those best-kept-village type of places with a duck pond, a village green, a cricket pitch, a bluebell wood and two pubs (The Nag's Head and The Lamb). There's a fine old manor house that was built in the times of William and Mary. William Pitt the Elder once owned it and, since 1947, it has been a residential adult education college.

The name Urchfont is said to come from the spring (fount) of the Urch, which never dried up. However, the pond does tend to dry out as it's more of a dew-pond than a stream-fed one, but has a kind of cistern system which detects when the level gets low and then summons up the assistance of a pump to draw water from a farmer's well. Apparently there was a time when villagers took it in turns to sit by the pond with a shotgun in order to guard the specially bred village ducks against marauding foxes.

Bear L past the pond and a standing sarsen, and follow the road round L to pass The Lamb. At the village green, turn R and shortly after (as the road bends L) go R up a drive signposted to Knights Leaze Farm. On reaching some farm land, go immediately L to walk on with a hedge close L. Continue in this direction, even after the hedge moves away L, to a stile. Cross a stile and a farm

The pond, Urchfort

road to the next stile and go down the field to a further stile near a power-cable pole. Cross a small stream and head straight uphill to a further stile. Don't cross it, but turn R to walk next to the fence to a stile in the far corner of the field. Cross this and then bear R to take a well-worn dirt road. Where this road bends R and goes down slightly, continue straight on with trees to R into a field. There's no distinct path but this leads to a stile about half way up the hill. Cross a stream and walk straight on around the contours to the far L corner of the field to enter woodland. The path now goes up steps to cross the London–Penzance railway, and then descends again to reach a field. Go half-L over the field to pass through a tractor-size gap in the hedge and on over the next field to a farm gate. Now turn R to walk with hedge close R with the village of Stert over to the L. Continue on the gravel drive, over a cattle grid and on to pass Fullaway Farm to a road. Turn R to a more major road. Go straight across and continue along a hedged path. The head-high stinging nettles finally end and we continue straight on up a clear grassy path. Views open out L to Stert and Urchfont and the woods of the New Plantation up on the Plain.

Cross the next road and go straight on with views L to Devizes but more stunningly straight views to the new Roundway White Horse, views slightly R to the Cherhill monument and views half-R to Tan Hill and Milk Hill. The clear path goes over a major cross-track and on to a cottage to R and a barn L. Immediately after, turn L into the trees and along another overgrown path. This goes on to a T-junction. Turn R to reach a road and then L to reach Coate Bridge. (I did this *once* and it's not worth it. You save a lot of time, scratches and nettle stings by simply carrying on to the lane, turning L and walking on to Coate Bridge that way.) Don't cross Coate Bridge, but take the path on the other side of the road that leads down to the towpath of the Kennet & Avon Canal. This continues along the L-hand side of the canal under Brickham Bridge before turning sharp R to go under the London Road Bridge. To continue immediately along the way, cross the next bridge over the canal (Park Road

Urchfont lays claim (over Bishops Cannings) to being the site for the Wiltshire moonrakers story. Some brandy smugglers took to hiding their illicit barrels in the village pond. One night, under a full moon, they went to retrieve their booty; but up popped the law, asking what they were up to. The smugglers claimed that they were dragging the pond for the big cheese. The officers saw that they were looking at the reflection of the full moon, and promptly dismissed the smugglers as idiots. And that's why Wiltshiremen are known as 'moonrakers'. The problem for Bishops Cannings is that apparently it doesn't have a pond; so Urchfont has laid claim that the smugglers were from Bishops Cannings, but were using Urchfont's pond!

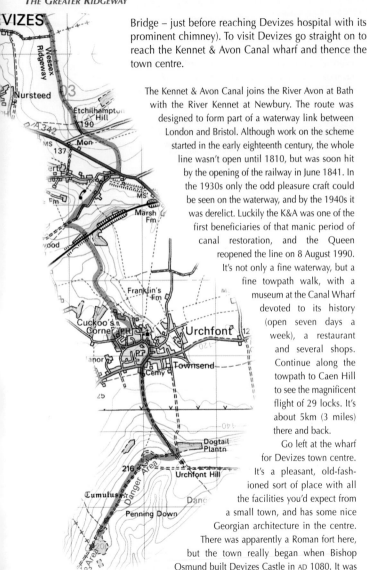

Bridge – just before reaching Devizes hospital with its prominent chimney). To visit Devizes go straight on to reach the Kennet & Avon Canal wharf and thence the town centre.

The Kennet & Avon Canal joins the River Avon at Bath with the River Kennet at Newbury. The route was designed to form part of a waterway link between London and Bristol. Although work on the scheme started in the early eighteenth century, the whole line wasn't open until 1810, but was soon hit by the opening of the railway in June 1841. In the 1930s only the odd pleasure craft could be seen on the waterway, and by the 1940s it was derelict. Luckily the K&A was one of the first beneficiaries of that manic period of canal restoration, and the Queen reopened the line on 8 August 1990. It's not only a fine waterway, but a fine towpath walk, with a museum at the Canal Wharf devoted to its history (open seven days a week), a restaurant and several shops. Continue along the towpath to Caen Hill to see the magnificent flight of 29 locks. It's about 5km (3 miles) there and back.

Go left at the wharf for Devizes town centre. It's a pleasant, old-fashioned sort of place with all the facilities you'd expect from a small town, and has some nice Georgian architecture in the centre. There was apparently a Roman fort here, but the town really began when Bishop Osmund built Devizes Castle in AD 1080. It was

a classic wooden motte-and-bailey of the sort favoured
by the invading Normans to subdue the Anglo-Saxons,
and was soon razed. Bishop Roger (Henry I's exchequer) rebuilt it in stone in 1138. The castle
demonstrated his power, and was considered to be one of the finest in the land.
The town developed, received its first
charter in 1141, was represented in

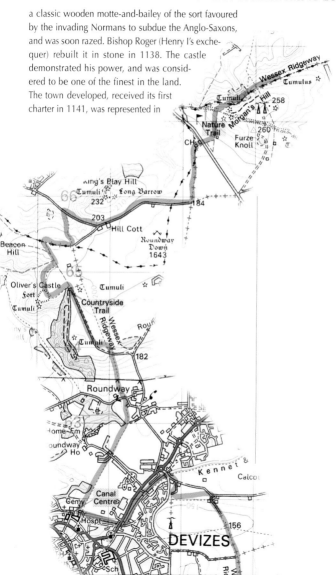

One of the most oft-repeated stories of Devizes is that of Ruth Pierce, which appears on a panel of the market cross. When Ms Pierce was accused of cheating on her market stall she said, 'May I drop down dead if am lying'. And she did. Devizes today has various agriculturally related industries. but is most famous for its brewery, the Wadworth company. Pilgrims will find the site in Northgate Street. Henry Wadworth started brewing in Devizes in 1875, and was the first man to cycle from London to Bath (it took him two-and-half days). And all done on iron tyres!

Parliament from 1295, and hosted an important medieval market. The castle remained only until the Civil War when, after a significant altercation, Cromwell had it demolished. The present 'castle' is Victorian and not open to the public. St Mary's in New Park Street was also built by the Bishop, and still bears the scars of Civil War cannon balls.

Sir Thomas Lawrence, 'the most fashionable English portrait painter of the late eighteenth and early nineteenth centuries', was brought up in Devizes. His father ran the Black Bear. Ale has been served in the Bear Hotel since at least 1599, but achieved fame under Thomas Lawrence senior, when customers included George III and Queen Charlotte, various foreign royals, David Garrick, the greatest actor of the age, as well the diarists and friends of Samuel Johnson, Fanny Burney and Mrs Thrale.

Market Place, Devizes

Stage 8: Devizes to Avebury

Start:	Devizes
Finish:	Avebury
Distance:	16.8km (10.5 miles)
OS:	Landranger 173 Swindon & Devizes
Route Features:	Hilly
Information:	Tourist Information Centre: Marlborough (01672 513989)

There is a new White Horse, officially opened with the burying of a time capsule on New Year's Eve 1999. This one differs from other Wiltshire white horses in that it faces right and is moving.

The two ends of this relatively short section are joined by a bus that runs regularly from Swindon (via Avebury) to Devizes. There are no facilities en route.

After crossing the bridge, pass through the pedestrian gate to R of the ornate main gates and along a tree-lined path with allotments R. Cross a minor road and continue in the same direction with a White Horse prominent on the hillside ahead.

On reaching the corner of a garden the main path goes R, but we go L up a field following some power lines. Continue on to reach a house fence R and then a road. Go L and follow the road round L and then, almost immediately, go R over a stile. Keep fence close L to reach a further stile and then go uphill past a pylon to reach a road. Turn L. The road bends R and goes on along a straight section of nearly 1km to a parking area. To R here is Roundway Down.

Things were very different at this peaceful spot on 13 July 1643, by which time the Civil War had been underway for a year. After the battle of Lansdown (at which the Cavaliers had forced the retreat of the Parliamentary troops), Sir William Waller, the Roundhead commander, received reinforcements and, on 7 July 1643, marched against the Cavaliers. The

Roundway near Devizes

Royalists were in no condition to fight again, and their commander, Sir Ralph Hopton, had been seriously wounded. They were only just able to stagger to the comparative security of Devizes with the Roundheads on their rear. Waller brought his army here onto Roundway Down in order to regroup. Hopton, apparently half blind and swathed in bandages, decided to hold the town with the infantry, while Prince Maurice, the Marquis of Hertford and the Earl of Carnavon, rode to Oxford for help.

The Roundheads, with their far larger numbers, maintained the bombardment of Devizes almost continuously for two days and nights. The Royalists' powder was nearing exhaustion; they were even melting gutters for bullets and resinating bed-cords for gun wick. Waller became over-confident, assuming that Prince Maurice's forces would be prevented from leaving Oxford. But on 13 July, 36 hours after leaving Devizes, the Prince brought some 1800 men over Morgan's Hill (the hill to the north with the radio masts). The Roundheads were trapped between the two groups of Cavaliers; Waller's infantry threw down their arms and ran. The majority of the Roundhead cavalry headed west, past where we now stand, and fell 100m (330ft) over the edge of Oliver's Castle into the 'Bloody Ditch'. The end was thus sudden and complete. To a force less than half his number, Waller had lost 1400 men, all of his cannon, all of his ammunition and all his baggage. The King at Oxford heard the news with great celebration. Meanwhile, Daniel Defoe wrote in 1724 that the people of Devizes were still calling it 'Runaway Down'.

Turn L. Ignore a gate into Roundway Hill Nature Reserve, but instead cross a stile to the R and walk around the headland of Oliver's Castle hillfort with views to the west.

> The views from this Iron Age hillfort (reputedly named after Oliver Cromwell) are fantastic, despite the often-ferocious wind. The castle itself covers some 1.4ha (3.5 acres). At one time there was a hill figure on one of the slopes, dating to 1845 and known as Snob's Horse because it had been cut by the shoemaker's apprentices, locally known as 'snobs'. There have been many attempts to re-cut the horse, but the hill is now protected as an SSSI.

The path eventually returns to a northerly direction with a fence to R. It then goes half-R through a gate. After 100m turn L at a signpost. After a short distance, the path goes to the R of a hedge and reaches a stile. Cross this and immediately turn R along a rutted, muddy track. At the end, bear L along a metalled lane that passes a house (Hill Cottage) and continues for 1.5km to reach a major cross-track. Turn L towards a golf clubhouse and cross the road. Cross the golf course via a series of white posts, which initially go slightly R and then bear L uphill with fence R. This path eventually winds round to go through a gate (and through Wansdyke) into a Nature Reserve.

Head half-R downhill towards some woodland (*not* R towards radio masts). Go through a gate and continue

Oliver's Castle

89

Originally the Wansdyke ran for 80km (50 miles) from near Inkpen to the Bristol Channel. Although much of it has gone, here on the Downs it can still be seen to be an impressive defensive work, even if the ditch and embankment are mere shadows of their former selves. No one knows what it's for or who built it. 'Experts' believe that it is a defence against attack from the north and probably post-Roman, say 5th century. At this time the Saxons held the area north of the Ridgeway, and it's possible that the Wansdyke was built by order of Ambrosius Aurelianus, the last Romano-British general, in order to hold the south and south-west against the invaders. This defence is said to have culminated in the battle of Mons Badonicus (see Walk 9 Avebury to Foxhill).

on along a rutted path through the woods. Follow the clear track with views L to the Lansdowne Monument on Cherhill Down. Follow the green road for 2km until reaching the second strip of trees to R.

This fine Roman road runs from Speen (Wickham) to Bath. From West Kennet it runs around Silbury Hill and then over this hill (Calstone Down). The road is a beautifully made turf terrace; usually about 6m (21ft) wide, but, in places, up to 9m (30ft). From Morgan's Hill, west to the hills above Bath, the Wansdyke was built on top of it.

Turn L through a pedestrian gate and on along a clear path that leads uphill to eventually go through a gate onto the top of Cherhill Down. Our way continues straight on. However, to see Oldbury hillfort, the Lansdowne Monument and the Cherhill White Horse, go L for a wander round with superb views west.

The 259m- (850ft-) high Oldbury hillfort provides views over the Avon valley and on to the Cotswolds. A nineteenth-century flint quarry lies inside. The earthworks enclose some 8ha (20 acres), and comprise double banks and ditches together with a turned entrance to make direct assault harder. It's unusual for such a large hillfort to have only one entrance, but this one is more than 30m (100ft) long and very deep. Such considerable defences suggest that this fort was of some strategic importance.

The Cherhill White Horse is in the north-west corner of the hill. The horse, the second largest in Wiltshire, is visible for 50km (30 miles), and was made by Dr Christopher Alsop, known locally as the 'mad doctor'. Supposedly he organised the workmen cutting the turf by means of a speaking trumpet from Cherhill about 2.4km (1.5 miles) away! The horse, 39.3m (129ft) long and 43.3m (142ft) high, is described as 'a typical eighteenth-century Stubbsian' beast, and faces left. The eye was originally filled with old bottles, bases up, so that it sparkled in the sun. The bottles disappeared over the years but were replaced in 1971. At various points in its life the horse has become a zebra, and has been given a 'sex-change' on several occasions!

The clue to finding the right way off Cherhill is to go back in the general direction of the path, which becomes progressively more sunken at its northern end. Keep an eye open for the route that heads in a northerly direction and downhill towards a light grey barn, a tumulus and the A4. After passing the barn, turn R at the tumulus. Bear R shortly thereafter and walk on along this Old Bath Road for 2.5km, at one point going to R of an earthwork.

In the eighteenth century the Cherhill Gang, stripped naked to avoid recognition, used to prey on folk passing along here. Eventually the locals tired of all this nonsense and set up a warning gibbet on the Cherhill-to-Beckhampton Road. Today this area is seemingly one of the most popular for crop circles, areas of flattened corn in the shape of everything from pocket watches to intricate necklaces. Recent studies suggest that 80 per

The prominent obelisk is the Lansdowne Monument, designed by Charles Barry (more famous for the Houses of Parliament), and built in 1845 for the 3rd Marquis of Lansdowne. The monument was built in memory of an ancestor Sir William Petty (1627–84). Petty was a physician, a professor of anatomy, a professor of music, an inventor, a founder of the Royal Society, a surveyor and landowner, an MP, a political economist and a statistician. The family home was Bowood Park, which can be seen in the valley due west and just south of Calne. The house and gardens, renowned for their rhododendrons and azaleas, have been open to the public since 1975. The house contains the laboratory where Joseph Priestley discovered oxygen gas.

Lansdowne Monument on Cherhill

cent of the circles are fakes (particularly the more elaborate ones) but that the rest are real and caused by some kind of disturbance in the earth's magnetic field. Curiously, 95 per cent of the world's crop circles have occurred around here.

Towards the end of this track, bear L through the centre of a stand of mature beech trees to reach a lay-by and the A4. Cross the road to a path and turn R. After 0.5km, bear L along a drive and past the gates of 'The Grange'. Take the L of two green lanes, passing a brick hut, to reach Beckhampton long barrow R covered with thicket.

Beckhampton long barrow dates from 4000–3500 BC, and is the first of

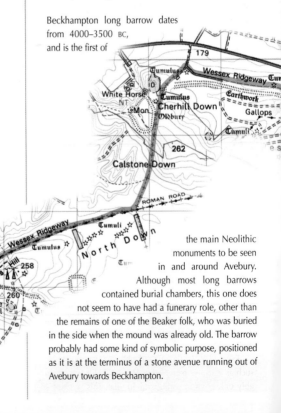

the main Neolithic monuments to be seen in and around Avebury. Although most long barrows contained burial chambers, this one does not seem to have had a funerary role, other than the remains of one of the Beaker folk, who was buried in the side when the mound was already old. The barrow probably had some kind of symbolic purpose, positioned as it is at the terminus of a stone avenue running out of Avebury towards Beckhampton.

The path bears R with the standing stones that mark the Beckhampton Stone Avenue in the field ahead. Our path becomes a metalled lane with the standing stones (called Adam and Eve) L and Windmill Hill, with its prominent tumuli, beyond.

Beckhampton Avenue was a ceremonial line of stones (Adam and Eve are the only remaining members) extending from the main Avebury stone circle west-wards, and erected *c.* 2400 BC. Windmill Hill, however, is likely to have been occupied by early Neolithic communities as long ago as 3700 BC. At this time, most of the surrounding country would

have been densely wooded; the hill may have been one of the few clear-ings and a focus of communal activity. The second phase of development (now called the Windmill Hill period), from 3500 to 3000 BC, saw the digging of three enclo-sures with ditches (the causeways) encircling 8.5ha (21 acres). There was a third phase, in the later Neolithic, when the hill was used less frequently, and by the time of the Bronze Age (1500–800 BC), the hill wasn't used as a camp, although a number of round barrows were built on it.

Excavation has shown that only temporary buildings, such as tents, were erected on Windmill Hill, and prob-ably only used in spring and autumn. This was not a place of permanent occupation, but one for trading and celebratory feasts. It's thought that animals were brought here from a wide area for dealing and butchering. At these times the people used pottery (Windmill Hill culture is noted for its round-based and rather 'sagging' pottery), built fires, made flint tools and ground flour on quern-stones. Animal skins were made into clothes, tents and thongs. There was also some burial of rubbish; animal and even human bones; skulls and long bones seem particularly popular, suggesting a kind of ceremonial purpose. A number of pits have also been found; filled with specially placed flints, stones and pottery, perhaps the remnants of sacred meals that have been ritually interred. Thus Windmill Hill may have had similar purpose to the later stone henges: a meeting point for widely dispersed communities, with an economic, ceremonial and symbolic role. But we must remember that Avebury and its related sites came into being because the Ridgeway was already there – and not vice versa.

Eventually the lane enters Avebury Trusloe with houses L and R. After a short distance, go L past two barriers and along a metalled path to reach a road. Go straight on to take a path to L of a green barn and to R of Manor Farm. Cross a stile and go half-L through a gate. Continue to another gate and follow a fenced path, over a bridge and into Avebury churchyard. Bear R through a lych-gate and turn L along Avebury High St. Within a short distance, we reach the centre of the village with a post office, the Red Lion pub, a few shops, visitor attractions and, of course, the Avebury stone circle.

Avebury was first recognised as a prehistoric site by the antiquarian John Aubrey in 1649, who recorded many of the features and even attracted the interest of Charles II, who came see it on his way to Bath in 1663. Aubrey considered Avebury to be the premier ancient site in Britain, and wrote that, 'It does as much exceed in greatness the so renowned Stonehenge, as a cathedral doeth a parish Church'. Regrettably, by the time William

Stukeley worked on Avebury (1719–24), the previously well-preserved circles had been desecrated by local builders who broke up the stones and dragged them off for use as building materials.

However, it wasn't until Alexander Keiller (heir to a Dundee marmalade fortune and keen archaeologist) bought the site that the stones were properly investigated. Keiller began excavation and restoration along the West Kennet Avenue in 1934–5. Stones were found, unearthed and restored to their original places. He found vast burning pits where stones had been plundered in the seventeenth and eighteenth centuries, and marked these with concrete posts.

Avebury is one of the largest stone circles in the

Avebury Stone Circle – Stone 10

Take a tour round the stone circle before continuing on along the Ridgeway. Start by visiting the National Trust's Alexander Keiller Museum, Avebury Manor, a shop and café. The manor is an Elizabethan house that was built on the site of an ancient priory. There are some fine gardens, with excellent topiary, a dovecote, and an eighteenth-century wishing well. There's also a great thatched threshing barn that contains an exhibition of crafts by the Wiltshire Folk Life Society. The church, significantly, lies outside the stone circle. Some authors suggest that Avebury was resistant to the new teachings of Christianity, and that when the village did finally 'succumb', the local clergy set out to deliberately suppress any lingering pagan beliefs. Much of the Avebury complex has been named after the Devil, and imagery on the font in →

world: 427m (1401ft) in diameter, and covering 11.5ha (28 acres). Originally the ditch was 6.7m (18ft) deep with vertical sides and a flat base. With the addition of the surrounding bank, rising to about 15m (50ft), the effect would have been even greater. It would also, of course, been gleaming white chalk. Enclosed within the bank and ditch were 98 standing stones in a circle. Another 27 stones formed a smaller north circle, 29 stones formed a south circle, and 12 made a Z-shaped feature. The stones, of which only 27 still remain in place, were dragged from the nearby Marlborough Downs and, unlike those at Stonehenge, were left rough. Each weighs about 40 tons or more. Although undated by modern methods, the site dates to between 2600 and 2400 BC, roughly contemporary with the first and second phases of Stonehenge. And just like Stonehenge, the process of construction is impressive, involving around 1.5 million man-hours. Some of the local chambered tombs are much older and would also have necessitated the transportation and erection of huge stones.

Most people agree that the great stone circle formed a kind of temple or religious centre for the Neolithic farmers of the Wiltshire Downs. It was here, perhaps, that they celebrated spring and harvest festivals, made laws and dispensed justice. William Stukeley suggested that the monuments formed a 'solar serpent' with The Sanctuary circle (see later) as the head, the West Kennet and Beckhampton Avenues as the body, and the Avebury circle, symbolising the sun, at its centre. Others think that Avebury was just a big burial ground, or linked with the Druids (who actually arrived in Britain a couple of millennia later). Another theory suggests that it was an astronomical calendar. Further mystical stuff has one of the longest ley lines in the country stretching from Land's End through Avebury and on to Bury St Edmunds. In a variation of this, it's said that 'Michael energy' runs through the village and many people believe that Avebury was, and still is, 'the energy centre of England'.

The Avebury stone circle is only one part of a much larger complex of Neolithic monuments. At the southern entrance of the main circle the West Kennet Avenue leads across the fields and up to the top of Overton Hill just over 1.5km (1 mile) away. The avenue originally consisted of 100 pairs of standing stones, approximately 15m (50ft) apart. It is magnificently wide and straight, with real sense of grandeur and ceremonial purpose. At the end of the Avenue, and not far from the official start of the Ridgeway National Trail, is another stone circle known as The Sanctuary. Originally there may have been some circular wooden-roofed buildings here, pre-dating the stone circles at Avebury. Then the Beaker people demolished the wooden buildings in favour of two concentric rings of sarsens. All this work would have been contemporary with the laying out of the West Kennet Avenue. William Stukeley named The Sanctuary in 1720, but in 1724 a builder broke up the stones. Concrete pillars now mark where stone holes have been found, while those holding wooden posts have been marked by round pillars. It seems likely that The Sanctuary was built for religious purposes.

A little to the west along the A4 stands another great enigma: Silbury Hill, the largest man-made mound in Europe, about 40m (130ft) high and covering just over 2ha (5 acres). If it were put in Trafalgar Square, it would nearly fill it and reach three-quarters of the way up Nelson's Column. In addition, the hill is surrounded by a ditch, dug out to construct the mound, and originally 38m (125ft) wide and 9m (30ft) deep. Excavations in

← the church perhaps refers to the battle between the serpent of the pagan temple at Avebury and the new Christianity.

The most notable stones in the circle include the Swindon Stone (the largest at 60 tons), the Devil's Chair and the Repaired Stone. The most famous is the Barber's Stone. When Keiller was resurrecting it in 1938, he found the skeleton of a man underneath. It appeared that he was a travelling barber-surgeon from the fourteenth century. The general view is that he was helping to move the stone when it fell and crushed him. His bones can be viewed in the museum.

Avebury Stone Circle – the Barber Stone

1968–70 suggest a date of 2500 BC – about the same age as the stone circle – but nobody is certain exactly why Silbury Hill was constructed. Legends and tales about its possible purpose abound: we can at least assume that it is the mound itself that is important as some kind of tribal marker or cenotaph (an empty tomb; a sepulchral monument to honour someone whose body is actually somewhere else).

How it was built is also a matter for discussion. Myth tells us that there was once a quarrel between the people of Marlborough and Devizes. The Devil agreed to help Marlborough by dropping a pile of earth onto Devizes. The people of Devizes appealed to St John for help and, following his advice, an elderly man carrying a sack of old boots went out to meet the Devil. The Devil, with a heavy load of earth, was in a foul temper when he met the old man, and asked him the distance to Devizes. The old man said that he had left there three years previously, and showed the sack of boots that he'd apparently worn out on the way, whereupon the Devil dropped his load of earth in anger and vanished. Thus, according to legend, was Silbury Hill formed. Archaeologists, of course, disagree. They've calculated that some 18 million man-hours went into building the hill; that is to say, 700 men working for 10 years, making Silbury one of the most labour-intensive projects in prehistoric Europe at a time when the Marlborough Downs had a population of just 10,000, with as many as 50,000 in the whole of Wessex.

Just to the south of Silbury is the West Kennet long barrow, one of the largest in Britain, measuring 100m (328ft) long and 2m (6.5ft) high. It contained 46 burials, including 12 children. The barrow was probably in use from 3700 BC and the entrance finally closed, using a huge standing sarsen flanked by smaller ones, by the Beaker people around 2200 BC. The final Beaker burial was of an elderly man in a crouched position. It has been suggested that some highly respected priestly dynasty was interred at West Kennet, attracting pilgrims from as far away as the Mediterranean… and from places along the Great Ridgeway! ←

East Kennet long barrow can be found about 1.5km (1 mile) to the south-west. It's covered with scrub and has never been excavated, even though it's just as big as West Kennet. The presence of sarsen stones at its east end might indicate a similar plan and purpose to its better-known neighbour.

PART 2: THE RIDGEWAY NATIONAL TRAIL

Stage 9: Avebury to Fox Hill

Start:	Avebury
Finish:	Fox Hill
Distance:	25.7km (16 miles)
OS:	Landrangers 173 Swindon & Devizes, 174 Newbury & Wantage
Route Features:	Remote country
Information:	Tourist Information Centres: Marlborough (01672 513989); Swindon (01793 530328)

Avebury is comparatively well served with buses (the Swindon-to-Devizes bus being just one); the stop is opposite the Red Lion. Fox Hill has a Thamesdown service between Swindon and Marlborough. With one change it is therefore possible to link the two ends of this section. There's a pub at about half way at Ogbourne St George and, in summer months, some kind of refreshment at Barbury Castle Country Park.

Smeathe's Ridge

If you walk along the path straight on here, you will, after 7km (4.5 miles) arrive in Marlborough. This fine town has one of the widest main streets in the country, enclosed by some splendid Georgian buildings and colonnaded shops. It also has Marlborough College, the public school built in 1843 on the site of an old castle. In the grounds is the Silbury-like mound called Maerl's Barrow, which gives the town its name.

Walk along the High St and past the Red Lion. Continue straight on and out of the village along Green St. This road becomes a path (the Herepath – a Saxon army road) and winds gradually up hill for a further 2.5km to reach the junction with the Ridgeway National Trail. This is well marked with a series of National Trail notice boards. Turn L.

This is Overton Down and we're now on the Ridgeway National Trail. The official start is in a rather unprepossessing car park on the A4 about 3km to the right. The Hobhouse Committee first muted the idea of a Ridgeway National Trail in 1947; this original proposal covered what we now also call the Wessex Ridgeway, and ran from the Chiltern Ridge to reach the sea at Seaton Bay. In 1956 Tom Stephenson submitted an even longer route, from Cambridge to Seaton Bay. The National Parks Commission considered this and, in 1962, came up with a proposal that was, more or less,

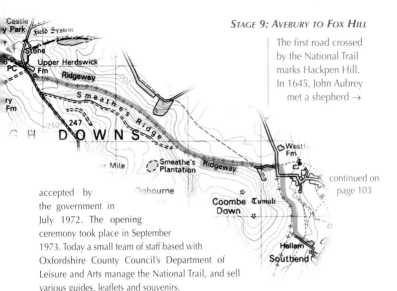

The first road crossed
by the National Trail
marks Hackpen Hill.
In 1645, John Aubrey
met a shepherd →

continued on
page 103

accepted by
the government in
July 1972. The opening
ceremony took place in September
1973. Today a small team of staff based with
Oxfordshire County Council's Department of
Leisure and Arts manage the National Trail, and sell
various guides, leaflets and souvenirs.

Follow the clear path for 4km to a country lane. Cross
straight over.

We're walking through some of the most ancient landscape in the country: a land littered with prehistoric sites
and large, curious stones, known as sarsens. It was these
stones that were used to build Avebury and Stonehenge.
The word 'sarsen' is thought to derive from 'saracen'
(meaning foreigner), as sarsen or saracen stones were
believed to have appeared by foreign magic. In fact,
these boulders which litter Fyfield Down are all that
remains, after erosion and glaciation, of a swaddling cap
of Tertiary sandstone that lay over the chalk. Sarsens are
also known locally as 'grey wethers', as from a distance
they look a bit like sheep; a wether is a castrated ram.
Freshly broken sarsen has a warm honey-colour similar
to Cotswold stone, but dulls to grey over time. There are
numerous round barrows on the Down, built for the
nobility, together with the, perhaps more proletarian,
non-barrow cemeteries. There are also extensive field
systems. Excavations on the Down have uncovered

← from Winterbourne
Bassett who claimed
that some fairies once
took him into an
underground cavern
just here on Hackpen.
The Hackpen White
Horse can be found on
the north-western
scarp, cut into the
chalk to celebrate
Queen Victoria's coro-
nation in 1838. It's on
the side of the hill just
a short distance down
the road to the left.
A better view, if
somewhat more
distant, can be had
from the A4361 near
Winterbourne Bassett.

successive layers of agriculture from Neolithic times right up to the third and fourth centuries AD.

The clear path continues for 2.5km to another small road. Don't take the lower path that goes straight on, but turn R and then, after 30m, L through a gate to head up the slope of Barbury Castle. Cross the centre of the hillfort and out through a gate. Walk on with fence R to a second gate and the information centre, car park and toilets.

It's worth noting that the L-hand path is the true route of the Ridgeway, marked on the OS map and running south of Chiseldon and along some metalled roads, north of Liddington Castle. The National Trail – our path – takes a much longer and more rural route. Barbury Castle stands at some 268m (880ft) on a spur of the Downs overlooking the valley of the River Ray. These great hill-forts are thought to have been sited to command the Ridgeway and to defend against attack from the north. The Ridgeway was an important trade route for the Beaker people, and had to be protected; although cultural links with Brittany may have made them feel

Ridgeway mud in April, Foxhill

secure to the south, they were vulnerable to the north. The camps of Barbury, Liddington, Hardwell (on Woolstone Hill), Uffington, Rams Hill, Letcombe and Blewburton all commanded positions to the north. Edward Thomas, in one of his more poetic moments, described the Ridgeway from here to Streatley as a 'battlement walk of superhuman majesty'.

The battle of Barbury Hill, fought on the slopes just below the hillfort, took place in or around AD 556 when the vestiges of the Romanised British were trying to repel the Saxons. The British commander Vortigern had invited the first Saxons into Britain as mercenaries, and they later rebelled. Some time around AD 500 a Saxon tribe, the Gewisse, had occupied the Hampshire valleys. By 552, led by Cynric, they had taken Salisbury, before moving on to defeat the British here at Barbury in 556. Saxon Cæwlin, who had brought the West Saxon forces from the Thames valley, joined Cynric. Exactly what happened next is not known, but Cæwlin went on to become ruler of both the Gewisse and the West Saxons. It was, therefore, on these slopes, that the foundations of the kingdom of Wessex were laid; and it was this Wessex of Alfred and Athelstan that formed the basis of what we now call England. There are better and bigger hillforts, archaeologically more important sites, and strategically more significant hilltops, but Barbury has a unique charm and wonder, and, in summer, usually has an ice-cream van.

From the car park, go out onto the narrow, metalled road and turn R. The road passes Upper Herdswick Farm and becomes a rough track. Shortly after the farm, take the sign-posted track L along a broad path, forking L to continue over grassland onto Smeathe's Ridge.

continued on page 104

The splendid vale on the left as we walk into Ogbourne St George was littered with army buildings left over from World War II. The red-brick dereliction stretched for over 1.5km north up to Lower Herdswick Farm in the near distance.

Follow the wheel ruts to a gate. The path then descends slightly into a dip. Bear L here to a gate and continue on to another gate below a reservoir.

Continue through a further gate to a road. Turn R. After 100m, the road goes sharp L into Ogbourne St George.

Ogbourne St George has a pub, The Old Crown, and a manor house on the site of an old priory (a short distance from the well-hidden parish church). The pub is on the far side of the village – walk all the way through (about 1.4km/0.9 miles) and turn left at a T-junction. If you don't fancy the walk back, leave the pub and turn left. Continue along this straight road to the main road. Turn right and walk on for about 200m to a minor road

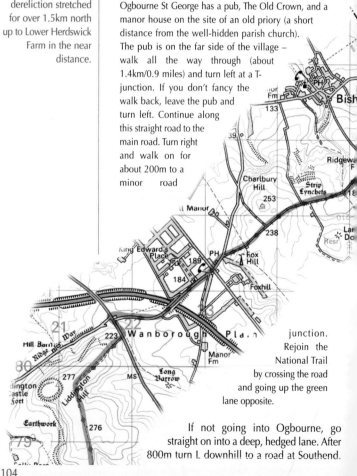

junction. Rejoin the National Trail by crossing the road and going up the green lane opposite.

If not going into Ogbourne, go straight on into a deep, hedged lane. After 800m turn L downhill to a road at Southend.

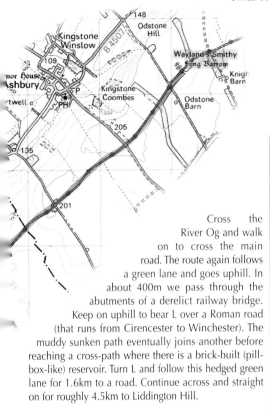

Cross the River Og and walk on to cross the main road. The route again follows a green lane and goes uphill. In about 400m we pass through the abutments of a derelict railway bridge. Keep on uphill to bear L over a Roman road (that runs from Cirencester to Winchester). The muddy sunken path eventually joins another before reaching a cross-path where there is a brick-built (pill-box-like) reservoir. Turn L and follow this hedged green lane for 1.6km to a road. Continue across and straight on for roughly 4.5km to Liddington Hill.

Liddington Hill, at 277m (909ft), has a commanding position and its Iron Age hillfort must have been formidable. The view was apparently a favourite one of local authors Richard Jefferies (keen naturalist) and Alfred Williams (poet and essayist). Jefferies was one of the first 'country diary' writers, and died from TB at the age of just 38. He once said that up here on Liddington he was 'utterly alone with the sun and the earth'. Whether he'd still say that is perhaps open to question: Swindon lies in the valley below. The town owes its origins to the Great Western Railway, and although the related works

Edward Thomas called Fox Hill Totterdown, a name which seems to have disappeared from the current range of OS maps. The Shepherd's Rest public house was originally a place where shepherds rested, and is said to be 500 years old. Luckily walkers are very welcome.

have been made into museums, other businesses have taken their place. It's a major growth area, helped by both the rail connections and the ever-raucous M4.

Many people believe Liddington Hill to be the site of the battle of Mons Badonicus, where Arthur defeated the Saxons. Fifty years after the end of Roman occupation, in the late 460s, the country was in a mess. Civil war between the native, largely Romanised Britains, and the Saxons went on for years, with the Saxon advance aided by fresh landings along the south coast. But there was a major halt to their progress when the British rallied under a leader called Ambrosius Aurelianus. At the end of the century (c. 490–9) a major victory at a place called Mons Badonicus heralded a generation of relative peace and order. The battle itself was probably more of a siege than open plain warfare, with either the Britons or the Saxons occupying a hilltop. According to a statement in the Historia Britonum, in a single charge the British killed 960 of the enemy, who were then defeated. A British victory over the advancing Saxons undoubtedly happened. But who lead the British forces, and where is Mons Badonicus?

Welsh tradition gives the commander's name as Arthur, a relative of and successor to Ambrosius. In reality, Arthur was not so much a king as a military commander for a number of kingdoms, and there's no mention of the round table or Guinevere or Lancelot. But, if Arthur did exist, this battle could be where the legend began: the successful defence of a beleaguered population. But was Liddington Castle the site of the battle? No one really knows.

The path bears R (north-east) and goes through a gate and down to a minor road. Turn L and take the next road R which goes over the M4. The route now rejoins the original course of the Ridgeway (as opposed to the National Trail). Continue to a crossroad (a junction with the Ermine Way Roman road between Silchester, Cirencester and Bath) and go straight on to the Shepherd's Rest.

Stage 10: Fox Hill to Scutchamer Knob

Start:	Fox Hill
Finish:	Scutchamer Knob
Distance:	25.6km (15.9 miles)
OS:	Landranger 174 Newbury & Wantage
Route Features:	Remote country
Information:	Tourist Information Centres: Wantage (01235 760176); Vale and Downland Museum and Visitor Centre in Wantage (01235 771447)

Fox Hill (or Foxhill) has a regular bus service to either Swindon or Marlborough. Scutchamer Knob, however, is some 3.2km (2 miles) uphill from the nearest village of East Hendred. East Hendred has a shop, pubs and buses, but you should allow for the extra miles. There are no facilities on the path, but there are pubs in a succession of villages about 1.5km (1 mile) or so to the north: Bishopstone, Ashbury, Woolstone, Kingston Lisle and, a little further on, Sparsholt and Letcombe Regis.

From the Shepherd's Rest, continue up the road. After about 200m, bear R through a parking area and out onto the downs. Our route is now a clear easterly one for over 40km (24.5 miles). The immediate objective, however, is Ridgeway Farm in approximately 2.5km, and a minor road from the village of Bishopstone.

About 0.8km after Ridgeway Farm, we enter Oxfordshire. About 2.5km after Ridgeway Farm we reach the B4000. (Turn L for Ashbury in 0.8km, or R for Ashdown House in 1.5km, and Lambourn a lot further on).

Ashbury no doubt owes its position to springs gushing from the chalk. Ridgeway travellers would have been keenly aware of available water sources on what otherwise would have been a very dry journey. The village

To the north (L) as we walk away from Fox Hill is Charlbury Hill. On the eastern side of the hill, and visible from a spot opposite a bridleway going R, are a series of strip lynchets or ancient field systems. Lynchets were formed through continuous ploughing around the contour to produce flat, cultivable terraces, and probably date to the late Bronze Age. This particular set consists of seven steps about 4.5m (15ft) wide and up to 4.2m (14ft) deep.

Ashdown House, to the south-east, was built in 1625 by a nephew of Inigo Jones for William, Earl of Craven, and described as 'the perfect doll's house' by Nikolaus Pevsner. In 1632, the Earl of Craven went to fight for Frederick V, King of Bohemia. There he met and fell for Charles I's sister (James I's daughter), the beautiful Elizabeth of Bohemia (aka 'The Wrater Queen' or 'The Queen of Hearts'. Although some say that he was an unre-quited lover, after her husband died she lived in Craven's house in Drury Lane until her death in 1662. He is said to have 'consecrated' Ashdown House to her. Ashdown House is now under the stewardship of the National Trust, but is infrequently open.

still offers liquid refreshment at the pub. On Swinley Down, just to the south, is a hillfort known as Alfred's Castle; it's quite small, but probably played a role in keeping open the lines of communication between the major forts. There is no evidence that the place was associated with King Alfred, but it does guard the road to the village of Baydon, which is situated on an area of high ground some 4km south. Some suggest that this, and not Liddington, is the site of battle of Badon Hill.

Just over 0.8km after the B4000, the path reaches Wayland's Smithy.

Wayland's Smithy

Wayland's Smithy is a Neolithic long barrow. Beneath the visible upper mound is a timber chamber covered with earth and faced with sarsens, built around 2800 BC. Fifteen skeletons were found here, and it appears that before interment the bodies were left to decompose or be eaten. The bones were then separated and the skulls arranged in ritualistic manner with food, pottery and flint tools. The Severn-Cotswold-type barrow was built later, on top of the original, with four large sarsens to mark the entrance. This barrow contained three stone-lined chambers and held the remains of eight people. Some Windmill Hill pottery has been found here.

'Wayland' can be traced in many cultures: Anglo-Saxon, Old English, Icelandic and Old French. The favourite tale seems to be that after the arrival of Christianity, Wayland, a Scandinavian god, was forced to shoe horses, but was never seen doing it. If a traveller's mount needed to be shod, the owner left the horse and a groat by the barrow and went away. Overnight the animal would be shod; if the horse owner tried to watch, nothing would happen. It's also said that if iron bars are left at the Smithy they're turned into horseshoes. Apparently when the site was first investigated some iron bars were found but, sadly, no horseshoes. Sir Walter Scott popularised these legends in 1821 in his novel *Kenilworth*. Wayland is also said to have shod the Uffington White Horse.

Uffington white horse

Until about 200 years ago, the Ridgeway was a much wider group of tracks, running along the top of the Downs or down in the valley on our left (where runs the western end of the Icknield Way). Various Enclosure Acts between 1750 and 1800 prescribed the line and width of the Ridgeway. For most parishes this was 12m (40ft), although in some parts it was as much as 20m (66ft). The banks and hedges that border the route date mostly from this time, and prevented driven animals from straying.

Continue in the same direction to a small road with Compton Beauchamp to L.

Compton Beauchamp has an Elizabethan manor house with a moat, gardens and terraced lawns. The hill just before the village is Woolstone Hill complete with small hillfort, Hardwell Camp.

We cross another small road (turn L for NT car park and, after nearly 2km, the village of Woolstone). The Ridgeway now goes uphill to the top of Whitehorse Hill. To visit Uffington Castle and the White Horse, go through the gate L.

The White Horse at Uffington is one of the most famous chalk hill figures in the country. Part of its attraction is that it is more abstract in

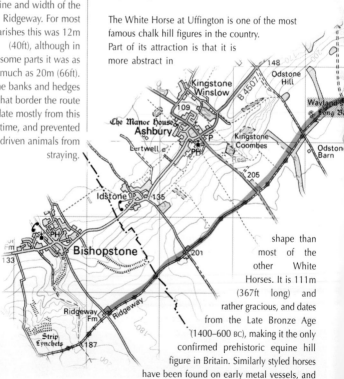

shape than most of the other White Horses. It is 111m (367ft long) and rather gracious, and dates from the Late Bronze Age (1400–600 BC), making it the only confirmed prehistoric equine hill figure in Britain. Similarly styled horses have been found on early metal vessels, and coins from the Early Iron Age Atrebate tribe show a similar design. A small, bronze horse of similar design was found at Silchester, south of Reading, the capital of the Atrebates. However a coin of the Dobunni (a Gloucester tribe) was found in Uffington Castle, which some think may link the horse with them.

The figure isn't terribly easy to see except from a distance or, indeed, from the air, and as a result its existence has been subject to all kind of alien or cosmic

The horse needs frequent rescouring to keep it white and to avoid weed growth. Today the National Trust does it, but in earlier times it was down to the people of Uffington, an event associated with all kinds of games and jollification.

theories. It is possible too that the horse was once lower down the slope and thus easier to see; an aerial view suggests that there is a darker area some 4.5m below the figure which implies the original shape. There are a number of theories and stories associated with the horse: it is, for example, considered lucky to wish while standing on the horse's eye. One of the more feasible reasons for its existence is its possible connection with a Celtic mythological culture called Tara. In this goddesses bearing the attributes of horses were prominent, and it is suggested that the Uffington figure was some kind of sacred site dedicated to this Celtic myth.

continued on
page 112

The view from the White Horse is spectacular. The cone-shaped mound just down in the valley is Dragon Hill, either after King Arthur's father, Uther Pendragon, or because this was where St George slayed his particular fire-breathing monster. There is a patch of bare chalk on the top that has been soaked with the doomed beast's blood, and on which grass never grows. The village below us is Uffington, marked by the fine thirteenth-century church known as 'The Cathedral of the Vale'. Uffington is most famous for two literary residents. Thomas Hughes wrote *Tom Brown's Schooldays*; he was born here and is buried in the churchyard. The village hall is called the Thomas Hughes

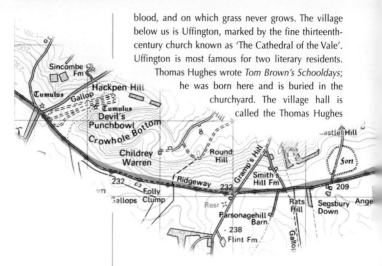

Memorial Hall, and the old school houses Tom Brown's School Museum (enquiries tel: 01367 820259). John Betjeman lived at Garrards Farm in Uffington with his wife Penelope just after their marriage in 1933. The Betjemans soon immersed themselves in village life, and their son, Paul, was born here in 1937. John Betjeman travelled up to London by train from, the now closed, Uffington Station, before moving to Farnborough in 1945. Uffington Hill also affords a view over Didcot Power Station, away to the north-east.

Back on the Ridgeway continue along the broad path east to a road.

About 1.5km (1 mile) after Uffington is Rams Hill, just off track to the right, a hillfort built around an earlier, possibly 1500 BC Bronze Age enclosure. The road we reach is Blowingstone Hill. To the north (about 1.5km/1 mile) is Kingston Lisle. About half way down the hill can be found the famous blowing stone (a sarsen stone brought down from White Horse Hill) in the garden of a cottage. If you stuff your face into a hole in the top and blow, you get a deep, raspberry noise. It's claimed that King Alfred, amongst others, used it to summon fighting men from the surrounding countryside. If all that blowing makes you thirsty, there's The Blowing Stone Inn (well signposted) which serves meals and has accommodation.

The clear track continues for 2.5km. Just after a trig point in a field L, there is a drinking water tap L. We eventually join a minor road from Sparsholt (2.5km). Bear R along this and, where it joins the B4001, go straight ahead on to the broad Ridgeway path.

Sparsholt's Star Inn is a 400-year-old pub with accommodation, set in the heart of this prime horseracing country. When James Edmund Vincent passed this way in 1906, he was able to find some locals who could remember the days when coal came by wagon from South Wales along the Ridgeway. Apparently the residents of the many villages down in the valley sent their teams up to the Ridgeway to fetch it.

The way continues for more than 3km through areas used for gallops. Cross the next road (go L for Letcombe Bassett).

The view to the left opens out beautifully, with a splendidly deep coombe known as the Devil's Punchbowl. Welcome to Letcombe Bassett, the village nestling down the hill to the left (north), renamed 'Cresscomb' by Hardy in *Jude the Obscure*, presumably because the brook was once known for its watercress. The seventeenth-century Old Rectory, with its early fifteenth-century thatched barn, also has literary associations: Dean Swift, author of *Gulliver's Travels*, spent his last summer in England here before going to Ireland in 1714. Alexander Pope visited him in his rectory garden on one occasion. More recently the racehorse trainer Capt Tim Forster trained three Grand National winners in Letcombe: Well to Do in 1972; Ben Nevis in 1980; and Last Suspect in 1985.

Excavations at the nearby Seven Barrows (south of here, near Lambourn) have revealed that the man-made barrows have sheltered the underlying natural chalk from weathering. As a result the base rock under the barrow is some 60cm (2ft) higher than the surrounding downland, implying that some 60cm of the downs have been washed away since Neolithic times. This may not surprise those tackling the route in winter months.

Beyond Letcombe Basset is Letcombe Regis, the latter a Royal manor of the kings of Wessex, where various kings had hunting lodges. Antwicks Manor, once an ancient moat house, was rebuilt as a neo-Elizabethan mansion at the end of the nineteenth century by one 'Boss' Croker, who had made fortune in New York. It was the headquarters of his racing stables. It's also where, in the early 1900s, the Riot Act was read for the last time in England following an incident in which a 'blazing effigy' of a later owner was driven up to the manor gates. There's also a pub, the Greyhound.

About 0.8km on, a track goes L (again to Letcombe) but the Ridgeway trail goes straight on to Segsbury Farm (where there is a track L which cuts across the middle of Segsbury – or Letcombe – Castle in the direction of Letcombe Regis).

Segsbury Castle (Segsbury Camp or Letcombe Castle) is an Iron Age camp, enclosing about 10ha (25 acres). Segsbury is a 2,300-year-old settlement with round houses, pits and other features which remain deep in the chalk, safe from damage by modern ploughing. The Oxfordshire Village Book tells the story of a great battle just here, in which the blood from the resulting massacre streamed down Castle Hill. The people in the village below shouted 'Let the blood come! Let it come! Let come!' – and so Letcombe was named.

Our way continues straight on to reach Manor Road. Turn L for Wantage (3.2km) and Court Hill Ridgeway Centre – a hostel and field studies centre (tel: 012357 60253)).

In the late eighteenth century Wantage was known as 'Black Wantage'. The industrial revolution had

brought ruin to the small local factories and mills; unem-
ployed workers, coupled with itinerant canal navvies
and others, turned Wantage into a pretty scandalous
place. Now-adays, Wantage is really quite pleasant, with
a number of shops and hostelries, and known primarily
as the birthplace of Alfred the Great. Lester Piggott, too,
was born here in 1935.

Alfred became King of Wessex in AD 871. He spent
the next seven years fighting the invading Vikings, before
facing complete defeat. He took refuge at Athelney in
Wiltshire, rallied his forces, and routed the Danes at
Eddington. Alfred's diplomacy at this time is seen as
masterly. His army was never strong enough to defeat
the Danes, but they agreed to sign the Treaty of
Wedmore in 878. The Danish leader accepted
Christianity and withdrew his armies to a line beyond
Watling Street. Although marked by a number of skir-
mishes (including Alfred's taking of London) there
followed a period of peace, during which Alfred rebuilt
churches, founded schools and applied himself to his
studies. He firmed up the defence of the country with a
network of garrison towns (burhs). He founded a navy.
He established the first common code of law. He developed a body of literature through translation and new
works including the Anglo-Saxon Chronicle. He died in
899 leaving a well run and united
country. His successors,
Edward the Elder and
Athelstan, were
then able

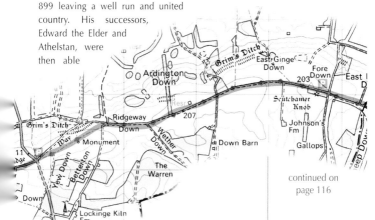

continued on
page 116

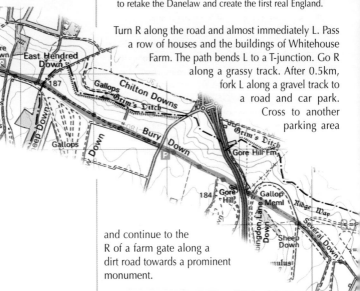

to retake the Danelaw and create the first real England.

Turn R along the road and almost immediately L. Pass a row of houses and the buildings of Whitehouse Farm. The path bends L to a T-junction. Go R along a grassy track. After 0.5km, fork L along a gravel track to a road and car park. Cross to another parking area and continue to the R of a farm gate along a dirt road towards a prominent monument.

> The Wantage Monument is said to be an exact copy of a fifteenth-century cross in Florence. Local landowner Robert Loyd-Lindsay became Baron of Wantage in 1885. He fought at the battle of the River Alma in the Crimean War, and was again 'conspicuous for his courage' at Inkerman, and was awarded the Victoria Cross. He went on to be an MP and was prominent in the founding of the Red Cross. He was also founder of the University College at Reading, and was said to have been a benevolent landowner for his time.

Continue along the broad track to a point where the route takes a slight turn R. The Ridgeway then continues east with East Ginge Down to L. The route passes a drinking water tap and goes on past a prominent reservoir (the Ridgeway Reservoir) L to a point where a bridleway joins from the L in front of a stand of trees.

> The Ridgeway is amazingly wide at this point, perhaps

30m (98ft) or so, airy and lofty and remote. Just on the other side of the gate near the bridleway sign and to the left is a sarsen stone with a plaque in memory of Lady Penelope Betjeman. If you, as a walker, remonstrate about the incursion of 4x4 vehicles up and along the Ridgeway, old Sir John was complaining about it in 1948! He described how, even before World War II, the track was getting boggy and worn by tourists 'too lazy to get out of their motor cars and walk'. The trouble is that where there was once the odd lightweight Austin 7 or even the heavyweight Rolls-Royce, there is now the multitude of mud-churning and macho 'All-Terrain' vehicles. In the mid-1970s, Betjeman supported moves by Oxfordshire County Council to ban motor vehicles completely from the stretch of Ridgeway between Uffington Castle and the B4001. This move was, sadly, unsuccessful.

There are various paths running left (north) from here to the small villages 3.5km (2.2 miles) away at the bottom of the hill: Ardington, Lockinge, West Ginge and West Hendred. Early eighteenth-century Ardington House is the home of the Baring family and open to the public several times a year, principally in May and August (tel: 01235 821566). It was once owned by Robert Vernon, born poor in 1774, who, by selling and hiring horses to the army, made himself a fortune. He then bought Ardington House and began amassing a fine

Penelope Betjeman's sarsen

East Ginge and the surrounding downs are littered with gallops, and if you're coming along here in the early morning you're likely to see a line of fine thoroughbreds going through their paces. Many of the villages hereabouts have racing stables, and East Hendred's Turnell stable had a Grand National winner, Maori Venture, in 1987.

art collection. Ardington also has a craft centre and the Boars Head pub, dating back some 400 years. Lord Wantage built a model farm and village at Lockinge, and resided there in Lockinge House. The estate was both employer and landowner and the village has the feel of control.

Continue onwards into an area of woodland atop Cuckhamsley Hill where there is a small parking area.

Scutchamer Knob (Cuckhamsley Hill, Scotchman's Knob or Scutchamfly Barrow) is a rather anonymous spot, comprising a slight bank coated in trees that were

The Wantage Monument

planted in 1965. However, there is evidence that this was once a major landmark and a prominent meeting place, or moot, for the men of Berkshire. Richard Colt Hoare measured it in 1819 as some 149m (490ft) in circumference and 23.5m (77ft) high; it was clearly much more impressive in days of yore. Some say that this was the burial place of Cwicchelm, the great Saxon king who died in 593. The place then became known as Cwicchelmshlaew – perhaps Cuckhamsley Hill? The Danes under King Sweyn are said to have gathered here in 1006, after ransacking Wallingford. The alternative Scutchamer name is said to derive from an old word for someone who beat out (or scutched) flax into a workable fibre. We do know that in the fifteenth and sixteenth centuries there was an 'almost' daily market for 'corn, victuals and other merchandise goods' here, prohibited when East Ilsley market was sanctioned in 1620. There was also a kind of cloth fair held here by the good peoples of the Hendreds in the valley below to our left.

The Hendreds are either named from the Welsh word hendre, a house used by farmers during the winter, or from the Anglo-Saxon hennerithe or waterhen brook. East Hendred, with village shop and a couple of pubs, can be reached by going left along what is called the 'Golden Mile', for, interestingly, about 3.2km (2 miles!). The Eyston family, related to Sir Thomas More, has occupied East Hendred manor house since 1453, and they also paid for the Victorian-Gothic church. In Thomas More's time the village was an important centre for the wool trade. A number of the old cottages, including that which now houses the shop and post office, date from that time.

Stage 11: Scutchamer Knob to Mongewell

William Cobbett was no great fan of the Berkshire Downs, describing them as 'very bad land and a very ugly country', but he clearly missed the sense of space, which is intoxicating. It's joyful walking country that was once well known for its hares and, sadly, its hare coursing. If you're lucky, hen harrier and marsh harrier can be seen, and buzzards visit regularly. The hobby and short-eared owl are also here.

Start:	Scutchamer Knob
Finish:	Mongewell
Distance:	24.5km (15.3 miles)
OS:	Landrangers 174 Newbury & Wantage, 175 Reading & Windsor
Route Features:	Remote country
Information:	Tourist Information Centre: Wallingford (01491 826972)

The Ridgeway at Scutchamer Knob is some 3.2km (2 miles) up from East Hendred. Mongewell is 1.5km (1 mile) from Wallingford, which has plenty of shops, hostelries and transport links. The route passes close to East Ilsley where there are two pubs, and through Streatley and Goring-on-Thames where there are shops, pubs and transport links (including a railway station). There's another pub at South Stoke.

After crossing a minor road the view opens out with East Hendred Down L and gallops R. We enter Berkshire with a view of Didcot Power Station and, in the foreground, Harwell Laboratory to L.

Didcot Power Station, built on an old army depot, was opened in 1970. The six giant cooling towers (some 112m/325ft high) are a major landmark, which seems to be visible from the Ridgeway for miles. Slightly nearer is the tall, slender chimney and barbed-wire fence of Harwell Business Centre.

Harwell used to be famous for its cherries. James Edmund Vincent, writing in 1906, describes extensive areas of cherry blossom in spring, and the difficulty of avoiding the various weapons used as bird scarers later in the season. They've probably been growing cherries here since the fifteenth and sixteenth centuries, but these days Harwell is famous solely for matters nuclear.

Harwell Business Centre is the headquarters and largest site of the UK Atomic Energy Authority. It was a RAF base in former times and became the Atomic Energy Research Establishment in the 1940s.

After another 1km, the path reaches a car park and road on Bury Down.

From the car park turn R for West Ilsley. Our route continues straight on from the car park to go under the A34 via a concrete tunnel. The path bends R out of the tunnel. Shortly after, turn L (away from the A34) across Several Down. The path bends R and comes to a point where two paths are signposted R. Both go to East Ilsley (in 1.8km).

A detour to East Ilsley is worthwhile and the village makes a good stopping point. It's a delightful place that was renowned for its corn market and its sheep fairs up to the 1930s. It's said that 80,000 sheep were driven into Ilsley and out again on the annual fair day. There were also smaller weekly markets. An average of 400,000

The Oxford-to-Newbury turnpike – now the A34 – was originally opened in 1776. The tunnel underneath has a mural painted by a number of artists from nearby Compton. Just after turning left, the path passes a stone commemorating Hugh Frederick Grovesnor who died here, aged 19, on military manoeuvres in 1947.

The A34 Mural

Ilsley remote amid the Berkshire Downs,
claims three distinctions o'er her sister t[...]
Far famed for sheep and wool, the not for
for sportsmen, doctors, publicans and s[...]

Sheep Fair   Royal Charter

sheep a year were sold in Victorian times. A large number of these would, of course, have been moved along the Ridgeway. The Ridgeway and Icknield Way were excellent drove roads; having ample roadside grazing and no tolls.

J.H.B. Peel in his *Along the Green Roads of Britain* reported a conversation with an old farmer who as a boy had 'sa 'undreds o' sheep travelling this road'. The same old farmer said that peddlers travelled the road carrying ribbons and needles and 'suchloike'. Just before World War I, Edward Thomas said the best time to meet travelling sheep was after one of the fortnightly markets at East Ilsley. He also said that sheep were driven to Tan Hill fair (a few miles south of the end of the Ridgeway National Trail) and Yarnbury fair (on Salisbury Plain). Thomas suggested that as many as 500,000 sheep might have been traded at Tan Hill Fair; which would have presented a fine spectacle (as well as a congested Ridgeway!). Flocks of sheep were driven along the Ridgeway around East Ilsley as recently as 1962. Many of the old pubs have gone, but there are still two right next door to each other: The Swan

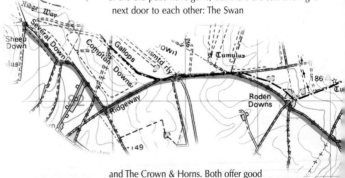

and The Crown & Horns. Both offer good beer, good food and en suite accommodation.

After passing a tap on Several Down, the path joins a concrete lane (to Ilsley Barn Cottages) and continues to a cross-path just before some overhead power cables. Here turn L. (Go straight on for Compton. Turn R for another way into East Ilsley.)

The original course of the Ridgeway would have run straight from Bury Down to the Roden Downs ahead of us. The diversion occurred in the eighteenth century when Churn Plain to our left came under cultivation. The railway later kept the route south of its proper course. The village of Compton is directly south of the Ridgeway, and is home to the Institute for Animal Health. IAH research infectious diseases as well as matters related to animal welfare and food safety. At this point the village is hidden behind the hill, but keep looking right and it will appear, eventually.

The Ridgeway now returns to being a broad open, airy path with gallops and Didcot Power Station to L. It then crosses an old railway bridge.

The Didcot, Newbury & Southampton Junction Railway (DN&SJR) was planned as a north–south link between Didcot and the line to Southampton at Micheldever (Hampshire), but actually only ever went as far as Winchester. The line opened in 1885, but was always quiet; it was closed to passengers in 1960 and to goods in 1966. Careful observers can still detect the remains of Churn Halt just north of the bridge.

Go straight on. After 600m, a track joins the Ridgeway from the L and our chalky eroded path

Just after the railway, a left fork takes a line on along what might easily have been the most convenient, and certainly shorter, route for early travellers. That way goes along the Fair Mile to fords or ferries at Moulsford, Littlestoke and Wallingford. In many ways the Fair Mile route would have been more obvious than that which the National Trail follows. The prime motivation for a detour to Goring may well have been its use as a port for goods or passenger traffic coming up the Thames.

continued on page 124

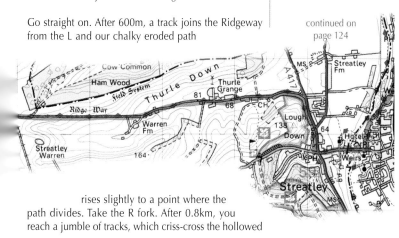

rises slightly to a point where the path divides. Take the R fork. After 0.8km, you reach a jumble of tracks, which criss-cross the hollowed

Ridgeway. Our route becomes more like a green lane with high hedges to each side and with the occasional glimpse of Lowbury Hill through the bushes to L.

It's easy to miss Lowbury Hill, which has a few Iron Age earthworks, a 'swallow hole' (a type of reservoir), a Saxon barrow and a Roman temple. Piles of roofing tiles, 872 Roman coins and thousands of oyster shells were found here in 1916, and a female skeleton buried in the mortar of the Temple's south wall. The theory is that this was some kind of human 'foundation sacrifice'. Lowbury is thought to be the site of the Battle of Ashdown in which the early English defeated the Viking invaders, although the precise locality of this battle has been a matter of debate. Recently, however, interest has centred here, on Lowbury Hill. The two armies met, according to chroniclers, at a point marked by 'a rather small and solitary thorn-tree', the site of which is unknown today.

The Vikings had been carrying out the odd coastal raid since AD 789, and in 865 the Danish 'Great Army' came to conquer the land. Led by Kings Halfdan and Ivarr the Boneless, they took Northumbria and East Anglia and headed south. By January 871 they were in Reading and set out to attack the (now) native Saxons whose army was just 24km (15 miles) away up on the Berkshire Downs. Saxon morale was high. They were led by King Aethelred and his brother and heir, Alfred, who was then just 22. At dawn on 8 January, the Danes prepared for battle. Aethelred decided to hold mass even though he knew that the Vikings were about to attack, so Alfred was forced to divert certain defeat by attacking and catching the Vikings on the hop. It worked. By the time Aethelred had finished his devotions, Danish casualties were mounting; with his return to the fray, the invaders gave ground and retreated to Reading to lick wounds and fight another day. For although Aethelred and Alfred had been victorious on this occasion, they were to be beaten at Basing and later at a site called Meretun. By April, Alfred was king. The Danes had reinforced and, after a year of further warfare, Alfred was forced to seek peace. But his reputation had been formed.

There is now a gentle straight rise. At the top of this there is another series of criss-crossing tracks. The National Trail waymarks help here, but where the track divides take the L fork (R will take you into Aldworth in 2.5km).

> The crossing track just before the fork was once a major route from Dorchester to Newbury. Evidence suggests that it is certainly pre-Roman in origin although it would have been developed by the Romans as an alternative route from Dorchester to Silchester. Some have suggested that a small community once existed up here.)

After a further short rise, the view opens out L with the large white mill building marking Wallingford in the valley below. To R the hills of Watership Down can be seen in the distance. The path continues for 3.2km to reach a parking area and join a country lane. Continue in the same direction for a steady, if dull, 2.5km trudge to the A417.

> We are now entering the vicinity of the Goring Gap, a great north–south slice through the chalk hills and the course of the River Thames, separating the Berkshire Downs from the southern Chilterns. It takes its name from the riverside village of Goring, but the Gap is not a river gorge as such but rather a broad cleft in the chalk ridge. The breach was made in the Ice Ages, before which the Thames flowed north-east to The Wash. As ice

It's quite a way south, but Aldworth is worth a visit if you're thirsty. The Bell pub is described as a haven for traditionalists and has been CAMRA Pub the Year. In Norman times Aldworth was the seat of the de la Beche family, who built a castle up on the Downs (now long gone); the tombs of its builders remain in the church. The de la Beche tombs were so famous that Elizabeth I rode here just to see them. There are nine rather battered stone knights and ladies. The men are so tall they were called the Giants, with three of them known as John Long, John Strong and John Never-Afraid.

At Streatley the National Trail joins two equally ancient tracks: the Icknield Way and the Port Way. Apart from the odd diversion we will now follow the Icknield all the way to Norfolk. Up to now, the Icknield has been running roughly parallel with the Ridgeway, but at the bottom of the chalk scarp. It has run through the villages of Wantage, Harwell, Upton and Blewbury, whereas the Ridgeway has stayed high up on the Downs. It has been suggested that one route was for summer, the other for winter, or that the lower way, the Icknield, was for the passage of trade and migration, whereas those on pilgrimage to Avebury took the faster, super-highway, route of the Ridgeway. The Port Way has followed a similar line to the Icknield. Port Ways in general date from the 9th century when trade restarted after the Dark Ages, and were tracks leading to a →

formed in the outflow at The Wash, the blocked river formed an enormous lake to the north of the chalk ridge and eventually it forced its way through a weak spot in the hills. The course of the Thames altered to its present one, and all routes of communication have flowed through the Gap ever since.

The Goring Gap has recently been identified as the 'crooked glen' of legend. It's suggested that King Arthur's last battle, the battle of Camlann (or Camlaun), took in the fields to the left here. The battle took place in AD 517 and followed Arthur's campaign to oust the Anglo-Saxons from East Anglia. Medraut, the only Arthurian knight recorded in factual history, sought to supplant Arthur and joined with the Saxons to challenge our hero somewhere on a line between Ipswich and South Cadbury which, broadly, coincides with the route of the Icknield Way. Could it be here that King Arthur was killed? Can we possibly imagine that his supporters would then have carried his body along the Ridgeway or Icknield Way to Avalon (said to be Glastonbury)? It's certainly something to think about.

Turn R along the A417 and walk on until this road joins the A329. Continue in the same direction to the traffic lights (and the Bull at Streatley) and turn L.

Streatley is a pleasant little place spoilt by the A329 with its constant flow of traffic. There are some Georgian houses, a nineteenth-century church with a fifteenth-century tower, a nineteenth-century malthouse, used as a village hall, and the fine Streatley Hill, with its wonderful view over the Goring Gap. Streatley was once home to the parents of the Bloomsbury painter Duncan Grant. It was also at Streatley that he had 'a sort of visionary experience' in which he heard a voice 'from outside of himself' telling him to go and become a painter.

The Thames Path National Trail goes through Streatley taking a route past the church to the river bank. It follows the river for 294km (184 miles) from the Thames Barrier in London right up to the source at

Thames Head near Kemble. Curiously perhaps, between Goring-on-Thames and Wallingford, the Thames Path takes the western side of the river while the Ridgeway and the Icknield Way take the east. The two routes can make a fine, full-day circular walk with a number of suitable watering holes at either end.

Continue on to cross the Thames into Goring.

The Ridgeway and Icknield Way both cross the River Thames into Oxfordshire (or in Saxon times from Wessex into Mercia) here at Goring-on-Thames. Local historians suggest that there's been a ford here since prehistoric times. Streatley and Goring were linked during the Roman occupation by a raised causeway. Drovers forced their sheep and cattle through the water en route from the West Country and Wales to the markets to the east. By the medieval period, travellers continued to use the Roman causeway or were shipped across by ferry. Goring Lock was completed in 1797 and the first bridge erected, upstream of the ferry, in 1837. The current bridge dates from 1923. In times gone by, Goring and Streatley acted as ports; goods or people travelling to or from the continent disembarked here for continuation along the Ridgeway or Icknield paths.

Although the prettiest section is by the river, Goring is worth a wander. There are some shops and a café as well as some pubs (the seventeenth-century John Barleycorn and the Miller of Mansfield, and the older Catherine Wheel, formerly a forge). There has been a corn mill on the Thames at Goring since the Dark Ages and, at one time, the Abbey of Bec in Normandy owned it. It was certainly recorded in the Domesday Book and painted by Turner. Later, the mill provided electricity for the village but it's now a private house. The church was once the chapel of a Norman nunnery, and has one of the oldest bells in the land, cast about 1290. It hangs on a bracket as it's too precious to be rung.

The Icknield Way takes a different course from the Ridgeway National Trail between Goring and North Farm, near Britwell Salome. The Icknield follows a minor

← particular port or town. They were normally reused ancient or Roman roads, and many were still called Port Ways right into medieval times.

road out of Goring heading north-east past Catsbrain Hill to Ipsden and then on footpaths to cross Grim's Ditch near Blenheim Farm: a total distance of 15.25km (9.5 miles). We take a riverside route to Wallingford, then along Grim's Ditch to Nuffield and up to North Farm: a total distance of 19.25km (12 miles). The Icknield Way wasn't chosen for the National Trail because it's covered with tarmac along much of its course, but we could assume that the original route followed the Icknield. The Swan's Way, incidentally, is a 105km (65-mile) long path from Goring to Salcey Forest in Northamptonshire. The original Swan's Way was an ancient byway that ran from Northampton to Knettishall Heath in Suffolk, a point we reach in 250km (150 miles) time. The Swan's could therefore be considered as an alternative route. The waymarked path, however, is a little contrived and is not an ancient way.

About 100m after crossing into Goring, turn L along Thames Road. Go straight ahead to a footpath and along this to another road. Turn L and then go straight on. Where the road goes R, go straight on, taking the R-hand of two parallel lanes. The path eventually reaches a lane going to the Old Leatherne Bottle pub/restaurant L. We

Weir and Lock at Goring

go straight on along the private road which progressively deteriorates to a gravelled drive and then a dirt path before heading over open fields with a railway embankment R. At the far side of the field, go L onto a road and into South Stoke. Walk on to pass the Perch and Pike pub and South Stoke church.

The Abbey of Eynsham near Oxford owned South Stoke until Henry VIII dissolved the monasteries. There are still the remnants of some monastic fish ponds to the north of the village. The Perch and Pike is a seventeenth-century Brakspear's pub that doubles as a restaurant. Brakspear's excellent beer is brewed in nearby Henley.

Further on, at the road junction, bear L and, after 200m, turn L along a dirt track towards the Thames. At the river, turn R through a gate and on to the river bank.

The towpath crossed just here to the Moulsford side; the horses being transferred by ferry, which was still in operation in 1962. The gastronomically renowned Beetle and Wedge Hotel occupies the opposite bank, a rambling old manor house named after a beetle (a mallet) used to hit the wedge which split trees for floating down river to London; a custom last seen here in 1777. George Bernard Shaw frequented the hotel and, seemingly, H.G. Wells used it as a model for his 'Potwell Inn' in *The History of Mr Polly*.

We now follow the pleasant and popular Thames-side path for just under 3km to pass under the railway and on.

God's Wonderful Railway (the Great Western) was engineered by Isambard Kingdom Brunel and first opened here on 20 July 1840. Moulsford Bridge, known locally as the Four Arches, was designed by Brunel and is a marvellous example of a skew bridge with its impressively slanting brickwork.

About 1km after the bridge, go through a gate and on to a point where the Thames-side path ends. We are forced R along a gravel drive towards some houses.

Edward Thomas believed there was something called the Papist Way that crossed the Thames here, having diverted from the Icknield Way at Ipsden. When he did his walk along the Icknield just before World War I, he crossed the Thames at this point by means of a ferry. The boy who rowed him over told him that the road up from the ferry on the western side was called Asylum Road as it was right next to 'a big, red lunatic asylum'. Both the road and the Fair Mile Hospital are still there. Why this route is called the Papist Way isn't clear. although the name could be connected with a monastery that was near where the railway line now runs at Cholsey. From there the Papist Way heads through Aston and Blewbury to rejoin the Icknield Way at Upton.

Turn L after roughly 30m onto another dirt path. Go through a gate and continue with a field R. After crossing a concrete footbridge, go through a gate and continue across the field to a further gate. The obvious path stays with field R through another gate and on along a narrow track. Go through two more gates into the churchyard at North Stoke and round to a lych-gate.

North Stoke's thirteenth-century church has a medieval door, thirteenth-century font and fabulous fourteenth-century wall paintings. Michael Caine has a house here, and the celebrated operatic and recital singer Dame

Clara Butt lived at Brook Lodge in the 1920s and 30s and is buried in the churchyard. Dame Clara might well have known the gentleman from the Grange who in the 1920s kept lions and who, apparently, took them for walks along the village street.

Walk on to a metalled road and then L at the T-junction. Continue along the street, past Brook Lodge (L) and over the millstream (the Drincan). Go straight on into a broad bridleway. For part of this way, there's a new golf course to L and R. The path leads to a metalled road at Mongewell Park.

In the first quarter of the twentieth century, Mongewell Park was celebrated as one of the finest of the smaller stately homes of England. Its grounds were famous. The Fraser family had owned the estate during the Victorian period and had built a new mansion. Mr A.C. Fraser loved trees and their preservation in his park was a great interest. The estate also had a fine Norman church and a sizeable lake. After World War I a wealthy American bought the estate, spent colossal sums on both house and grounds, and added various luxury features including a sports pavilion and a boathouse. After occupation by the RAF in World War II, the house and grounds were almost taken over by the National Trust, but Carmel College (a Jewish boarding school) occupied the site up to 1997. Now, it seems, bits are being sold off as luxury apartments.

Continue straight ahead and past buildings and a lake to R. Where the road turns R keep straight on to a bridleway indicated by a concrete post. Take this path until just before Wallingford bypass (carry straight on here for Wallingford). Turn R parallel with the road and through some trees for about 0.7km to the B4009.

Wallingford offers a full range of shops and hostelries, as well as buses north to Oxford or south to Reading. Agatha Christie moved here in 1935, to Winterbrook House, with her second husband, archaeologist Sir Max

THE GREATER RIDGEWAY

On the north side of the bypass is the headquarters of CAB International; one of the world's major research and information organisations in agriculture, forestry and public health. CABI actually originated in the days of Empire when they concentrated on controlling the pests and diseases of crops in the colonies. They've expanded over the years and are now fully international although remain focused on third-world problems.

Mallowan. They lived here off and on for the rest of their lives. By the 1970s the house was gradually becoming dilapidated and the garden was going to rack and ruin. Agatha died here in January 1976 and was buried in Cholsey churchyard; her husband died not long after.

It's highly probable that the Icknield Way crossed the Thames at Wallingford as well as at Goring. In some ways it's a more obvious and shorter route. It was (and is) also on a main north–south route to Oxford as well as being on the river. Thus, with its surrounding rich agricultural land, the town became important. There's a possibility that the Romans were here, and it's likely that King Alfred fortified Wallingford's earthworks as a defence against the Danes. In AD 1006 the Danish King Sweyn burnt and almost razed the place but it was rebuilt by Edward the Confessor who used it as a royal residence. The strategic importance of the town and its river crossing became more apparent during the Norman invasion. After the Battle of Hastings, William marched his army northwards to London but was strongly repelled. Baulked by the river, William came 80km (50 miles) upstream to cross the Thames at Wallingford. The army then marched back to the capital on the northern side and entered the city unopposed.

William allowed Robert D'Oillis to build Wallingford Castle, accentuating its strategic value. Wallingford Castle was finished in 1071, and at its zenith was one of the most important castles in the country. During the civil war between Matilda and King Stephen, it was to Wallingford that Matilda came after a dramatic escape from Oxford. Stephen besieged her there before, in 1153, agreeing the Treaty of Wallingford, which conferred succession to her son. That son, Henry II, held his first Parliament here in 1154, and the following year presented the great Charter to the town, thus officially recognising it as one of the first English boroughs. King John used the castle as a palace and the Black Prince was married here. The Prince's son, Richard II, was brought up in the castle Dower House. Katherine de Valois also lived here for 15 years after the death of her husband, Henry V. The last royal occupant was

132

Henry VIII, but by Tudor times the town had suffered severely from the plague of 1349 and only 44 houses remained. Henry VIII dissolved the Priory, and the bridge over the Thames virtually collapsed. The Civil War finally brought the town to its knees. Wallingford was one of the last places to surrender to the Roundheads and was besieged by the Parliamentary army under Sir Thomas Fairfax for 16 weeks before surrendering in July 1646. Cromwell then demolished the castle. What is left can still be seen just to the north of the bridge.

Despite a history of war, plague and fire, Wallingford has kept many of its fine old buildings. The church of St Mary le More was partly rebuilt about 1650, and the similarly vintaged town hall is a splendid structure with its stone pillars and imposing façade. Perhaps it was here that local criminals in James I's time were brought. It is said that for a first offence a villain could elect to have his eyes put out and be mutilated rather than receive the normal punishment – which for 'larceny' was hanging.

Woodland on Grim's Ditch near Nuffield

Stage 12: Mongewell to Chinnor

Start:	Mongewell
Finish:	Chinnor
Distance:	24.1km (15 miles)
OS:	Landrangers 175 Reading & Windsor, 165 Aylesbury & Leighton Buzzard
Route Features:	Easy country
Information:	Tourist Information Centres: Wallingford (01491 826972)

The Ridgeway path at Mongewell is 1.5km (1 mile) from the town of Wallingford with its excellent facilities and bus routes. Chinnor has all the facilities of a large village including buses to Princes Risborough, Thame and High Wycombe. There's a pub on the main road at Nuffield, several in Watlington and one in Lewknor.

Cross the road to a gate. Walk on along the course of Grim's Ditch in a straight line (over two roads) for 5.2km.

Grim's Ditch is the largest monument left by early man in the Chilterns. It ran originally for about 80km

(50 miles) from the Thames past Nuffield towards Henley and then from Marlow to Ivinghoe Beacon and Dunstable. In fact, roughly the way we're going. The name Grim's Ditch was used by the Anglo-Saxons for any number of linear earthworks that they supposed were the works of a god or the Devil. Recent work has dated this ditch to the fourth century BC. The bank was originally 3m (10ft) high and 6m (20ft) wide – and still is in places – topped by a wooden palisade and fronted by a pair of ditches. It's now thought that it was a frontier of an Iron Age tribe based at Sinodun hillfort (near Wittenham Clumps north of Wallingford). The Icknield Way between Goring and North Farm, incidentally, crosses the Ridgeway National Trail at the second road.

Eventually you reach a T-junction. Here go L to a road. Turn R to Nuffield church.

The nave of Holy Trinity church at Nuffield has walls dating from AD 634 containing Roman tiles; the rest is Norman. One of the inmates of the churchyard is William Richard Morris, first Viscount Nuffield, who died in 1963. After starting a bicycle repair shop,

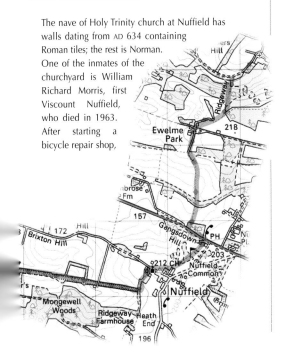

*Ridgeway path on
Grim's Ditch*

We are now 212m (700ft) above sea level on one of the south-ernmost hills of that Area of Outstanding Natural Beauty known as the Chilterns. The Chilterns are basically chalk, capped with as much as 4m (13ft) of clay and flint. The whole area is broadly a plateau, with a steep scarp at its north-western end facing onto the Vale of Aylesbury. The Ridgeway follows that scarp from here through Oxfordshire, Buckinghamshire, Hertfordshire and Bedfordshire to Ivinghoe Beacon. The rest of the Chilterns are characteristically smooth, rounded hills, often cloaked in extensive woodland, and particularly rich in beech which was planted here in the eighteenth and nineteenth centuries to supply the furniture industry. →

Morris sold and maintained motorbikes, before setting up a factory in Cowley. The first Morris Oxford was produced in 1913. Morris revolutionised the car industry in Britain, and his company formed the basis of, in 1952, the British Motor Corporation, the third largest car company in the world. He lived in nearby Nuffield Place (see below).

Continue along the road to the end of the churchyard. Look for the Ridgeway sign in the hedge L and take the path over a stile onto Nuffield Common Golf Course. Follow the white posts across two fairways and into a copse. The path leads to Fairway Cottage and the main road (A423). Just up the road to the R are the Crown pub and Nuffield Place.

The Crown is a seventeenth-century coaching inn, and has a range of home-made food. Nuffield Place, built 1914, was home to Lord Nuffield from 1933–63. Several of the rooms are decorated in 1930s fashion, and classic and veteran cars are often on show. For opening times tel: 01491 641224.

Our route bears L over the road to enter a small wood through a gate. After leaving the wood, continue over a field towards a white post. Continue straight on through a narrow strip of woodland and uphill, heading for the white post across the field. Continue in broadly the same direction, past a stagnant pool R to a junction. Bear R along a rutted farm track with views L to Didcot Power Station and a white building (Culham Laboratory). Continue past the impressive Ewelme Park to L and on past the gatehouse. Go through the farmyard, passing some barns before turning R at the end.

Culham Laboratory, more properly the Culham Science Centre, is home to the Euratom/UKAEA Fusion Power project. Britain contributes to fusion research with its own work and through its contribution to Euratom's 'flagship' experiment the Joint European Torus (JET). JET is situated at Culham. Fusion power involves fusing hydrogen isotopes together to release energy: it's basically how stars produce theirs. The potential is for an almost limitless, more controllable and comparatively pollution-free source of energy.

← These hills have a wonderful sense of place: a landscape of deep valleys, picturesque villages and great pubs. They also have a vigorous conservation organisation in the shape of the Chiltern Society, founded in 1965. Their office is in Chesham, tel: 01494 771250 (or www.chiltern-society.co.uk).

Chiltern Hunt used on Nuffield Church

In the olden days, the Icknield Way through this part of Oxfordshire was variously known as Icknel, Acknil, Hackney and Hackington. Another version of the name was used in a south Oxon rhyme, said to date from 1717: 'Henley-on-Thames and Ackington Way, Are never without a thief night or day'. Robert Plot also recorded this reputation for villainy in 1677 in his *Natural History of Oxfordshire*. He noted the isolation of the route and the fact that "tis much used by stealers of cattle'.

There's a treat in store between here and Lewknor in roughly 11km (7 miles) time – you will see red kites. These magnificent birds used to be widespread, but persecution led to their extinction in England and Scotland. Throughout most of the twentieth century just a few pairs survived in central Wales. The English red kite reintroduction project started in 1989 when kites from Spain were released in the Watlington area. It's been a huge success. In 1999, 81 pairs of red kite reared 153 young; the Chilterns population is now large enough to provide nestlings for release in other parts of England. Watch for a gliding buzzard-size bird, with a gorgeous russet-brown body and diagnostic forked tail. The reintroduction has been hugely popular. And you will see at least one. Promise.

The path continues along a green lane and around the R-hand edge of a field. Don't take a footpath R, but continue to follow the headland path to another wood. The path now descends steeply. At the end of the wood, go through a gate and over a field to another gate. At a lane (known as Ladies Walk), turn R. After about 0.4km go through a gate with Swyncombe House to R. The bridleway now goes R to pass St Botolph's church.

Ridgeway path north of Nuffield

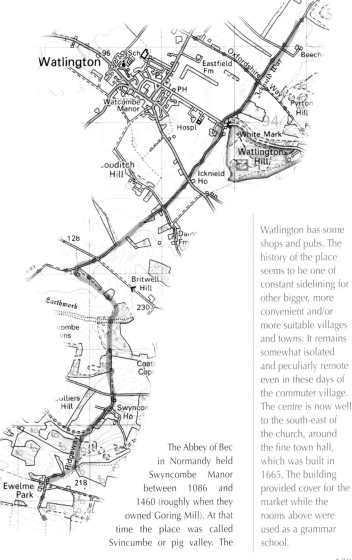

Watlington has some shops and pubs. The history of the place seems to be one of constant sidelining for other bigger, more convenient and/or more suitable villages and towns. It remains somewhat isolated and peculiarly remote even in these days of the commuter village. The centre is now well to the south-east of the church, around the fine town hall, which was built in 1665. The building provided cover for the market while the rooms above were used as a grammar school.

The Abbey of Bec in Normandy held Swyncombe Manor between 1086 and 1460 (roughly when they owned Goring Mill). At that time the place was called Svincumbe or pig valley. The

The Oxfordshire Way runs for 105km (65 miles) from the Thames Valley to the Cotswolds. It starts in Henley and goes via Blenheim Park to Bourton-on-the-Water. It's a well waymarked route through some delightful country.

present house is an Elizabethan manor extensively rebuilt in Victorian times. The lovingly restored St Botolph's dates back to the eleventh century.

After passing the church, the lane turns L. We pass the Rectory and then cross a minor road to go through a gate. The path takes the L edge of the field. We descend and then rise into woodland. After a short distance, a path leaves L but we go straight on downhill. The view opens out to Britwell Salome House in the distance L. The path goes half-L and, in 0.8km, passes some farm buildings and turns sharp R to rejoin the Icknield Way. After about 0.4km cross a minor road and walk on to Lys Farm House where the path continues along a metalled road. Cross the B480 to Icknield House R. The path now offers views to Watlington Hill R. Continue along the track until the next road, Hill Road. (Turn L here for Watlington in 800m.)

Ridgeway path near Lys Farm, Watlington

Britwell Salome has been inhabited for at least 800 years and is said to have a yew tree that's 7m (23ft) round. To the north, there's a farm called the Priory that once

housed 25 nuns driven from France during the Revolution. Local tradition has it that the Icknield Way used to be popular with priests travelling between Lincoln Cathedral and cities to the west (such as Plymouth). The Priory, along with Watcombe Manor near Watlington, is supposedly one of the 'hostels' used by these journeying clergy.

On the other side of the trail is Watlington Hill and Christmas Common, so named after a Civil War truce here in 1643. The 38ha (96 acres) of Watlington Hill are owned by the National Trust and are a popular place for a Sunday stroll. Much of the hill is chalk grassland and scrub, and it's a good birding spot. On its north-western face, Watlington Hill bears the 'White Mark', an 82m (270ft) high obelisk cut into the chalk by Edward Horne in 1764. It is alleged that Horne felt that the church should have a spire and so had this one cut.

Continue along the clear track that soon crosses the Oxfordshire Way.

The Ridgeway National Trail now seems to spend the entire stretch to Ivinghoe intertwining with the Icknield Way. Just along here that name is used for a number of parallel paths that run north-eastwards. The northern-most Lower Icknield Way (which runs north of Watlington) was 'improved' by the Romans. The Middle Icknield Way follows the B4009. The National Trail follows the southernmost Upper Icknield Way. It has been suggested that there might have been a further route along the ridge of the Chilterns and that this was the true Ridgeway. It's clear that this Greater Ridgeway didn't originate as confined roads or bridleways but was probably a series of paths spread over 1km (0.6 miles) or so. With enclosure, these would have been made into the three narrow, parallel tracks we see today.

The lane continues uphill through trees to pass Shirburn Hill to R.

Shirburn itself can be just made out to the left. There's a

A worthy organisation is based in Lewknor. Hearing Dogs for Deaf People train dogs to alert deaf people to sounds which hearing people may take for granted. The organisation has placed more than 600 hearing dogs since 1986, and now trains 275 dogs a year. If you want to know more, they have a web site or ring 01844 353898.

Steam fans should check out the Chinnor & Princes Risborough Railway (The Icknield Line). This formed part of the Watlington & Princes Risborough Railway; built in 1872. The last passenger train ran in 1957, and the last section from Chinnor to Princes Risborough served the cement works until 1989. The Railway Association was formed that year with the aim of preserving what remained. The line from Chinnor to Thame has been bought and that to Princes Risborough restored. If you want to ride into Princes Risborough, the timetable can be heard on tel: 01844 353535. There's also the Chinnor Windmill Restoration Society which aims to rebuild the Chinnor Windmill and then use it to grind wheat. It's occasionally open for public view.

castle (or more accurately a fortified house), a deep moat and a church (with a Norman tower) together in an 80ha (200-acre) park. It isn't open to the public and seems to have had a difficult history for visitors: when Dante's tutor stopped by he was 'waylaid by robbers' and had to run for his life. The castle was once home to the Earls of Macclesfield, one of whom became Lord Chancellor in 1718. As George I couldn't speak any English, Macclesfield read his speeches from the throne. The king showered him with honours, but Macclesfield was found to have been selling various high government positions and was promptly sent to the Tower. His son was one of the best-known astronomers in Europe, and it was mainly down to his calculations that the calendar was altered in 1752.

The straight, hedged green lane continues, eventually opening out to a wider, grassier track that heads towards the M40. Just before reaching the motorway, the Ridgeway crosses a metalled road. (For Lewknor, and the fine Olde Leathern Bottel pub, go L here for 0.8km). On the other side of the M40 tunnel, Beacon Hill and the Aston Rowant National Nature Reserve rise up to R.

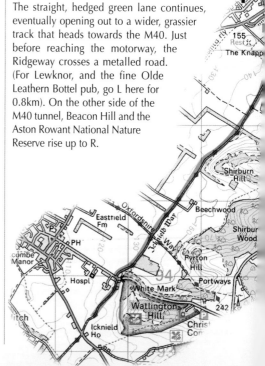

continued on
page 144

English Nature manages 134ha (331 acres) at Aston Rowant. The reserve has some typical short-sward chalk grassland, rich in flowering plants and featuring a number of wild orchids such as white and narrow-lipped helleborines and common twayblade. The rest comprises some typical Chiltern beech woodland. There are over 45 bird species and fallow and muntjac deer are common. All this despite the fact that the site has been cut in two by the 21m (70ft) M40 ravine. The village of Aston Rowant can be seen over to the left (due north). The oldest part of the village lies by the twelfth-century church of St Peter and St Paul. In Henry VIII's time, the bell ringers of the church were put in the stocks for ringing the honour of Princess Elizabeth as she rode past on her way to imprisonment at Rycote. The village has a delightful village green surrounded by eighteenth- and nineteenth-century farmhouses and cottages. Aston Rowant is often the venue for top-class cricket as Oxfordshire commonly play one-day cup matches here.

The path goes on to cross the A40 and

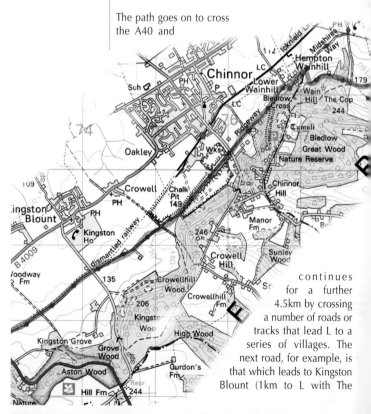

continues for a further 4.5km by crossing a number of roads or tracks that lead L to a series of villages. The next road, for example, is that which leads to Kingston Blount (1km to L with The

Cherry Tree pub) and the cross-track after that leads L to Crowell (The Shepherd's Crook pub). The broad, grassy track continues straight ahead towards the chimneys of Chinnor cement works. The path ascends with Oakley Hill R before descending to a road. (Go L for Chinnor, 0.8km away.)

There's probably been some kind of settlement at Chinnor for centuries because of its proximity to the Icknield Way. It became a centre for lace making, chair making and agriculture. In the early nineteenth century there were 268 lace makers in the town, and a number of 'bodgers', men working the surrounding beech woods. The cement works opened in 1908. The town was certainly involved in the Civil War: it's said that there was a skirmish in the High Street involving Prince Rupert before the battle of Chalgrove Field in 1643. Nowadays, as with a lot of these villages along the Way, it's mostly a commuter base.

Chinnor Hill (to the left immediately after Chinnor) is a 28ha (70-acre) SSSI, owned by Berkshire, Buckinghamshire and Oxfordshire Wildlife Trust (BBOWT). The reserve is right on the Chiltern escarpment and has chalk grassland as well as an area of oak and ash woodland, and some mature open-floored beech wood. Apart from its wildlife there are two Saxon burial mounds and, perhaps significantly for us, three ancient sunken trackways.

Stage 13: Chinnor to Wendover

Start:	Chinnor
Finish:	Wendover
Distance:	18.2km (11.3 miles)
OS:	Landranger 165 Aylesbury & Leighton Buzzard
Route Features:	Easy country
Information:	Tourist Information Centre: Wendover (01296 623056)

Chinnor has all the facilities of a large village including buses to Princes Risborough, Thame and High Wycombe. Wendover is a small town with a number of bus services and a railway station. Princes Risborough (some 8km/5 miles from Chinnor) is another small town with plenty of facilities including a railway station. The route passes a pub at Cadsden.

The National Trail continues across the road and climbs steadily with Wain Hill (R). Eventually you reach a red-brick house after which the Ridgeway bends R.

Rupert Brooke once surveyed 'the slumbering Midland Plain' from Wain Hill. Brooke stayed several times at the Pink and Lily Inn, near Lacey Green, south of Princes Risborough. On Wain Hill, and impossible to see from the Ridgeway, is a cross cut into the turf, thought to have been made in the seventeenth century. Some have suggested that it was a waymark for travellers along the Icknield Way. Lord Carrington owns this land, and the former Foreign Secretary lives in the Manor House at Bledlow, a village just over 1km away to the north-east. It's a rather lovely place with a thirteenth-century church, a rippling stream with water-cress beds, herringbone-brick houses and the Red Lion, a seventeenth-century inn that was once a row of cottages.

At the start of the next stretch we leave Oxon for Bucks. The path winds round a series of bends to a prominent cross-track. About 30m further on, follow the advice of a Ridgeway signpost (partly hidden in hedge R) and leave the main track, through a gate into a field. Bear L downhill into a hollow and then walk uphill with fence L to the corner of the field. Just before this go through a gate in the fence L and turn R. Continue, with fence R, to go through a gate to a road. Bear L over the road to enter another field via a gate. The clear path crosses the field, goes through a gate and over a cross-track. Go through the next gate and turn R. Follow the path with trees R and up the steep slope onto Lodge Hill. Continue across the ridge with views L and R towards a line of trees. After a gate, bear L along a grassy path before going downhill to a further pair of gates. Continue downhill through a gap in a hedge. Ignore the prominent stile R and go downhill following a hedge R. Continue under some power lines to a road.

Cross the road on to a driveway that leads to a house (Longwood). Take a path to R of the house and on over a field towards a white post in front of some trees. Go through a gate and turn R to follow a hedged path through a golf course. This path bends R, through a gate and over a railway. Go through a gate and into a field. Continue uphill, keeping a line of trees to L. After another gate, cross the top of Saunderton railway tunnel and then through a further gate into a field. Go between two pylons to a minor road. Turn R along the road (Upper Icknield Way) downhill and over a crossroads (with Shootacre Lane). Whiteleaf Cross is visible on the hill ahead.

In recent years Whiteleaf Cross has become more of a dirty scar than a prominent chalk mark. This is a pity, as apparently you can see seven counties from it, and it's said to be visible from the tower of Magdalene College, Oxford, and from Uffington, (now 50km/80 miles away). It's certainly big enough to be seen, at 26.5m (87ft) long and 15m (50ft) wide. Its origins are less than certain. A boundary mark is thought to have existed here since

You may remember that after the Battle of Hastings, William marched his army up the Thames to Wallingford where he crossed the river and then marched them back to the northern side of London. It has been suggested that William actually marched his army along this part of the Icknield Way to somewhere near Tring, effectively conquering the Chilterns.

The painter Sir Peter Lely (1618–80) was once a resident of the town. When Van Dyke died, he became court painter to Charles I. Despite this closeness to royalty, he managed to survive the various political to-ings and fro-ings of the time and, most curiously, even went on to paint a portrait of Oliver Cromwell. Another former resident was Amy Johnson who lived in a cottage near the church.

The Market house, Princes Risborough

AD 903, called Weland's stock (or pole), but this particular cross was first documented in 1742. We can definitely say that in 1947 the cross was incorporated into the Buckinghamshire county arms. And, as with Uffington, it was regularly scoured by the villagers in the eighteenth and nineteenth centuries with much 'junketing' and general debauchery.

Continue along Upper Icknield Way to major road and turn L to walk along the pavement towards Princes Risborough. After Culverton Manor Farm and about 0.8km on, turn R into another lane called Upper Icknield Way. The rough track passes along the back of Princes Risborough, before going downhill to Brimmers Road. (Here turn L for Princes Risborough.)

Princes Risborough has a wide range of shops as well pubs, buses and a railway station. The village (or town?) owes its name to the Black Prince who owned land here and, according to legend, had a small palace near the church. Many timbered and thatched cottages remain, and there is a splendid brick market house. Important to Great Ridgeway travellers is the puddingstone, a strange sarsen boulder, near the Budgens roundabout.

Pudding Stone, Princes Risborough

Puddingstones are believed to have been used as waymarkers by prehistoric travellers. We will pass another at Royston and there are more in East Anglia. It seems that there could well have been a succession of them along the course of the Ridgeway and Icknield Way.

We continue along a green lane. Just opposite some playing fields, leave the Icknield Way at a clear signpost by turning R uphill towards woodland, keeping the fence close R. Go up a stepped path and over a footpath. Before the top, go through a gate into a field. Continue uphill towards the R edge of a wood to a road (Kop Hill). Don't go through the gate but go L with woods R. Go through a gate and on to another road.

Kop Hill (also known as Soldier's Mount or Plum Pudding Hill) became famous in the 1920s for car and motorbike hill-climb races. There may have been a Roman lookout post here, and it's been suggested that there may be a Roman villa here too. If you're here on the night of a mid-winter full moon, tradition says that you should circle the hill seven times. You will then see a Roman soldier on a white horse who will present you with a bag of gold. The view from the hill is magnificent, with Didcot Power Station visible in the west together with the twin cones of Wittenham Clumps prominent to the south of that.

The National Trust owns Pulpit Hill, designated as an SSSI in 1972. The grassland area was ploughed during World War II and is only slowly restoring itself. The 20ha (50-acre) reserve is predominantly chalk grassland with scrub, with some woodland on the hill (basically beech with whitebeam and yew, but also some conifer). The birds here are typical of the Chiltern escarpment. In winter there's mistle thrush, fieldfare, and redwing with occasional flocks of siskin, redpoll, goldcrest and firecrest. Apparently you can see ring ouzel in springtime and spotted flycatcher, nuthatch, treecreeper and, even, hobby in summer. And in June there is a virtual carpet of orchids.

The democrat John Hampden made his protest against ship money (a tax imposed by Charles I without the authority of Parliament) at Great Kimble. At a parish meeting there in 1635, he met the assessors and stoutly refused to pay the £1 due. His subsequent arrest and trial caused further tension between king and Parliament immediately prior to the Civil War. Great Kimble, incidentally, also has a pub: the Bernard Arms (see below).

Turn R along the road and then, after 20m, L (with a car park to R). Follow the broad dirt track to a clearing with a Neolithic long barrow L. This is the top of Whiteleaf Hill. About 20m further on, turn R to go through a gate. Follow the dirt path that eventually goes sharply downhill through a wood. At the bottom, go through a gate and bear R to the Plough pub. Continue with pub L to the Cadsden Road. Turn L. After 200m (and opposite a golf course), go R through a gate. Walk on up the steps to reach a field with Pulpit Hill ahead.

Go straight across the field to the far corner and then continue along a narrow path. At a point where bridleways cross, turn L to go through a gate and over the grassy hillside with fine views L. Eventually bear L to go up an eroded slope into some woodland. Go up some steps to a sunken footpath. (Turn L here for Great Kimble 0.8km north). Turn R and, a little further on, go through a gate L into a field. The tumulus on the hill L is called Chequers Knap.

Great Kimble is said to have got its name from the British king Cunobelin, king of the Catuvellauni at the time when Roman eyes were turning to Britain (c. AD 40). Cunobelin and the Romans seemed to have had some degree of mutual respect (or toleration?), in that it was only after his death that the Romans decided to invade. In the woods almost due north from here is a motte-and-bailey earthwork known as Cymbeline's Castle. It seems improbable that this mound by the Icknield Way was anything to do with him as his capitals were first at St Albans and subsequently at Colchester. The only certainty here is that if

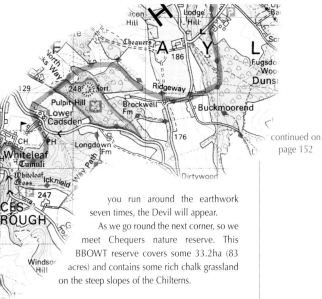

continued on
page 152

you run around the earthwork
seven times, the Devil will appear.

As we go round the next corner, so we
meet Chequers nature reserve. This
BBOWT reserve covers some 33.2ha (83
acres) and contains some rich chalk grassland
on the steep slopes of the Chilterns.

Continue across the valley following a clear path to
a fence. Follow the track that bears R following the
fence. Go through a gate and over a field for 300m to a
gate (with Chequers visible straight ahead). The path
bears R. Continue with woods (Maple Wood) R.

Chequers is the official country retreat of the Prime
Minister. It was built in 1565, altered and enlarged in
the eighteenth and nineteenth centuries, and finally fully
restored by Lord Lee of Fareham in 1912. He created a
trust in 1917 so that the place could be used by PMs
from then on. Lloyd George is reported to have said that
the house was 'full of the ghosts of dull people'. The
house is still furnished with much that was left from Lord
Lee's collection as well as some souvenirs from other
periods of occupation. In 1565, the then owner, William
Hawtrey, was given the job of imprisoning Lady Mary
Grey, Lady Jane's sister, as she had angered Queen
Elizabeth I by marrying in secret. There's a room on the

Chequers

second floor of the house where Lady Mary was imprisoned for two years. Later the estate was linked to one of Oliver Cromwell's children, and it still contains an extensive collection of relics of the period. The fine avenue of beech trees that stretches up to the big house along 'Victory Drive' was planted for Sir Winston Churchill. A somewhat later incumbent John Major once held talks with the Russian leader Boris Yeltsin at Chequers.

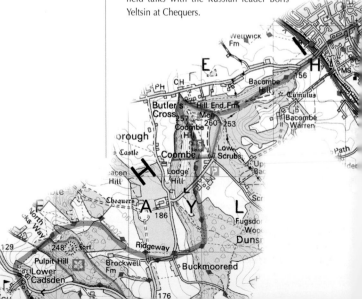

At the end of Maple Wood, turn L at a prominent sign-post. Go downhill through two gates and on to the drive of Chequers itself. Cross the drive and walk on to go through a gate into the next field. Follow the path round to a gate. Cross the road, bear L and follow the track past some farm buildings. Take the R-hand of two tracks into the wood. The next section is complicated and you should keep your eyes open for waymark posts. Continue uphill. At the brow of the hill, with a small pit just R, go L along a sunken path. Shortly thereafter go half-R into the wood. The path now follows a zigzag course through the wood with waymark posts every 50–100m. Eventually you reach a post-and-rail fence. Cross a stile R and turn L to continue along a woodland path. Go over the next stile and then L to reach a minor road. Turn R to go uphill along the road. Opposite a house (R), turn L and walk into the wood following waymarked posts as before. Continue through a gate and turn L towards the edge of the hill. The path now continues along the edge to the top of Coombe Hill.

Before he gave Chequers to the nation, Lord Lee presented Coombe Hill to the National Trust. At 257m (845ft), it's almost the highest point in the Chilterns, with an impressive view over the Vale of Aylesbury, with Aylesbury itself in the middle distance. There's also a topographical plinth with pointers to show where places are. One of these is Ellesborough, with its flint-faced parish church on top of a high mound, used by visitors to Chequers. The imposing monument on Coombe Hill is dedicated to the men of Buckinghamshire who died in the Boer War. The opening ceremony for the Ridgeway National Trail took place on Coombe Hill on 29 September 1973. Lord Nugent of Guildford declared the path open, and the official party then proved what keen long distance walkers they were by strolling the 3km(1.8 miles) into Wendover.

From the monument, bear half-R, taking the lower path towards a hedge. This path is marked by a waymark post

Coombe Hill Monument

about 100m from the monument. It leads to a gate, goes over a sunken bridleway and on through another gate into woodland. The track now descends gradually down Bacombe Hill. Towards the end of the ridge, go through a gate and down to the B4010. Turn R and walk over a bypass and a railway line into Wendover.

> Wendover's new bypass was opened in October 1997 after first being mooted in 1935! The town itself has a number of shops and hostelries, as well as a railway station and buses.
>
> Wendover's name comes from the Anglo-Saxon wand (winding) ofer (bank). Henry VIII once gave that winding bank to Catherine of Aragon as a present. Associations with Henry also extend to a row of thatched terraced cottages on the Tring Road (turn L at the clock tower then R at the roundabout), known as Anne Boleyn's cottages because they were a marriage gift. In 1600, the town had one pub for every 50 inhabitants. Although most have gone, you'll be relieved to know that the old coaching inn, the Red Lion, is still in the High St. Oliver Cromwell slept there in 1642, and Robert Louis Stevenson stayed in 1875, and described Wendover as a 'struggling purposeless sort of place'.

Collectors of little known and otherwise useless information will want to know that the children's nursery rhyme 'Jack be nimble, Jack be quick, Jack jump over the candlestick' is reputed to come from Wendover. The town's lace makers celebrated the feast of St Catherine, their patron saint, every 25 November. After a good deal of feasting and jollification, they would set off fireworks and play 'leap-candle'. In this a candlestick with a lighted candle was put on the floor, and if you could leap over it without extinguishing the flame you would have good luck for the following year.

Stage 14: Wendover to Ivinghoe Beacon

Start:	Wendover
Finish:	Ivinghoe Beacon
Distance:	18.5km (11.5 miles)
OS:	Landranger 165 Aylesbury & Leighton Buzzard
Route Features:	Some hills
Information:	Tourist Information Centre: Tring (01442 823347)

Wendover is a small town with hostelries, shops, buses and a railway station. The end of the Ridgeway National Trail at Ivinghoe Beacon, however, is in the middle of nowhere. Ivinghoe, some 2km (1.25 miles) from the Beacon, has a pub but only a sporadic bus service into Aylesbury. You may prefer to use Tring (or Tring Station) for the end of this section. Alternatively, the village of Whipsnade (8.8km/5.5 miles) further on has buses to Luton. The latter would extend the day to 27km (17 miles). There's a pub about half way at Wigginton. Central Tring is a smidge too far to recommend as a pub stop although it has plenty to offer. If doing the longer stretch to Whipsnade, there are two pubs at Dagnall.

Go past the car park and Red Lion pub and just before reaching the clock tower turn R along a narrow lane (Heron Path). The path winds through some parkland before joining a stream. At the end the path bears R and then L towards the church with a pond R. At the road, turn L in front of the church.

The actual route of the Icknield Way goes straight on at Wendover along the A4011 to Halton Camp and then to Tring. That route is labelled as the Upper Icknield Way on OS maps. Meanwhile, you may notice that Wendover parish church is somewhat peculiarly placed some 0.8km (0.5 miles) south of the town. The story goes that it was to have been built on a more central field, but every time the work began all the building materials were whisked off by witches, or maybe fairies, and left here. The original field is still called Witches Meadow. Almost identical tales are known for Christchurch Priory, Alfriston church and others. One of Wendover's vicars, the Rev Joseph Smith started the England's first-ever savings bank in the vestry of this very church in 1799.

Follow Church Lane round to a major road. Go straight on along a no through road. Just after some farm buildings the lane becomes a dirt track known as Hogtrough Lane. Go past Boswells Farm and continue past a tiny cottage buried in woodland L. Continue along a dirt road. After 250m, turn L along a clear woodland path. After a further 20m, fork L keeping a wooden post to R. After a further 100 m, fork R to walk up hill into the wood. As the slope starts descend again, bear L. This clear path continues for roughly 2 km to a road near Uphill Lodge. Turn R and then L. Walk on through the woodland to a cross track and turn L. Go down hill to a deep gully and turn R. Walk up the gully which eventually bends R to continue past a cottage to reach Aston Hill Road.

Go roughly straight on, over the road, and through a gate in the hedge. Head towards the jutting corner of a hedge and then towards the radio mast; crossing two fields. Go through a gate to a road at the base of the mast. Turn L for a short way and then R into woodland. Follow the clear dirt path through the wood to reach a minor road. Turn L along Gadmore Lane and down hill into Hastoe. At a crossroads, go straight on along Church Lane to eventually reach a more major road at Hastoe Cross. Cross the road to go up the gravel drive opposite. Continue straight on and past Wick Farm. Just before reaching a metalled road, turn L over a stile (go straight on for the Greyhound pub in Wigginton). Walk on until the path takes you R over a stile and then bends L to a minor road.

Wigginton was originally an agricultural community, with links to straw plaiting and lace making. The Rothschilds occupied the local 'big house' and they were responsible for many of the estate workers' houses built here.

You may well have heard of the 'health resort' of Champneys, which is housed in a big mansion (set in 69ha/170 acres of parkland), about 2.5km (1.5 miles) south of where you now stand. The first mention of the house occurs in 1307 when Ralph de Champneys owned it. The original house was pulled down in Victorian times and rebuilt by the Valpy family. After various owners, the 'naturopath' Stanley Lief moved into Champneys and, in 1925, he turned it into a 'nature cure resort', the first in Britain. Today, Champneys describes itself as 'one of the worlds leading health resorts'.

Nowadays it has become just another commuter village. Although the name is Saxon, about 160 years ago a third-century Roman house was found near the parish church. Some 15 rooms have since been excavated; at least 10 of which have tessellated floors. There are also remains of geometric pattern mosaics, probably designed and made by the Corinian School at Cirencester.

Continue straight on with a laurel hedge R and woodland L. The path soon runs alongside a brick house with fancy Tudor chimneys and out to a drive. Turn R to a minor road. Cross the road to go through a gate and along a fenced path. Pass a trig point and go through two gates into a field. Keep along the L edge to go through another gate. After a further gate, the path bends L and passes two gates close together (bypassed to R) to reach yet another gate and then a road. Turn R and shortly after L through a gate. Walk on, with views to Ashridge ahead. After a while, the path goes through a gate to L, continues in the same direction to another gate and round to cross a footbridge over the A41(M). At the end turn R and then, 50m on, L through a gate and onto another gate and the A4251 (the old A41). Cross the road and turn R. After 100m, the route passes Pendley Beeches Lodge. Turn L through a gate just after the lodge and walk along this hedged/fenced path for 800m with Pendley Manor L.

In the fourth century there was a village of Pendley. But in 1440 Sir Robert Whittingham got permission to enclose 81ha (200 acres) of the area. He seized the land, tore down the houses and had a mansion built on the site. In more recent times the lords of the manor of Pendley (in a rebuilt late-Victorian pile) have been the Williams family, of which the equestrian commentator Dorian Williams was a member. Pendley Manor is now a hotel; the rest of the estate was sold as Pendley Farm, now a stud and training stables.

Continue along the fenced path to eventually cross a gallop, go through a gate and reach a road. Turn L to a T-junction. (Turn L here for Tring.) Turn R to cross the Grand Union Canal.

Tring started as a market town, particularly noted for its fine veal and veal pies. If you look at the map you can see that for some reason the Roman Akeman Street (now the B4635) is peculiarly diverted north at Tring for about 2km (1.25 miles). In the eighteenth century, Sir William Gore, a Lord Mayor of London and Director of the Bank of England, acquired Tring Park and moved the town north away from his mansion. The modern bypass goes plum through the middle of the Park. The first house at Tring Park was designed by Christopher Wren, and visited by Charles II and so, possibly, Nell Gwynne. The Park was later bought by Baron Lionel Walter de Rothschild and he had the house rebuilt. The second Baron Rothschild was a Fellow of the Royal Society and a keen zoologist, and he filled the Park with animals and used a carriage drawn by zebras. He also founded the Tring Museum (since 1938 part of the Natural History Museum), open most of the time, but check on tel: 0207 942 6171.

The Grand Union Canal near Tring

159

Aldbury Pond

The Grand Junction Canal was built at the height of 'canal mania', with the intention of providing a fast navigable link between London and Birmingham. Up to that time, the quickest way from the Midland canal system at Braunston (north-west of Daventry) to London was by a combination of the Oxford Canal and the Thames. The GJC was to be nearly 100km (60 miles) shorter. Work on the route started in 1793 and the line, including a major terminus at Paddington, opened in 1805. From then until 1838, the canal was a huge success; however, with the opening of Robert Stephenson's London & Birmingham Railway, income declined by 43 per cent in just six years. The company managed to keep traffic levels up into the 1870s and was able to make a number of significant improvements but the writing was clearly on the towpath wall. The 1890s saw amalgamation with some of its neighbours, and by 1929 the company became the Grand Union Canal Company. Although business continued to be lost to rail and road, the line remained open, although nowadays its prime function is as a cruising waterway. At Tring, the Grand Union reaches its 5km (3-mile) long southern summit. The builders reached here in 1799 and the resultant cutting is 2.5km (1.5 miles) long and 9m (30ft) deep. It took five years to dig! It's also a jolly good path and was the first officially designated long-distance towpath walk.

Our route passes the Royal Hotel and then the railway station. Cross the railway and continue on to pass a minor road L. After a further 100m or so, turn L (go straight on for Aldbury) up a metalled drive.

The pretty village of Aldbury is 2.5km (1.5 miles) further along Station Road, complete with village green, duck pond, fifteenth-century church, really gorgeous houses and, of course, some old stocks and a whipping-post. The stocks provided the name for a big eighteenth-century house just outside the village, home of a Victorian novelist, Mrs Humphrey Ward, from 1892 to 1920. For such a peaceful setting, it's perhaps more shocking to modern sensibilities to find that a brutal killing in Aldbury village formed the basis for one of her novels, *Marcella*, in 1894. Mrs Ward was also one of the first women magistrates and was fiercely opposed to the suffragettes. She was the niece of Matthew Arnold, mother-in-law of the historian G.M. Trevelyan, and aunt of Julian and Aldous Huxley. They, along with Henry James, often used to visit. Huxley said that she was his 'literary godmother'.

Further up the hill to the east is the Ashridge Estate which dates back to the times of the crusades. Edmund Crouchback, Earl of Cornwall, built a palace here with a surrounding deer park. He also installed 20 monks who guarded some precious drops of Christ's blood that

Duchie's Piece at Aldbury Nowers is also known as the Queen Elizabeth the Queen Mother Nature Reserve and was so designated in 1990 to celebrate HM's 90th birthday. Come here in summer and you will soon realise that it's a fabulous place for butterflies; half of all the butterfly species recorded in the UK have been seen here. The most notable, and extremely rare, are the Duke of Burgundy (of which only one was seen in 1998) and the dark green Fritillary.

Ivinghoe Beacon, at 230m (756ft), is a celebrated viewpoint. It was established as a beacon during the reign of Elizabeth I, to rouse local men in case of a Spanish invasion. The summit is ringed by a Late Bronze/Early Iron Age hillfort. There's a Bronze Age barrow at the highest point inside the fort and others on the hills nearby.

had been 'liberated' during the crusades. The place thus became an important destination for pilgrims and, in 1290–1, Edward VI held his Parliament here. Henry VIII knocked down the monastery and took the house for himself; Elizabeth I sold it in 1575 to the Egerton family (later the Dukes of Bridgwater and Earls of Brownlow). National fame came to the third Duke, Francis Egerton, when, in 1761, he asked the engineer James Brindley to build the first canal, the Bridgwater, between the family's coalmines in Worsley and Manchester. This was a fantastic commercial success, and stimulated canal mania.

James Wyatt designed the current Gothic Ashridge House in the early nineteenth century. Humphrey Repton and Capability Brown designed the surrounding park. When the third Earl of Brownlow died in 1921, the estate was sold, and served as a hospital during World War II, then as a store for the Public Records Office. The house is now a management college while the

continued on page 164

park, including the woods and commons right up to Ivinghoe Beacon, are owned by the National Trust. The park covers over 1,600ha (4,000 acres) and includes some of the most lush and beautiful woodland in the country. There's plenty of wildlife, including a herd of 200 fallow deer, many

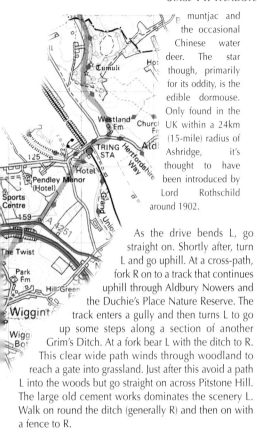

muntjac and the occasional Chinese water deer. The star though, primarily for its oddity, is the edible dormouse. Only found in the UK within a 24km (15-mile) radius of Ashridge, it's thought to have been introduced by Lord Rothschild around 1902.

As the drive bends L, go straight on. Shortly after, turn L and go uphill. At a cross-path, fork R on to a track that continues uphill through Aldbury Nowers and the Duchie's Place Nature Reserve. The track enters a gully and then turns L to go up some steps along a section of another Grim's Ditch. At a fork bear L with the ditch to R. This clear wide path winds through woodland to reach a gate into grassland. Just after this avoid a path L into the woods but go straight on across Pitstone Hill. The large old cement works dominates the scenery L. Walk on round the ditch (generally R) and then on with a fence to R.

There's plenty to see from Pitstone Hill, which is a nature reserve covering 22ha (54 acres) of chalk grassland. Grim's Ditch runs over most of it, and there are pits on top which are thought to be the remains of prehistoric flint mines. You can see Pitstone Windmill in the field to north, the Marsworth Reservoirs away in the distance to west, and the column of the Bridgwater Monument just visible amongst the trees to east. Most prominent, however, are the Castle Cement workings at the base of the hill. The cement works closed in 1991 and ever since there's been a battle over what'll happen next. At the time of writing, the matter is still in the air. A date of 1627 was found inscribed on Pitstone windmill which would make it one of the oldest surviving mills in England. The mill worked right up until 1902 when it was damaged in storm. It was given to the National Trust in 1938 and restored, and is open on summer Sunday afternoons (check on tel: 01494 528051). The Marsworth Reservoirs were built to

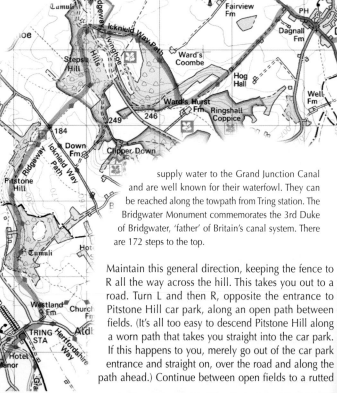

supply water to the Grand Junction Canal and are well known for their waterfowl. They can be reached along the towpath from Tring station. The Bridgwater Monument commemorates the 3rd Duke of Bridgwater, 'father' of Britain's canal system. There are 172 steps to the top.

Maintain this general direction, keeping the fence to R all the way across the hill. This takes you out to a road. Turn L and then R, opposite the entrance to Pitstone Hill car park, along an open path between fields. (It's all too easy to descend Pitstone Hill along a worn path that takes you straight into the car park. If this happens to you, merely go out of the car park entrance and straight on, over the road and along the path ahead.) Continue between open fields to a rutted track. Bear R and up the hill to a gate and stile. Do not cross, but take the parallel path to the L and walk on with fence to R. Head firstly towards and then into some low woodland. As you leave this, go down the hill and turn R through a gate. Continue across open ground to a road. From here there are a number of well-worn paths to the top of Ivinghoe Beacon. The official route crosses straight over and forks R. Shortly after, turn L and walk up the well-trod route to the top.

Edward Thomas reported seeing men droving sheep along the Icknield Way here, taking their flocks from Berkshire and Dorset to Dunstable, Royston and the farms of Cambridgeshire and Suffolk. He would have been about half way along his walk at that point, and wasn't enjoying it much. He took about 10 days to walk the path: he tried both Upper and Lower Icknield Ways before following the route through East Hendred to Wanborough. He also took the higher, Ridgeway, route to see the White Horse and Wayland's Smithy. He started before six in the morning and often walked 25 or 30 miles a day. It was a tough regime and a good walk but you can't help read the book and wonder why he did it.

Thomas was born in 1878 and made a somewhat precarious living as a writer. He wrote his book on the Icknield Way just before World War I. In 1914, he met with a group of poets and started writing the poetry that made his name. He published 143 poems, and mixed with Robert Frost, Walter de la Mare and W.H. Davies. He was described as the 'reluctant poet' and was apparently quite shy about his work, which was principally what we might now call war poetry. An exploding shell killed him on 9 April 1917 (the first day of the Battle of Arras).

The village of Ivinghoe is a quiet sort of place which, story has it, provided Sir Walter Scott with the title for *Ivanhoe*. It has a couple of watering holes (although The Kings Head is more of a restaurant than a pub) as well as sporadic buses into Aylesbury. The Beacon, of course, marks the end of the Ridgeway National Trail and the start of the Icknield Way path. We are now 333km (207 miles) from Lyme and 249km (154.5 miles) from Hunstanton.

PART 3: THE ICKNIELD WAY

Stage 15: Ivinghoe
Beacon to Luton Leagrave

Start:	Ivinghoe Beacon
Finish:	Luton Leagreave
Distance:	20.9km (13 miles)
OS:	Landrangers 165 Aylesbury & Leighton Buzzard, 166 Luton & Hertford
Route Features:	Country and town
Information:	Tourist Information Centre: Luton (01582 401579)

Things start to get serious again. After the cosy comforts of a National Trail, you'll quickly notice that the waymarks aren't quite as thorough and the paths not quite so clear or well trod. The long-distance path known as the Icknield Way has a hard time following the original prehistoric route. Take a glance at any road map and the original line is easy to follow: it's now called the A505. This is an extension of the Romanised Icknield Way that we saw just after Watlington, going through Tring, Dunstable, Luton, Hitchin, Baldock and Royston to cross the M11 just north of Great Chesterford. The line (if not the A505) then continues through Newmarket and Thetford to The Wash. Why the Romans should have 'improved' the Icknield in this fashion is a puzzle; suggesting only that having a good road to The Wash (and hence Lincoln or York) was important. Clearly the A505 is not good walking territory. We therefore follow the Icknield Way, as devised by the Icknield Way Association, which weaves around the original along a somewhat quieter line. In 1992, the Countryside Commission designated the Icknield as 'a Regional Route' to connect the Ridgeway with the Peddars Way.

As mentioned, Ivinghoe Beacon is in the middle of nowhere and Ivinghoe village poorly served by public transport. You may prefer therefore to start at Tring Station or at Whipsnade. Luton Leagrave is a railway station just one stop from central Luton. Pubs will be found en route at Dagnall and Dunstable.

From the top of Ivinghoe Beacon retrace your steps to the road. Turn L to take a path to a gate near the Icknield Way milestone. Go over the stile ahead and walk on with fence to R. You should cross the next stile to continue with fence R. Recently, however, this has become grossly overgrown and the 'popular' route switches to the National Trust field to R. If taking the correct route, keep fence close R to the next stile which then enters the NT field. The de facto route keeps the fence close L to a gate where the fence moves away L (with the entering stile). We continue by bearing slightly R to follow the contour of the hill to a gate and stile. Continue along a woodland path. After a cross-track, the route enters a dark cypress plantation. Eventually the clear path leaves this and enters a slight clearing with a view over fields to L towards the Whipsnade Lion.

After about 100m, go straight on, keeping the fence close L and ignoring the obvious track which bends R. Our path goes up the Hanging Coombe to a stile and a farmyard. Keep the fence close L to a gate and turn L immediately after along a dirt drive to a gate and stile. The route now continues in this general direction, along the R-hand edge of a narrow stand of trees and over several stiles, to the metalled driveway of Hog Hall Farm. Turn R and walk on to reach the A4146. Turn R to a roundabout (the centre of Dagnall). Go straight on, passing the All Saints Chapel of Ease, to the Golden Rule pub. Just after this, turn L with school L.

It's a strange place to find an Italianate basilica, but the All Saints Chapel of Ease was built in 1863 under the patronage of the last Earl Brownlow of Ashridge. At the time it served as a church, a day school and a mission room for the people of Dagnall.

The Whipsnade White Lion is on a hill below Whipsnade Wild Animal Park, and was made in 1933 as an advert for the zoo. It's 147m (483ft) long, making it just about the largest chalk hill figure in the UK. You get a much better impression of its size from the B4506. Interestingly, it's claimed that the lion is home to a colony of guinea pigs.

All Saint's Chapel of Ease, Dagnall

This path goes uphill, at first with hedge and then fence L to a stile and a road. Turn R and, after 100m, L through a gate next to the drive to 'The Bungalow' (which it isn't!). Go over the stile L and up the path to a further stile onto a golf course. Go straight on, over (or round) the first tee to the L side of a hedge ahead. Bear slightly L to walk on with trees to L to a narrow strip of trees separating two fairways. Bear slightly R to continue with trees close L until there's a bunker close R and a waymark post in the trees. Turn L and walk straight, following the waymark posts (at roughly 100m intervals) over several fairways to a fence surrounding Whipsnade Zoo.

> Whipsnade Wild Animal Park is part of London Zoo, and opened in 1931 in what was then a rather remote spot in the Bedfordshire hills. Nowadays it's all very accessible and more like a theme park. It does, however, make the normal zoo look a little cramped and inhumane, and focuses on the conservation of 2500 endangered species. Whipsnade is open all year (tel: 01582 872171).

Turn R. This path now follows the fence. The path goes L, then R into a wood, L at a T-junction, rejoins the fence and continues on to a metalled path. Turn L. Continue along the path, bearing R when it becomes a lane to reach Whipsnade green. Turn R to walk around Chequers House (ex Chequers Inn) to a drive. Follow the drive to the main road. Cross over and follow the lane opposite into the Tree Cathedral car park. Go through the gate and bear L to walk on with fence close L, and Tree Cathedral R, to a gate.

> The curious Tree Cathedral is made up of trees and hedges planted in a pattern inspired by Liverpool Cathedral; there are cloisters, transepts and chapels. Edmund Kell Blyth designed it in the 1930s as a memorial to three of his friends who were killed in World War I, and later presented it to the National Trust. It's a rather wonderful, calming place that seems to have all the solemnity of a real cathedral.

Continue with fence L to a gate. This leads over the drive of a bungalow to a path. Turn R and follow the path to a point where the view opens out over the Aylesbury plain ahead. Turn R, with hedge close R, and then take a path L that goes downhill to meet a cross-path. Turn R and just before the gate ahead, bear R uphill to another gate. Cross the field ahead along a worn grass path, staying in the centre (despite a popular path uphill to R). At the far side, go through a gate and walk on to the top of Dunstable Downs. From here bear R to the car park and visitors' centre.

> Dunstable Downs is a country park, owned by the National Trust, and the highest point in Bedfordshire at 242m (794ft). There are some dazzling views over the Vale of Aylesbury, as well as a Countryside Centre (open all year at weekends, most days during the summer – tel: 01582 608489). The country park attracts hordes of people, including hang-gliders and sometimes balloonists. There's also the London Gliding Club down in the valley. There is a custom of rolling oranges down Dunstable Downs on Easter Monday. But Dunstable Downs had a far more serious role in the past: look for

If you've seen the signs hereabouts, the Chiltern Way is a circular route of 200km (125 miles) which takes in Ewelme in the south-west through Bledlow, south of Wigginton, up to Streatley (Beds) in the north, then south again via Harpenden, Chorleywood and Hambledon. The walk has been beautifully signposted throughout by Chiltern Society members, and locally funded.

We'll be leaving the countryside behind for the next 14.5km (9 miles). The idea of walking straight through Dunstable and Luton may be a bit daunting, but it's not as bad as you might think. Honestly. If you just can't stand pavement bashing, the Icknield Association has devised a northern alternative (it's described in their route guide and marked on OS Explorer Maps) but it's further and seems even more contrived. You could also consider just getting a bus into Luton and then out again. But that's a bit of a cheat. No, you should try it – choose a sunny Sunday and you'll have numerous chats with numerous dog walkers. It'll also make you really appreciate the walk out of town.

the Five Knolls, a series of grave barrows on the northern fringe (or the hilly bit to the right as you look at the gliders). These are thought to be as much as 5000 years old and once part of a much larger group. There are also Roman and Norman burials here. The sheer prominence must have made the site significant and a place at which to honour the dead. The Five Knolls site was also used by the Saxons as a place of execution; 40 bodies have been found there with their hands tied behind their backs.

From the visitors' centre cross the road to a drive opposite with a fenced path half-L. Go down this path and onto a golf course. Follow the line of young trees ahead to reach the club car park. Go straight on. The path eventually leaves the course along an enclosed footpath (Buttercup Lane). This joins a drive and then descends to a road (Hurlock Close). Cross this and walk straight on for a short distance before turning L along Meadway. After 150m (and just before a bus stop) turn R along Cemetery Lane. At the end, pass some bollards and continue into Bennett Close. Now walk on with a recreation field R to reach another road. Cross this and go straight on with a Salvation Army Hall R. Pass a Baptist Chapel R. Bear R and then L to pass a Methodist Church. Now turn L along a shopping precinct, and shortly after, turn R to go through a passageway to reach Dunstable High St (aka Watling St) at a pedestrian crossing.

'The crossing of the Icknield Way and Watling Street makes Dunstable,' wrote Edward Thomas. Watling Street was one of the prime Roman roads running from London to Chester. The Romans had a settlement here and we might suppose that this would have been one of the stopping places for armies marching north. The town of Durocobrivae lay in the civitas of the Catuvellauni. Archaeologists have found a huge timber building in Friary Field, near Watling Street, over 30m (100ft) long and probably one of a pair. Numerous Roman burials have also been discovered. But the town itself was founded by Henry I for the purpose of guarding the safety of the ways against bandits who inhabited the surrounding woods.

Dunstable was one of the 12 selected towns where the body of Queen Eleanor (wife of Edward I) was brought on its way back to London. The queen had died in Nottinghamshire and the distraught Edward ordered that each night on the return the coffin should rest at a place capable of appropriate reverence and ceremony. To commemorate the event, the king had a cross erected in each town; sadly Dunstable's no longer exists.

It was as a coaching town that Dunstable came into its own. By the early eighteenth century this was a busy spot on the way from London to Holyhead and Ireland, with as many as 80 coaches a day coming along Watling Street and stopping here. The road was often improved at great expense, and in the first half of the nineteenth century Thomas Telford engineered what later became the A5. There are some fine old coaching inns in the centre of Dunstable, such as the Saracen's Head and the Sugar Loaf.

Cross the High St and turn R. After 100m, and just after No 33 (Priory House), turn L into Priory Gardens. Follow the path that bends L in front of the church and then round R to the L of it.

St Peter's Church was once the Augustinian Dunstable Priory founded by Henry I in the 1130s. Sadly only parts of the original survive, most notably the nave. Two Norman west towers were blown down on the same day

Dunstable Downs in August

during a storm in 1222. It was here that the first divorce in England was announced when Henry VIII 'dumped' Catherine of Aragon.

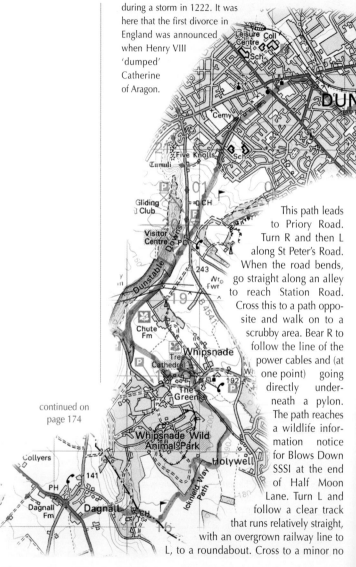

This path leads to Priory Road. Turn R and then L along St Peter's Road. When the road bends, go straight along an alley to reach Station Road. Cross this to a path opposite and walk on to a scrubby area. Bear R to follow the line of the power cables and (at one point) going directly underneath a pylon. The path reaches a wildlife information notice for Blows Down SSSI at the end of Half Moon Lane. Turn L and follow a clear track that runs relatively straight, with an overgrown railway line to L, to a roundabout. Cross to a minor no

continued on page 174

172

through road (Chaul End Road). This road becomes a metalled path (an overgrown road) and then bears L down into a field. Continue straight on in the direction of a pylon in the distance. Just after this bear L to cross a pedestrian railway bridge.

This reaches a road. Turn R along Bradley Road and over the M1 motorway. Turn first L along Halfway Avenue. This meets the A505 near a Travelodge Motel L. Cross the main road (pelican crossing). On the other side, turn L and then R along Stoneygate Road with Challney High School to L. Just after the school, turn L along a footpath that's enclosed with some ferocious looking fencing. At one point, the path bears R to pass a children's play area and then R again bordered with that metal fencing. At the end, turn R along Ely Way. Continue straight over a crossroad into School Lane. Eventually this narrows to become a path that soon arrives at Beechwood Road near a newsagents. Turn L to a T-junction then R along Compton Avenue to reach Leagrave railway station.

This is as close as we get to the centre of Luton, which is about 4km (2.5 miles) south-east of here. There's been a rich vein of archaeological finds in and around the town, which has been occupied since the Stone Age. The Romans and the Saxons were here too, albeit mostly in the northern fringes. The real growth of Luton began in the seventeenth century when a number of manufacturing industries were established, the most notable being straw plaiting. The surrounding country was, and is, fine arable land and the use of straw to make hats probably started about 1600. By the middle of the nineteenth century there are said to have been 30 factories making straw hats and importing fine Tuscan straw. But by the turn of the twentieth century the industry was

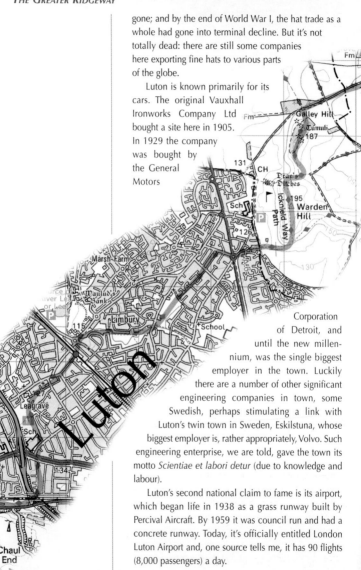

gone; and by the end of World War I, the hat trade as a whole had gone into terminal decline. But it's not totally dead: there are still some companies here exporting fine hats to various parts of the globe.

Luton is known primarily for its cars. The original Vauxhall Ironworks Company Ltd bought a site here in 1905. In 1929 the company was bought by the General Motors Corporation of Detroit, and until the new millennium, was the single biggest employer in the town. Luckily there are a number of other significant engineering companies in town, some Swedish, perhaps stimulating a link with Luton's twin town in Sweden, Eskilstuna, whose biggest employer is, rather appropriately, Volvo. Such engineering enterprise, we are told, gave the town its motto *Scientiae et labori detur* (due to knowledge and labour).

Luton's second national claim to fame is its airport, which began life in 1938 as a grass runway built by Percival Aircraft. By 1959 it was council run and had a concrete runway. Today, it's officially entitled London Luton Airport and, one source tells me, it has 90 flights (8,000 passengers) a day.

Stage 16: Luton Leagrave to Letchworth

Start:	Luton Leagreave
Finish:	Letchworth
Distance:	21.3km (13.3 miles)
OS:	Landranger 166 Luton & Hertford
Route Features:	Town and country
Information:	Tourist Information Centre: Letchworth (01462 4878681); e-mail: info@letchworth.com; Letchworth First Garden City Heritage Museum (01462 482710)

Luton Leagrave has a railway station and bus services into central Luton. Letchworth also has a railway station and numerous bus services. However, if you wish to travel between the two, you have to change bus at Hitchin. There are a couple of convenient and pleasant pubs on the way at Pirton and Ickleford.

Turn L along Station Road and then R to go under the railway to a roundabout. Go straight on along Bramingham Road (passing a petrol station and Macdonalds R). Continue with Marsh House Community Centre (and Waulud's Bank) L and the River Lea R. As the river swings R, take the tarmac path R which marks the route of the Upper Lea Valley Walk.

Leagrave is more than just a town suburb. It's home to the source of the River Lea which runs from here to the Thames at Docklands. The Lea Valley Walk follows the river for 80km (50 miles). It also has Waulud's (or Waulaud's) Bank which is Neolithic in origin (various flint arrowheads have been found) and once bore a henge (a sort of wooden Stonehenge). Its religious or ceremonial significance must therefore have been quite great. Excavations suggest that it dates from 2000 BC, similar to Avebury and Stonehenge. Waulud's Bank is one of the features named along the Michael/Mary line, and is included in at least one local ley line. A ley is a peculiar, and disputed, feature of the landscape in which sites of ancient importance can be joined on a map by straight lines. The local ley here is relevant because the points along it are mostly included in the route of the Icknield Way as it runs north-east: Waulud's Bank; Dray's Ditches; Galley Hill; Deacon Hill; Pirton Church; Holwell Church. It's an interesting observation that warrants some investigation.

There are two paths through Limbury Park. My route was to walk on and at a fork take the path R over a bridge. Follow this as it bends L and over the next bridge L. Then bear R to a third bridge. At the path turn L and follow this line to reach Neville Road. Cross the road, turn L and then R after the end house. After 100m, turn L over a bridge and go straight on up the grassy hill with no clear path. Aim for the L-hand of two roads visible ahead at the far end of the recreation ground. This is Gooseberry Hill and we walk up it, over a crossroad and on to a T-junction at Grasmere Road. Turn R to reach the A6 Bedford Road. Cross by the pedestrian crossing and go L to turn R up Weybourne Drive. Follow this to its end and continue along the track ahead. At the

River Lea, Limbury

Luton from Warden Hill

summit of the path turn L onto a path that runs over Warden Hill with views of Luton and the golf course L.

The path rises to a gate and the top of Warden Hill. Continue along a worn grassy path, which winds downhill to reach two kissing gates. Take either to reach a cross-path. Turn R (Drays Ditches are to L – part of the Waulud ley) along part of the John Bunyan Trail. Go uphill and then turn L at the field corner. Continue with fence L round the hill, through a gate and onto Galley Hill (the next part of the Waulud ley). Follow the path down to a gate and enter a golf course. Go straight on through the gap ahead with hedge R and green L. When the hedge comes to an end, turn half-L to a green lane. There is an Icknield Way information notice L.

Drays Ditches date from the seventh century BC and are the remains of a frontier fence: a series of post-holes cut into the chalk, with a now silted-up ditch, have been located. Galley Hill is a popular spot for local birdwatchers, and there are brown hares here too. There were gallows here in the fifteenth century, and some 24 burials, variously dating from prehistoric times, through Roman to late or post-medieval.

The John Bunyan Trail commemorates the fact that the author was born at Elstow, just south of Bedford. This trail runs for 72km (45 miles) around Streatley, Sharpenhoe, Harlington, Ampthill, Cranfield, Stevington, Clapham and Bedford. Some of the places visited are linked with his travels as a tinker; others are thought to be places where he preached. This was actually illegal, and he was put in Bedford gaol for a while on account of this and for his non-conformist views, and he wrote *Pilgrim's Progress* there. Bunyan described the hills between here and Pirton as those 'delectable mountains'.

Turn R and follow the green lane to a road. Continue in the same direction along the road to the Treasures Grove picnic area and car park. Continue straight on, through the car park and on to the green lane straight ahead.

The lumpy hills to the north of this section are the Barton Hills, and one of those (cloaked in trees) is Ravensburgh Castle, a classic Iron Age hillfort covering about 9ha (22 acres), dating from the fifth century BC. Reinforcements were added in the middle of the first century BC, at a time when the eastern ramparts were breached, interesting when you consider that Julius Caesar had invaded Britain in 54 BC. Cassivelaunus, king of the Catuvellauni, led the main opposition against these Roman forces. After some initial success, the Britons were beaten back into their stronghold, which was around the Hertfordshire/Bedfordshire area. As the other tribes submitted to the Romans, or even helped them, Cassivelaunus retreated into his oppidum (town or centre). With local assistance, Caesar then succeeded in capturing it. The precise location has been a matter of hot debate, but Ravensburgh is a prime candidate. Cassivelaunus went on to organise uprisings in Kent before Caesar took his army home to avoid the British winter.

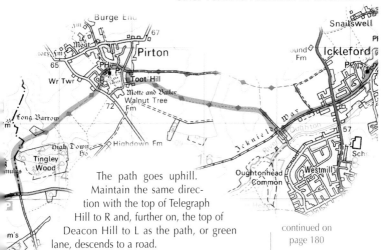

The path goes uphill. Maintain the same direction with the top of Telegraph Hill to R and, further on, the top of Deacon Hill to L as the path, or green lane, descends to a road.

continued on page 180

In Napoleonic times, Telegraph Hill bore one of the stations built as part of a rapid communication system from Great Yarmouth to the Admiralty in London. This was a kind of early-warning system against the threat of invasion, based on a kind of semaphore. Each hut had a lookout man who would record the message from the previous hut, and pass it to the next by opening and closing a series of shutters on the roof. It was cumbersome and depended on clear weather, but significantly quicker than using a horse and rider. The Icknield Way Association tell us this telegraph chain followed the Icknield Way, at roughly 16km (10-mile) intervals, for much of its route (there is a Telegraph Road near another site at Icklingham).

Turn R along the road for 250m and then go L (at a waymark post) along a bridleway. Walk uphill to the corner of a field and then go half-R to a road. Cross and walk along Great Green to reach the village green at Pirton with the Motte and Bailey pub to R. Go R after the pub, down Crabtree Lane. Opposite No 16, go R along a path. At the church gate go R and then L, before

It is recorded that at Ickleford in 1590 there was a man named Harding, who claimed to be a witch – a capital offence. However, his charms and potions were so bad and so frequently failed to cure ailments that he was sent to prison for fraud.

179

The Spirella building was originally the factory for the famous Spirella corset company. It's now a Grade II Listed Building, and was reopened in October 1999, after a £11m refurbishment, as a 'state-of-the-art' business and conference centre.

an information board, to walk on with fence close L. (For the Fox pub, the village stores and the village pond, continue along Crabtree Lane, which bends L and then turn R – following the Icknield Way Riders Route signs.)

The information board outlines the history of Pirton and gives an artist's impression of what the motte-and-bailey castle – Toot Hill – must have looked like in its prime, when it was surrounded by a moat and looked rather grand. Toot, or moot, hills are common throughout Britain and are probably prehistoric meeting places. Silbury Hill is thought to be one. The

church is built within the bailey of the old castle, and is included in the Waulud ley line. Although largely rebuilt in 1877, the tower is essentially twelfth century. Legend has it that there's a horde of gold at the bottom of Pirton village pond.

At the end of the field, walk on into Walnut Tree Road and turn R. After a short distance, take a path (with a metal gate) that runs between house Nos 11A and 13. This path passes some allotments to reach a sports ground. Bear L to walk on with field to R. Continue in this same general direction for nearly 2km to a green lane known as Mill Way. Turn R and walk to some cottages and turn L along Westmill Lane. This leads to the A600. Cross straight over and go along Turnpike Lane to a road junction near the Old George pub in Ickleford. Bear L, past the pub, the church and Ickleford Stores.

Just after the stores and bus stop, turn R along a gravel drive that leads to a field. Bear L to cross one of the two bridges over the River Hiz. The path then goes over the railway footbridge and on, along an obvious course through some pleasant countryside, for 1.5km to a road at Wilbury Hill. Continue, over the road, and along a path that reaches a gap in the hedge in the corner of a field. This leads to a road (Icknield Way). Turn R and walk on for about 1km to reach Spring Road. Turn R down here and, just before a railway arch, go L along a path that eventually leads to a road near a railway bridge and the Spirella building. (Go R here for Letchworth and the railway station.)

Spirella Building, Letchworth

181

In 1903 Sir Ebenezer Howard and his associates formed a company called First Garden City Ltd and began to build a town at Letchworth, the first of Hertfordshire's garden cities, with wide boulevards and plenty of green areas. Everything was carefully controlled in terms of town planning and industrial development. Industry, for example, had a balanced need for men and women workers, as well as skilled and unskilled labour; there was also a rich diversity, including engineering and food production, printing and furniture manufacture. The town's physical openness must have been a stark contrast to the claustrophobic inner-city crowding that the people came to escape. Some ridiculed it. The fact that it was a 'dry town', a haven of temperance, probably didn't help the image. Even today, it's said to be bland, to lack soul, to lack city excitement or village closeness.

But Letchworth certainly appealed to the painter Spencer Gore, born in 1878 and a founder of the Camden Town Group in 1911. They were prominent post-impressionists who used bold colours, strong outlines and textured paint surfaces in their depictions of the urban landscape. Perhaps it was the novelty of the place that brought Gore to Letchworth in 1912. He stayed with a friend in Wilbury Road and painted numerous paintings of the new town. They all tend to have intensely bright colours and stylised forms.

We'll leave the last word about Letchworth to dear old Edward Thomas who, as he plodded his wearisome way out of town along the Icknield, wrote, 'Letchworth was still in sight, like so many wounds on the earth and so much sticking-plaster.'

Stage 17: Letchworth to Royston

Start:	Letchworth
Finish:	Royston
Distance:	23.4km (14.7 miles)
OS:	Landrangers 166 Luton & Hertford, 153 Bedford & Huntingdon, 154 Cambridge & Newmarket
Route Features:	Town and country
Information:	Baldock Visitor Centre (01438 737373)

Both Letchworth and Royston have railway stations, and you can travel from one to other using the regular train service. There are shops and other facilities at Baldock. The path passes pubs at Sandon and Therfield.

From the railway bridge, turn L. Pass the Spirella building and take the first R along Nevells Road. After a short distance, turn L into The Quadrant. Cross the main road onto Norton Common and then turn R along the first metalled path to walk between tennis courts and bowling greens and then past the open-air swimming pool. Bear R up the drive to a roundabout. Turn L and then R along Icknield Way for about 1km. At a round-about go L and then R into Blackhorse Road. After

Almshouses, Baldock

passing some factories, turn R along Knapp Close and over a railway bridge. The path winds round to the A1(M) and bends R to a footbridge over it to L. Cross the bridge and go straight on along West Avenue and down to a T-junction. Go L and immediately R into Pond Lane. Turn R at the next major road bearing slightly L at the end into the broad Baldock High St.

The 25ha (63 acres) of Norton Common are famous for their black squirrels, first seen here in 1944 and not elsewhere in England. Baldock marks the point where the Icknield Way crosses the old Great North Road, and there has been town here since the time of the Romans and Saxons. It was the Knights Templar who, having settled here, named it after Baldach, a city of their order near Babylon, now called Baghdad! In more recent times, the town has been known for malting and brewing, and of course for that all-important location as a staging post on the route north.

Go along High St to the roundabout with Tescos to

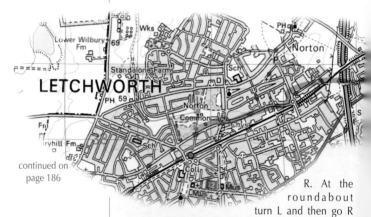

continued on page 186

R. At the roundabout turn L and then go R into Limekiln Lane. Pass a convent and a school and take a small metalled lane with Hillside (caravan) Park immediately L. When this lane bends L into the park, continue straight uphill along a footpath and up to a field. Maintain this general direction for about 2km, past some old farm buildings and on to a cross-track and a field in front of you. On the other side of the field is a low mound of a hill and our line over the field is towards the low point on the right side of that low mound. This is the exact course of a Roman road and heads towards the village of Clothall.

On the other side of the field, cross a stile. Immediately turn L and take a clear path with hedge L to a road. Cross and go uphill over a lane. Our way now continues in a gentle R curve for 2km to a road. Turn R to enter Wallington. The 'official' Icknield Way route turns R into a bridleway and then L past the church and L again to a duck pond. This is daft as it deliberately avoids the whole point of coming to Wallington. So go straight on into the village to a road junction and look L to see No 2 Kit's Lane.

> Wallington would be a fairly unremarkable place if it wasn't for the fact that in early 1936, one Eric Blair rented the (rather run-down) village stores at 2 Kit's Lane, right next to the (long-closed) Plough Inn. He, of course, was George Orwell. Although he only really lived here for four years, it was a busy time in what was then a rather remote spot and a rather primitive cottage. He was broke, and he came here with a view to writing in the

If you hate walking through towns you'll be pleased to know that it's mostly country from now on. There'll be the odd village, but Royston's about as big as it'll get – and that's pretty small. We don't actually go to Clothall, but it's famous for a Roman lead plate on which a message is written backwards: 'Tacita is hereby cursed, and this curse shall reveal her to be putrefying like rotting blood'. Such plates would have been nailed to posts at the temple, or thrown into a

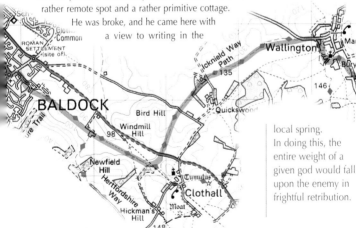

local spring. In doing this, the entire weight of a given god would fall upon the enemy in frightful retribution.

mornings and opening the shop in the afternoons in order to top-up his literary earnings. He wrote several novels here, including *Road to Wigan Pier* and, after fighting in the Spanish Civil War, *Homage to Catalonia*. He also married Eileen O'Shaughnessy in the village church. But the Orwells were always outsiders and it's said that they didn't mix much. Perhaps that's why he included various Wallington villagers in *Animal Farm*. Even though the Orwells still rented the cottage until 1947, they actually moved out in May 1940 when he got a job with the BBC. And in the front garden he planted a sixpenny Woolworth's rambler rose, which still flourishes as a large hedge.

Follow the road round as it bends R and walk on up to the aforementioned duck pond. We now go straight on,

Icknield Way near Wallington

186

George Orwell's house, Wallington

over a stile and up the hill to another stile just to the L of a grain silo belonging to Bury Farm, which some people think might have been the original setting for *Animal Farm*; others suggest Manor Farm, also in the village, or Chalk Farm, near Eastbourne.

The path continues to the far L corner of the field. Here four substantial mature hedges meet. Go through a gap and bear L. This path goes downhill to cross a ditch. Turn half-L and walk towards a thatched cottage on the other side of the field. At the road, turn L and then almost immediately R. The track enters a field and we continue with a hedge L. Eventually this path bends R to face some farm buildings and the path ahead becomes more overgrown. Here a waymark post indicates the position of a plank bridge over a ditch to L. After crossing, walk over the next field aiming for a stile just to L of a bungalow with solar panels on its roof. Cross the stile and walk along the drive to a road. Our way now bears R past the sign for 'The Aylwins' to a footpath sign near the village pond. Go through a gate and then keep to the R-hand side of the field to another gate. There is now a succession of kissing gates past and through some paddocks. Eventually the fairly obvious route goes down a field and takes another gate onto a

drive. Yet another gate enters the next field and the path bears R to a stile and plank bridge with two kissing gates. Our way now bears slightly R towards a cottage and a prominent footpath sign. Cross the stile and turn L along the road into Sandon and The Chequers pub. Turn R along the road to reach the green and the church.

Go through the lych-gate. Take the path to the L of the church and then bear L along a path through the graveyard to a road. Turn R and where the road turns L, continue straight for a short distance and then go R along a path labelled 'Park Lane'. This reaches a road. Turn L and then L again at a junction. After a short distance, take a further L along the drive to a house and bear R after about 50m to follow a path through the trees to a T-junction. Turn R here to go along a green lane to a further T-junction. Turn L to walk along this path to join a farm track. When this turns sharp L continue straight ahead with a ditch L. Continue along the path to a gate and stile L. Cross this and bear R along the field edge to a gate and stile. Cross into a field, and continue to another gate which takes the route into the next field. Go straight on with trees L to a stile. This leads to the road at Therfield village.

Turn L to reach the Fox and Duck pub. Go up the drive on the R side of the pub to a footpath to L just before a house. This leads to a field. Cross to the far L corner and a plank bridge after which turn half-L towards the middle of the next hedge. Now bear L slightly to a green lane. Follow this line for 2km as it becomes a path, then a green lane again, then a path again and then a chalk road. During this last phase, the road turns suddenly R, but we go straight on along a

The ancient custom of 'maying' was observed in Sandon every May Day well into the second half of the nineteenth century. In this some groups of men, presumably after a visit to The Chequers, were dressed in top hats with ribbons down their backs. They then toured the local villages singing traditional Mayers' songs. At the door of each house they would leave some may blossom and they would collect 'gifts'.

path with a hedge close R (the waymark post here is tucked in the hedge). This path soon leads to a stile onto Therfield Heath.

Therfield (Anglo-Saxon for 'dry place') was cleared 6,000 years ago by Neolithic farmers. There is a Neolithic long barrow and 10 Bronze Age round barrows here, one group of which is known as the Five Hills, and to the west are a number of Iron Age earthworks known as the Mile Ditches. The cleared Therfield Heath (aka Royston Heath) was much favoured by James I for its excellent hunting. He even established a hunting lodge called King James' Palace at Royston which became his country residence (he signed the death warrant for Sir Walter Raleigh there). The king enjoyed shooting dotterel and great bustard here, and hunting hares. In the eighteenth century Royston Heath became a popular spot for hare coursing amongst Cambridge undergrads, much to the displeasure of local farmers. But the place has always been a popular sporting venue. In the thirteenth century medieval grand tournaments were held here. In 1827, 15,000 people came to watch a prize fight between the champion Jem Ward and Peter Crawley. Royston Cricket Club was established just

continued on page 190

189

three years after the MCC. King James started races on the heath, and horses are still exercised here. It's also noted that the golf club (to R) once had Nick Faldo as its junior champion. The heath has featured in more important historical events, too. In 1455, Richard Duke of York, the Earl of Warwick and the Earl of Salisbury gathered an army of 3000 men here before the first battle of the Wars of the Roses at St Albans. The heath housed Italian and German POWs during World War II. Nowadays Therfield Heath is a nature reserve and SSSI covering 169ha (417 acres). It's an important area of chalk downland and, famous for its pasque flowers in April. Amongst its notable fauna are the chalk hill blue butterfly, the common lizard and the hooded crow.

Continue in approximately the same direction, following a chalky path down towards the Heath Sports Centre car park and the main road. Turn R to walk into the main road junction in Royston town centre (turn L here for the railway station).

Like Dunstable and Baldock, Royston's existence is based on the Icknield Way crossing a major north–south route, in this case Ermine Street (nowadays known rather

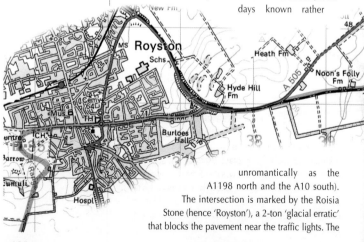

unromantically as the A1198 north and the A10 south). The intersection is marked by the Roisia Stone (hence 'Royston'), a 2-ton 'glacial erratic' that blocks the pavement near the traffic lights. The

The Roisia Stone, Royston

stone is thought to have been used as the base for a cross erected by (or, perhaps, for) William the Conqueror's sister, Lady Roisia. Here travellers could offer prayers for a safe journey. The cross has gone, but its base remains to this day. The Lady's cross may also have given us the hot cross bun, long thought to have originated in the area; the theory goes that Royston's cross may well be where the buns were invented. Ermine Street was a Roman road built to link London, Lincoln and York. Later the town became an important staging post on this road north. At one time there were 55 pubs in Royston to serve this passing traffic; a mere eight now exist. Dick Turpin's favourite pub, the Hoops, was demolished in 1961; the oldest, The Bull, dates from 1520.

One of the most curious places in the town is Royston Cave in Melbourne Street. It's actually a man-made cave, cut out of the chalk. The walls are partly covered with medieval carvings (dating from around 1310), thought to have been made by the Knights Templar. One theory is that it was probably a kind of secret meeting place used for initiations or other special ceremonies. It was discovered accidentally in 1742 and soon became a tourist attraction, being promoted as 'the greatest curiosity of the kind in Europe'. It is now open on summer Saturday and Sunday afternoons.

Stage 18: Royston to Great Chesterford

Start:	Royston
Finish:	Great Chesterford
Distance:	20.9km (13 miles)
OS:	Landranger 154 Cambridge & Newmarket
Route Features:	Easy country
Information:	Tourist Information Centre: Cambridge (01223 222640; 3222640 e-mail: tourism@cambridge.gov.uk

Both Royston and Great Chesterford have railway stations, and are linked by train via Cambridge. There are pubs at Heydon, Chrishall and Elmdon.

Continue along the road, past the Roisia Stone and on over a roundabout. Continue along the road for 1.2km until the pavement on the L comes to an end near a Greenwich meridian notice. Turn R and cross the road. Go up the drive opposite and then, almost immediately, go L up a clear path into the woods. This is a permissive path and is closed every 1 February. This line continues through woods to a field and then goes on with hedge and A505 close L. Go over two farm tracks to the road to reach the L-hand corner of the furthest field and a path that leads round L to a gravel road. Turn R. The road passes some houses and then turns L. We, however, go straight on along a path and over two roads for a total distance of roughly 4km (passing from Hertfordshire into Cambridgeshire). After the second road (if you reach a third you've gone too far), there's a small wood L. Opposite this a waymark post directs us R along the clear line of Heydon Ditch which runs between fields and up the far slope. We share this with the Harcamlow Way. At the top of the hill, turn R along the road into Heydon. Turn L at next road junction (turn R for the pub).

The well-manicured Heydon is one of the highest villages in Cambridgeshire. Curiously the church was bombed during World War II. The King William IV pub, an attractive old country inn with rambling rooms, showing beams, log fires and lots of ornaments, was crowned Vegetarian Pub of the Year in the Good Pub Guide 2000.

The road bends R and then L to pass a pond. Here turn R along a farm drive. Where this eventually goes sharp R in front of a small wood, bear L over a field (a waymark post helps here). The path arrives at a hedge, turn L and shortly thereafter R over a small footbridge. For those who didn't like Cambridgeshire, we are now in Essex. Walk on with hedge L to a drive and a road. Turn R and shortly after L. In this small field, go half-L through a gap in the hedge opposite a road. Turn R and walk into Chrishall.

The Harcamlow Way is a figure-of-eight walk that runs from Harlow via Standon through Saffron Walden, returning via Melbourn and Chrishall to Newport and Hatfield Forest.

Heydon Ditch

Chrishall is pronounced 'Krissle' or 'Kriss Hall'. The village is on relatively high ground for the area – 130m (427ft) above sea level – and locals have a joke that it qualifies as a 'Marilyn' (a name derived from the 'Munros' of Scotland). The village sign shows the Holy Trinity church and the graves of the Brand family who left a trust for both the village and the church. Beneath this on the left is The Red Cow pub.

At a road junction (with The Red Cow pub away R) go L and then almost immediately L into Loveday Close and a small cluster of new houses. Take a path to the L of the garage of the first house. This leads to what looks like a dead end but goes on to a field. Walk on with hedge close L, then a fence R and then between fields to a tiny gap in the hedge ahead. Go through this and you find a green lane. Turn R

and then L along the next green lane. This leads to a road. Turn R into Elmdon.

Elmdon typifies the fate of England's villages. Within a few months of each other in 1998, the fifteenth-century King's Head pub as well as the village's shop and post office were closed. The properties are simply worth much more as houses in this Cambridge commuter belt.

At a road junction near the church (where the pub used to be), turn R and go uphill. Just after some speed limit signs, and as the road bends R, turn L along a lane. This leads to Freewood Farm. Turn L just before a red-brick building and continue on to a metalled farm drive past a wood R. As this drive bends L, go R along a path with wood R and a field L. This soon changes to a wood L and a field R, but continue along the increasingly windy track to reach some houses. Just after a rather ornate, cream-coloured house, turn L along a path which provides a fine view of the Saxon St Mary the Virgin church at Strethall.

After arriving at a road, turn R and go downhill to a T-junction. Turn L, across the next junction and then, about 250m on – and just before a passing place on the road – go half-R diagonally over a field towards the far corner. Now bear L along a hedged path that, after 1.2km arrives at the M11. Bear R and then go L over the motorway bridge. The track bends L and then goes R along an enclosed path that soon becomes a drive and bends L to a road. Turn R to go over the level crossing and follow the road round to the road junction with Great Chesterford railway station to R. Turn L to cross the River Cam (or Granta) to 'The Crown House' and then turn R along Church St to reach Great Chesterford church.

continued on
page 196

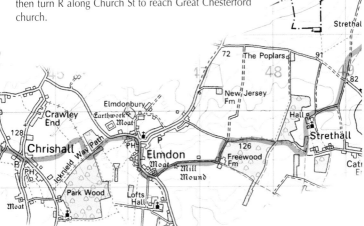

Great Chesterford isn't big, but it has at least two pubs, of which The Plough in the High Street dates from the eighteenth century. The Romans constructed a large fort here covering some 14–15ha (35–7 acres), probably built by order of Suetonius Paullinus in AD 61 after the Boudicca uprising. It appears that very quickly a vicus (or village) developed outside the fort on the eastern side of the river. This soon became a walled town which covered 16ha (40 acres). Apparently the walls were robbed for building stone in the eighteenth century. There

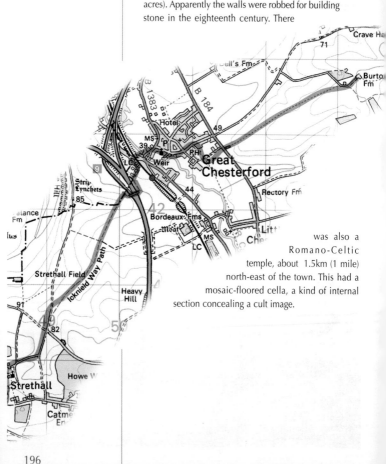

was also a Romano-Celtic temple, about 1.5km (1 mile) north-east of the town. This had a mosaic-floored cella, a kind of internal section concealing a cult image.

Stage 19: Great Chesterford to Stetchworth

Start:	Great Chesterford
Finish:	Stetchworth
Distance:	28.9km (18 miles)
OS:	Landranger 154 Cambridge & Newmarket
Route Features:	Easy country
Information:	Tourist Information Centre: Newmarket (01638 667200)

This section and the next are strangely remote. Some planning is needed, depending on how far you want to walk and where you want to stay. The proximity of Cambridge and Newmarket is useful, but can be misleading in terms of ready access. Buses do visit the various villages between Linton and Stetchworth, but they're not frequent and may not be conveniently timed.

The Dog & Duck, Linton

Great Chesterford has a railway station and Linton is well served with buses. Stetchworth has spasmodic buses and is relatively close to Dullingham station and only 5.5km (3.5 miles) from the centre of Newmarket. Luckily the route goes through several villages and each seems blessed with at least one pub.

Church St becomes South St and, after the Crown and Thistle, it bends L and becomes the High St. Not far after the pub, turn R along Rose Lane (go straight on The Plough). The lane leads to a barrier and footpath sign. Walk on for 100m and, at a cross-track, turn L uphill with hedge L to a road. Turn R for 50m, then L up a waymarked track.

The area to the right along here is Chesterford Park. This former mansion and grounds is home to a pesticide company called BioFocus. The multi-millions needed to bring a new pesticide to market these days have meant a constant series of mergers. The history of research at Chesterford Park illustrates this perfectly. In 1952 there was a company called Pest Control Ltd, which was taken over by Fisons Pest Control. Fisons merged with Boots to form FBC; in the 1980s FBC was, in turn, taken over by

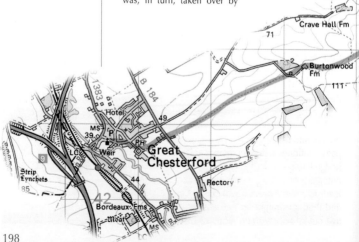

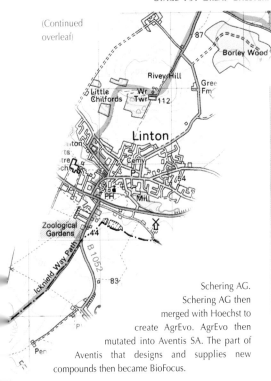

(Continued overleaf)

Schering AG. Schering AG then merged with Hoechst to create AgrEvo. AgrEvo then mutated into Aventis SA. The part of Aventis that designs and supplies new compounds then became BioFocus.

Continue for 2km along the top of the hill to reach a minor road. Turn R and follow the lane round to Burtonwood Farm. The path continues with farmhouse R. Just after the house go R along a track that bends L (with hedge L) and crosses two fields. Go through a gap in the field corner and turn R. After a junction of four hedges and paths, go half-R to a gap between fields. The path continues with electricity cables R. Continue with hedge L to go under the cables. We now go downhill to enter a green lane, which becomes a farm track that leads to a minor road. Bear L past a Cambridgeshire sign and then go straight on into Linton; passing the zoo L. Just before a busy main road, go L along a no through

Connoisseurs will note that the 8ha (18-acre) Chilford Hundred Vineyard is situated on a south-west facing slope, ensuring that the vines get the most sunshine during the summer and are protected from the winter's north winds. The wine itself is made and blended on site. It's said that the Chilford wines have a good clean flavour, a fragrant nose, a fruity body and good acidity. If you don't believe me then they welcome visitors between 11am–5pm from May to October, seven days a week. It's worth a stop as they also have an art gallery.

In AD 1010, marauding Vikings massacred the Saxon settlement of Balsham after the village had made a stand against the Danes. Just one man survived after defending himself so fiercely in the church tower doorway that the Danes gave up. The whole affair is celebrated on the village sign. The church itself now has a thirteenth-century tower and a 400-year-old bell. The village has two pubs.

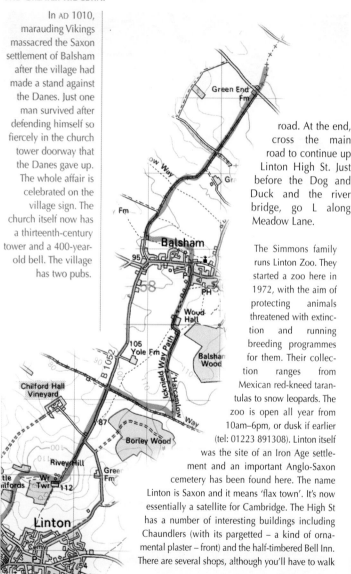

road. At the end, cross the main road to continue up Linton High St. Just before the Dog and Duck and the river bridge, go L along Meadow Lane.

The Simmons family runs Linton Zoo. They started a zoo here in 1972, with the aim of protecting animals threatened with extinction and running breeding programmes for them. Their collection ranges from Mexican red-kneed tarantulas to snow leopards. The zoo is open all year from 10am–6pm, or dusk if earlier (tel: 01223 891308). Linton itself was the site of an Iron Age settlement and an important Anglo-Saxon cemetery has been found here. The name Linton is Saxon and it means 'flax town'. It's now essentially a satellite for Cambridge. The High St has a number of interesting buildings including Chaundlers (with its pargetted – a kind of ornamental plaster – front) and the half-timbered Bell Inn. There are several shops, although you'll have to walk

Village Green, Balsham

a bit beyond the Dog and Duck to find the supermarket and, further on still, the post office.

Meadow Lane leads to a recreation ground. Take the path straight on and then turn R to walk past a sports pavilion and over the river. The path now goes straight on between houses into Symonds Lane. Go over this and along a path with bungalows (L) to a T-junction. Turn R for 50m, then L along a bridleway that goes uphill. Near the top of the hill, the path bends R to reach a substantial water tower. It then bends L to a minor road.

Walk along the road (past the vineyard entrance) to a signposted gap in the hedge R. Go half-R over the field to another hedge gap. Continue across the next field to a green lane. Turn R.

This green lane is actually the Roman road from Colchester to Godmanchester. It was given the name 'via Devana' in the eighteenth century by a Dr Mason, a Cambridge geologist. He mistakenly thought it went all the way to the Roman town of Deva (Chester).

In just under 1km turn L to go along a byway (shared with the Harcamlow Way) that eventually bends L (ignore footpath R) and then R to pass Wood Hall. Now follow the drive into Balsham.

The original course of the Icknield Way doesn't go through Linton and Balsham, but follows on from the A505 to take a line now used by the A11. That route runs along a comparatively narrow ridge of chalk that's an extension of the Chilterns and forerunner of the chalk that surfaces in north-west Norfolk. To either side of the ridge the chalk is covered with a layer of boulder clay;

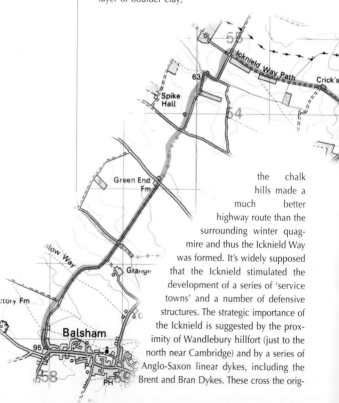

the chalk hills made a much better highway route than the surrounding winter quagmire and thus the Icknield Way was formed. It's widely supposed that the Icknield stimulated the development of a series of 'service towns' and a number of defensive structures. The strategic importance of the Icknield is suggested by the proximity of Wandlebury hillfort (just to the north near Cambridge) and by a series of Anglo-Saxon linear dykes, including Brent and Bran Dykes. These cross the original route but don't all reach the Icknield Way Path. Fleam Dyke, for example, ends just north-west of Balsham but we shall meet the Devil's Ditch just after Stetchworth.

continued on page 204

On reaching the main road in Balsham (turn R for the Black Bull and The Bell pubs), continue past the post office and stores on to the village green where there is an Icknield Way milestone. This tells us that we're 63 miles (101km) from Ivinghoe Beacon and 43 miles (69km) from Knettishall Heath. Go straight on along Church Lane. This goes R. Turn L at the church gate to a sports ground. Turn L and go round the field over a series of stiles. After passing some houses R, turn R along the green lane (Fox Lane). Continue on this for nearly 5km; crossing two roads. At the end, the lane turns R to reach a minor road. Turn L and walk on for about 300m. Then turn R by an Icknield Way post along a farm road to Crick's Farm. Eventually, where this track bends R by a pond, go L uphill along a footpath. Make for a gap between a hedge L and a fence R. Walk on with fence R to a road. Bear R along the road for 100m to a road junction. Go L, through a gate and follow the path that heads towards the church in Brinkley (coming out via Coles Lane).

Brinkley has the Red Lion pub (turn L and then straight on at two junctions). To continue the walk, however, go R along the road and then, just before a telephone box, L at an Icknield Way sign. This path runs alongside a stream R to a bridge and double stile.

Continue across the next field with wood L to a stile and bridge L. Walk on uphill and then go half-R along path between fields to go over a small bridge and through a gate. Continue with hedge R then go R through a gate and over yet another small bridge. Now turn L and walk on to the pub in Burrough Green.

Burrough Green is a small place with the convenient Bull pub. The eleventh-century flint church

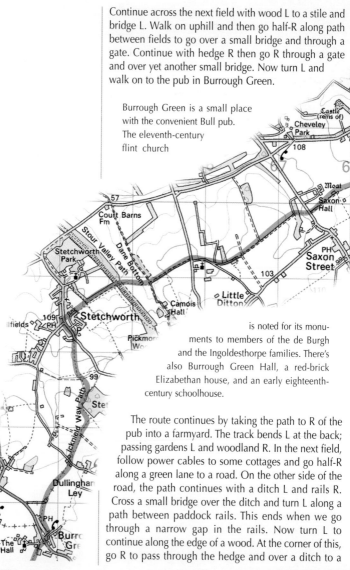

is noted for its monuments to members of the de Burgh and the Ingoldesthorpe families. There's also Burrough Green Hall, a red-brick Elizabethan house, and an early eighteenth-century schoolhouse.

The route continues by taking the path to R of the pub into a farmyard. The track bends L at the back; passing gardens L and woodland R. In the next field, follow power cables to some cottages and go half-R along a green lane to a road. On the other side of the road, the path continues with a ditch L and rails R. Cross a small bridge over the ditch and turn L along a path between paddock rails. This ends when we go through a narrow gap in the rails. Now turn L to continue along the edge of a wood. At the corner of this, go R to pass through the hedge and over a ditch to a path with ditch R. A short way on, follow another ditch that goes L downhill. At the bottom, go over a bridge and stile into a paddock. Walk on with fence L. This goes up to a stile and a green lane cross-roads. Go straight on to reach a road. Turn L to walk into Stetchworth.

Stetchworth has the Marquis of Granby pub. From there, there are occasional buses to Newmarket or even back to Linton. Glance at an OS map and it's possible to walk to the railway station (Dullingham), but it's a rather unpromising 3km (1.8 miles) away. Newmarket is just 5.5km (3.5km) to the north.

Stage 20: Stetchworth to Icklingham

Start:	Stetchworth
Finish:	Icklingham
Distance:	27.3km (17 miles)
OS:	Landrangers 154 Cambridge & Newmarket, 155 Bury St Edmunds
Route Features:	Easy but long
Information:	Tourist Information Centre: Bury St Edmunds (01284 764667)

Stetchworth isn't easy to get to, although there are buses and Dullingham railway station is reasonably close. Newmarket (and its railway station) is just 5.5km (3.5 miles) to the north. Icklingham doesn't connect with Newmarket on a public transport level but does have ready access to Bury St Edmunds where there is a railway station. Pubs are at Cheveley, Dalham and Tuddenham.

Just opposite the Marquis of Granby, go along a path signposted for the Devil's Ditch and Woodditton. This takes you over a road. Turn half-R to go along a path between bungalows. At the end, continue along the edge of a field, downhill with trees L. Keep on into the woodland straight ahead and over the Devil's Ditch.

The Devil's Ditch (or Dyke) runs dead straight for just over 11km (7 miles) from south-east to north-west across Newmarket Heath. Its position takes advantage of the higher ground. The associated ditch is still 6m (20ft) wide in places with a rampart of roughly 9m (30ft) above it. It was clearly built to defend land on one side, and the defences suggest that it was used by the people of the north-east against those from the south-west. Opinion varies on precisely who built it and when, but the most likely date for its construction is sometime between AD 300 and 750. One observation is that Iceni coins and artefacts occur north-east of the Dyke, but not (much) south-west. Was this the limit of Iceni territory? Or just coincidence? Its construction was a huge undertaking: one estimate sets the number of man-days at over one million. We can definitely conclude that it was seen as important to have control of the Icknield, and that this was thus a strategically important spot. Incidentally, the Stour Valley long-distance path runs along the length of the Dyke. The route follows the river valley south from Newmarket to Cattawade in Suffolk.

From the Devil's Ditch, go straight on between fields down into Dane Bottom. Turn R and then L along a farm track to a stile and a road. Turn R and then L along Maypole Lane with church to R.

Hop Drier, Dalham

This is about as close as the path gets to the famous horseracing town of Newmarket (about 5–6km/3–3.7 miles north-west). Newmarket has been the Mecca of horseracing since the seventeenth century when James I played a role in starting the 'sport of kings' here. The Jockey Club, the controlling body of British racing, also started here. They're still in a building in the High St right next to the National Horseracing Museum.

The gravestone of William Symons in Woodditton churchyard has indented into it an iron dish that it bears the following inscription:

Here lies my corpse, who was the man,
That loved a sop in the dripping pan.
But now believe me I am dead,
See here the pan stands at my head.
Still for sops till the last I cried,
But could not eat and so I died.
My neighbours they perhaps will laugh,
When they do read my epitaph.

Dalham main street

After the church, the road bends to Church Hall Farms North and South. Here fork L. Continue along the road, which becomes a farm track, for 1.5km. Where the track bends L before a wood, cross a stream R, and walk through the wood and into a field. The path goes uphill to a stile. Cross the road (turn L for The Reindeer pub in Saxon Street, about 1km away) to go along the bridleway ahead. Continue in this general direction into Cheveley. Turn L (R for Red Lion pub and the post office and stores).

Continue along the village street, passing the church R. About 250m after that, go R along a path that leads to a road in Ashley. Turn L and then at the Crown pub, go R to pass a pond R. Follow this road, which bends and twists, to go downhill to reach a crossroads. Continue straight on and just before a bridge over a river, turn R into woodland R. This path continues with the River Kennett L for about 1.5km to Dalham. Just before the road,

continued on page 210

All Saints church is an oddity in that it appears to be mostly redundant; some of its contents have been moved to St James. All Saints dates from the thirteenth century and is thatched.

the path goes over the river. On the road, turn L (turn R for the Affleck Arms). Just after a road signposted to the church (R) and a curious conical hop drier (L), go R through a gate and along a tree-lined avenue leading to Dalham Hall. At the church go R along a road and go L at a fork. This goes uphill. Near the top, turn L into some woodland where a sign says: 'Public Footpath Only. No Riders'.

The hop drier – hopbine – was built in the eighteenth century, and was apparently used to dry hops for the brewers at Dalham Hall. The Hall itself was once owned by the Rhodes family, of which Cecil was the most famous. The church bears along the north arcade some depictions of the seven deadly sins dating from medieval times (there's also the seven works of mercy). Its tower used to be 12m (40ft) higher, but a gale removed the spire in September 1658, on the same day that Oliver Cromwell died.

After passing through some woodland, the path continues with field R. At the corner, go L into some more woods and then R following a track just inside the wood. At the end of a clearing, follow a series of waymarks that show the path through a succession of turns. The route then leaves the woods and heads for Gazeley church. After passing some houses to reach a road, turn L to reach the church and the Chequers pub (to L). Now turn R to walk along the road to pass Gazeley School L. The road eventually bends R. Here fork R along the road signposted to Needham Street and Lackford. When you reach the small cluster of houses that comprise Needham Street go L opposite a red postbox and over a field. Cross a stile into another field and walk on to the corner of a wood. Continue with wood L to the field corner and a road. Cross and turn R for 100m and then bear L to go firstly under the dual-carriageway bridge (the A14) and then a railway bridge.

> This is Kentford. It could be a useful stopping/starting place. If you'd turned L on reaching the road, you'd have found hostelries and transportation into Newmarket. Kennett railway station is about 2km (1.25 miles) in that direction and offers trains to Cambridge and beyond. Edward Thomas came through here just before the first war. 'At Kentford motor cars tyrannically owned the road. Here were men going into the Fox and Bull, or standing contented by the Old Cock. In the shade of the old flint church tower and the chestnuts of the church-yard someone was cheerfully clipping grass at evenfall.'

Just after the railway, go L along Slade Bottom and past a sign for Lafarge Aggregates. This passes some gravel pits L and bends R to continue roughly straight for 2.5km to a T-junction in Herringswell. Turn R. After about 700m, go straight on, over a stile, at a gate labelled 'Hall Farm Private Road'. After a further 1km, this path ends and we go over a stile and along a path which bends R over a stream and into Tuddenham. (Turn L for a shop and the White Hart pub.)

> The earliest known inhabitant of Tuddenham was a pleiosaur (a kind of swimming dinosaur), dating from 120,000 BC. The earliest known humans are compara-tively recent, dating from 40,000 BC. Despite this, it was probably the Saxons who made it a permanent village; some dozen or so sixth- and seventh-century graves have been excavated. The name is certainly Saxon (Tudden-ham: Tudda's home or enclosure). The place came to be dominated by one family as the first Earl of Bristol bought the watermill and manor in 1698. Broadly, that same family then owned and expanded the property right into the twentieth century.

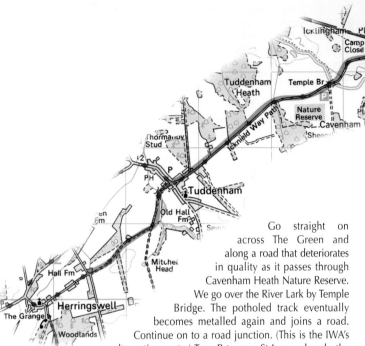

Go straight on across The Green and along a road that deteriorates in quality as it passes through Cavenham Heath Nature Reserve. We go over the River Lark by Temple Bridge. The potholed track eventually becomes metalled again and joins a road. Continue on to a road junction. (This is the IWA's alternative route.) Turn R to pass St James church, the Red Lion pub and then on to a second church (L). Here, just before the Plough pub, turn L to take a path to the R of this church, All Saints. About 150m after the church, turn R to resume the Icknield Way.

This is central Icklingham, which got its name from the Iron Age Iceni, or from the Icknield Way, or both. Coins from the Iceni tribe have been found here, together with those of their neighbours, the Catuvellauni. This suggests that Icklingham was once a border town situated at an important point for crossing the River Lark. The Temple Bridge is thought to be the earliest crossing of the river, on what was the old London-to-Norwich road. According to the OS the Icknield Way after Newmarket runs slightly south of our line; it follows the B1506 to

Kentford (at the point where we went under the A14). Then the route takes the minor road that goes straight to Lackford. This suggests that the earliest crossing of the Lark might have been there.

Icklingham has a couple of pubs and offers some transportation to Bury St Edmunds, which is just down the A1101. The cathedral town of Bury was where they buried what was left of St Edmund, the last Saxon king of East Anglia, after he met the Danes in AD 869. They made a shrine there and then built a great altar in 1214, so creating a popular pilgrimage destination. The Benedictine monastery, originally set up by King Cnut was, at the Dissolution, the richest in the country. Today, the town has its cathedral and some fine Georgian buildings around Angel Hill. Bury has a range of shops, accommodation and busy transport links.

Stage 21: Icklingham to Knettishall

Start:	Icklingham
Finish:	Knettishall
Distance:	26.5km (16.5 miles)
OS:	Landrangers 155 Bury St Edmunds, 144 Thetford & Diss
Route Features:	Easy but long
Information:	Tourist Information Centre: Thetford (01842 752599)

Icklingham is on the main A1101, just a few miles north-west of Bury St Edmunds, which has accommodation, a railway station and numerous bus links. Knettishall is in the middle of nowhere. The IWA obviously decided to head to the end of the Peddars Way National Trail rather than go through Thetford. The latter may have been better. It's easier for the walker in terms of accommodation and

*Abbey remains,
Bury St Edmunds*

transport, has relevant sites and, more importantly, is truer to the real Icknield Way. There is no refreshment opportunity en route for this section. You'll have to carry it with you.

The village of Lackford just to the south boasts some old gravel pits that have been turned into the Lackford Wildfowl Reserve, managed by the Suffolk Wildlife Trust. Edward Thomas stopped at Lackford on his walk. His description seems to sum up the different worlds of the leisured and working classes: 'There was no inn; but the shop was better than the inn could have been. My hostess was one of those most active, little, stoutish and cheerful women who never go out if they can help it. Being descended from suffering and sometimes roofless generations, they seem to see no reason for returning to inclement nature when they have a good digestion and a water-tight roof; they make good jam and tea.'

The Great Abbey Gate, Bury St Edmunds

215

We are now in Suffolk: famous, along with Norfolk, for being flat. 'A line of distant hills is all we want in Suffolk. A landscape should have that image of futurity in it.' So wrote Edward Fitzgerald in 1845. In Daniel Defoe's time his was an area 'wholly employed in daryies', famous for 'the best butter, and perhaps the worst cheese, in England'. In former days Suffolk and Norfolk were famous for their geese. 'They have within these few years found it practicable to make the geese travel on foot,' says Defoe, 'and a prodigious number are brought up to →

This path goes over a drive, then a stile to continue over a field with hedge R towards the R end of a line of pine trees. Once there, go half-R over a stile and turn R for a short distance and then L to continue with field R. This ends at an unmade farm road. Walk on for 20m and then go L along a path for a further 50m or so. Now go R into a field and walk with hedge and farm buildings to R. Eventually, the path leaves the fields and goes over a cross-track. Go straight on to reach a T-junction. (Turn R here for Lackford and the West Stow Country Park.)

West Stow Country Park is the site of a Saxon village and Anglo-Saxon cemetery. The site has been developed so that you can get a feel for what a small Saxon settlement might actually have been like. At the time of writing there are six Anglo-Saxon buildings that have been rebuilt on their original site, using authentic tools and methods. They've even remade some of the furniture. In the visitor centre some objects from the original village are on display. The 50ha (125-acre) country park has its own play area, visitor centre, shop and café. Special events and re-enactments take place during the year. The Saxon Village is open from 10am–5pm daily (tel: 01284 728718).

Turn L and walk along the forest track, through an area known as the King's Forest, for 6.5km.

The forest here was planted in 1935, so the king in question was George V. Conifers were growing here before then, though, and Edward Thomas walked through them on a hot

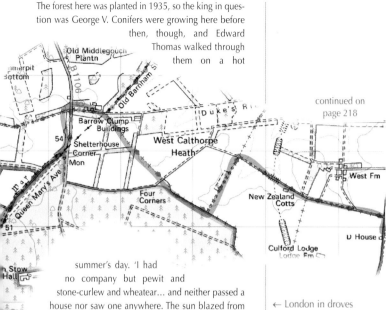

continued on page 218

summer's day. 'I had no company but pewit and stone-curlew and wheatear... and neither passed a house nor saw one anywhere. The sun blazed from the sky overhead and the sand underfoot; it burnt the scent out of the pines as in an oven; it made the land still and silent...'

← London in droves from the furthest parts... with a thousand, sometimes two thousand in a drove.'

Apparently this massive goose and turkey drive began in August after harvest and the beasts fed off the stubble as they made their way south.

This stretch ends at Shelterhouse Corner and a road (the B1106). Turn L on a path that runs alongside the road for 500m. Cross the road and turn R along a metalled lane (Duke's Ride). After 400m, at Barrow's Corner, a signpost points L for a route to Thetford. We, however, go a little further on and bear R near some power lines. The route now continues through some trees before going L into a field. Cross diagonally to the far corner and go through some more trees. Continue in this general direction to a waymark post. Here a track goes on along the edge of the forest R. After 0.8km, turn L along a grass track. This leads to a T-junction; turn R and walk on to meet a major road (the A134). Turn R for 250m to the 'D House' (unmistakably shaped like a D).

Just before it, go L along a drive (Euston Drove). Follow this clear track for 4.3km to another major road (A1088). Turn L. Cross a road junction and follow the main road as it bends R to go over a river bridge. Continue to the entrance to Euston Park (R).

Euston Hall has been the home of the Dukes and Duchesses of Grafton for centuries. It was actually built in the 1660s for the Earl of Arlington, Secretary of State to Charles II. He was responsible for foreign policy and was partly to blame for the idea of political parties as he helped form the 'Court' party, which later became the Tories. He also introduced Louis-Renee de Keroualle to Charles

II and she quickly became the king's mistress. Seemingly the whole business was pre-planned by Lord Arlington and the French Ambassador as a way of promoting Anglo-French relations. The first Earl died at Euston in 1685. It became the home of the Graftons when the Earl's daughter Isabella married Charles II's son, Henry Fitzroy, the first Duke of Grafton.

The hall itself houses a large number of seventeenth- and eighteenth-century paintings, including a number of portraits of Charles II, his family and court. Amongst the artists on show are Sir Anthony Van Dyck and George Stubbs. The hall is surrounded with some splendid grounds and parkland, through which meanders a tributary of the Little Ouse. Euston Hall is open from June to September, on Thursdays and Sundays from 2.30–5pm (tel: 01842 766366).

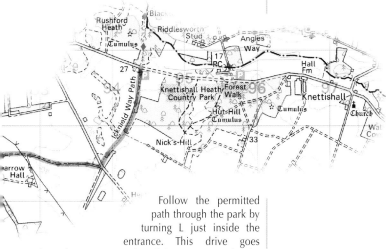

Follow the permitted path through the park by turning L just inside the entrance. This drive goes through a caravan park and then turns R. Take the first L near a barn to walk along Duke's Ride: a broad tree-lined track. This continues for 3.2km to a road. Go half-L over the road to take a path uphill. Walk straight on to a car park and road at the Knettishall Heath Country Park. The Peddars Way starts on the opposite side of the road.

PART 4: THE PEDDARS WAY

Stage 22: Knettishall to Little Cressingham

Start:	Knettishall
Finish:	Little Cressingham
Distance:	23km (14.3 miles)
OS:	Landranger 144 Thetford & Diss
Route Features:	Easy country
Information:	Tourist Information Centres: Thetford (01842 752599), Watton (01953 881440); Ancient House Museum, Thetford (01842 752599)

Knettishall has a couple of car parks, and the taxi companies in Thetford know it. Beyond that... Little Cressingham gets occasional buses and isn't far from Watton, a busy small town with all the usual facilities. On the way, there's a very convenient pub at Stonebridge.

We now enter the final part of our Greater Ridgeway walk; we leave the Icknield Way behind and take to the Roman Peddars Way. In doing this, we have opted for convenience and simplicity rather than historical accuracy. Many authors claim that there are faint signs of an ancient track a little to the west of the Peddars. But it's all a bit vague, has little or no historical authenticity and goes roughly the same way anyhow. Dr W.R. Rudge determined his version of the Icknield Way by following a series of puddingstones similar to the one we saw at Princes Risborough. The sheer rarity of these stones in this part of the world might indicate their significance in marking particularly important places. Based on puddingstones, Rudge's Icknield Way leaves from around Euston, to pass through Thetford at Nun's Bridges. From there the route goes via Two Mile Bottom (on the banks of the Little Ouse) to Grimes Graves (see later). The puddingstones can then be found at Cockley Cley,

Cranwich and Cowell (west of Swaffham). The next stone is at Narborough hillfort followed by East Walton and Gayton. The route then runs through Grimston, Snettisham to finish at Heacham just south of Hunstanton. It's an eminently sensible route, if tricky for modern-day walkers to follow.

The Peddars Way has military origins. Before the coming of the Romans, this was Iceni (or Eceni) territory. The Iceni were a client tribe, and signed an agreement with the Romans; an agreement of co-operation or,

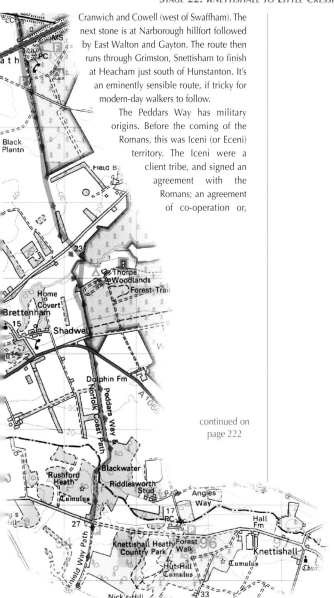

continued on page 222

some say, subservience. Meanwhile Roman forts and settlements were established at sites such as Camulodunum near Colchester, and Verulamium (St Albans). When Prasautagus, who had made the agreement, died in AD 60, the inherited lands were left to his two daughters. But the Romans thought differently; they withdrew loans and imposed their own authority on the territory. Prasautagus's wife, Boudicca, resisted. In reply, the Romans stripped and lashed her. Her daughters were raped. Iceni lands were seized. Boudicca and the Iceni fought back. While the bulk of the Roman forces were otherwise engaged in Wales, Boudicca formed an army, joined with the Trinovantes, advanced on Camulodunum and then on London. Her armies slaughtered and destroyed virtually everything they came across. But after destroying Verulamium, the Roman forces under Paullinus were ready; 15,000 well-organised Roman foot soldiers cut swathes through the opposition and the revolt was over. Boudicca apparently took her own life, by poison, at Battle Bridge, and that is where she is buried – the site now, according to some, occupied by Platform 10 at King's Cross Station.

After the revolt, the Romans laid waste the Iceni lands and the whole area put under much stricter military control. Part of this process was the construction of a number of military roads, one of which is now called the Peddars Way. In its original form this ran from Stane Street, near Colchester, to Long Melford, Ixworth and Knettishall. From there it ran along what is now the course of the National Trail to reach Holme. There was a second branch that went from Gasthorpe, just 2km (3.2 miles) east of Knettishall Heath, towards north-east Norfolk. The Romans used the main route for transporting troops to Lincolnshire. There's no recorded Roman

continued on
page 225

name, and it's suggested that 'Peddars' may simply have been a general word for a path or track. This road was used throughout the Middle Ages as a market route and drove road. It was also important as part of the pilgrims' route to Walsingham. After that it was metalled or was simply forgotten and just grew over.

A long-distance footpath route along the Peddars was first talked about in the 1960s. In 1982, J.F. Wilson put forward a feasibility study on the route. Although he died not long afterwards, the plan went ahead, and on 8 July 1986 the route was officially opened as a 74.4km (46.5-mile) long National Trail by The Prince of Wales. This southern end of the Peddars is marked by an information board in the car park at Knettishall Heath, and various waymarked circular walks begin here too. It's also the start of the Angles Way, a 124km (77-mile) path to Great Yarmouth. There it finds the end of the Weavers Way, which goes to Cromer. If you then take the Norfolk Coast Path, you can walk to Holme and then back here along the Peddars. The complete circle of Norfolk totals roughly 370km (230 miles). Knettishall Heath itself covers some 160ha (400 acres) of heath and woodland, and is a designated SSSI. There's a small visitor centre that opens on Sundays and Bank Holidays a bit along the road to the east.

The Peddars Way starts at an information board in a car park (note that the country park car park is nearly 1.5km to the east of the Peddars car park). Cross the road and walk roughly straight on. After 700m the path bends R and crosses the Little Ouse.

The route continues along the L-hand edge of some woodland and bends L. The woods R soon end and the route continues with a narrow belt of trees to L. Continue straight on to cross two roads, the first of which is the A1066.

You can reach Thetford in just over 5km (3 miles) by turning left here along the A1066, or you can phone for a taxi. It's worth the trip. Thetford developed where the Little Ouse met the River Thet, and it's probable that the

To the west of Knettishall is Rushford which has a fine old hall (c.1700) as well as a fourteenth-century church. To the east is Riddlesworth. The Riddlesworth Stud was opened by the horse magnate Sheikh Hamdam Al Maktoum, but perhaps more famous is Riddlesworth Hall School, where the late Diana, Princess of Wales, was a pupil in the late 1960s.

Icknield Way passed through the town on its way to the north coast. Edward Thomas certainly thought that one of the lanes that run through the castle was part of the Icknield. Others say that Nun's Bridges (so called because they led to a nunnery) is one of the few river crossings along its entire length. The importance of Thetford to the Iceni was established in the early 1980s, when archaeologists found a fortified site with buildings and ramparts dating to AD 40 at Gallows Hill. It was suggested that this was the Iceni headquarters at the time of the Roman invasion and thus home to Prasutagus and Boudicca. Was it from here that Boudicca's rebellion was launched? There are certainly indications that the site was destroyed shortly after that date.

Thetford became really important in Saxon times. The Danes quartered here in AD 869, and moved south-west along the Icknield Way the following summer. Being on the front line, so to speak, the next hundred years or so saw a succession of burning and rebuilding, and Thetford became a place of some significance. There was a mint here in the tenth century, and by 1071 it was the seat of a bishop. There were iron, copper and pottery industries, as well as spinning and weaving. The Normans built a castle on a mound which is reputedly second only to Silbury Hill as the largest man-made hill (probably Iron Age) in England. The fact that both are (approximately) on the route of the Greater Ridgeway can only stimulate further speculation. The castle itself was dismantled in the twelfth century, when the town lost precedence to Norwich, and by Elizabethan times it was pretty desolate. But recovery was slow but sure; by the middle of the nineteenth century there were four breweries, three foundries, a tannery, several malt and lime kilns, several corn mills and a paper mill. All this was aided by the arrival of the railways; indeed, the steam-engine firm of Charles Burrell was the main industry at this time. After Burrell's closed in 1932 decline once again set in until, in 1959, Thetford became one of London's overspill schemes.

Things to see in Thetford include the priory, established in 1104 and destroyed by Henry VIII, and the

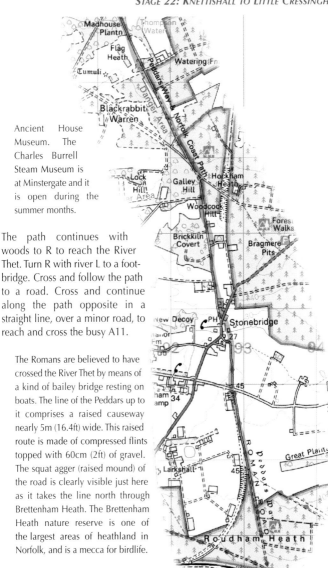

Ancient House Museum. The Charles Burrell Steam Museum is at Minstergate and it is open during the summer months.

The path continues with woods to R to reach the River Thet. Turn R with river L to a foot-bridge. Cross and follow the path to a road. Cross and continue along the path opposite in a straight line, over a minor road, to reach and cross the busy A11.

The Romans are believed to have crossed the River Thet by means of a kind of bailey bridge resting on boats. The line of the Peddars up to it comprises a raised causeway nearly 5m (16.4ft) wide. This raised route is made of compressed flints topped with 60cm (2ft) of gravel. The squat agger (raised mound) of the road is clearly visible just here as it takes the line north through Brettenham Heath. The Brettenham Heath nature reserve is one of the largest areas of heathland in Norfolk, and is a mecca for birdlife.

Thetford is known primarily for being the birthplace of Tom Paine, whose statue stands in front of the King's House. Paine (1737–1809) is principally known for his book *The Rights of Man* in which he attacked hereditary government and argued that all power be derived from the people. He demanded the immediate establishment of government by a representative chamber. He also suggested a type of graduated income tax and pensions for the needy. He proposed both free education and maternity grants. This was all a bit radical in 1790, and he found a more natural home in North America. His idea of universal suffrage and democracy was taken up around the world and Paine played a part in both the American and French Revolutions.

The British Trust for Ornithology has its headquarters here.

The route continues along the same straight course. Cross the Ely–Norwich railway line by the level crossing or a tunnel to R.

This whole area of Brettenham Heath is rich in archaeology. At an undisclosed place somewhere on the Peddars Way, aerial photography has revealed the site of an early Roman fort, perhaps built to impose order on the Iceni after Boudicca's revolt. The wooden fort was apparently surrounded by a series of defensive ditches; the outer one some 10m (33ft) wide. Inside the fort, there's indication of a couple of streets, some buildings and a compound of some sort probably used for horses. The most significant archaeological find in the area, however, is some 16km (10 miles) west of here (near Weeting on what may be the original course of the Icknield). Grimes Graves is the largest and most famous group of Neolithic flint mines in Britain dating back to 1800–2000 BC. The 800 filled-in shafts, many 10m (30ft) deep, and once thought to be burial chambers, cover some 8ha (20 acres) of Thetford Forest heathland. The shafts lead to tunnels that radiate out to follow the seams of high-quality flint. The main tunnels are about 2m (6.6ft) wide and 1.5m (4.9ft) high. On the surface, it all looks like a pock-marked series of bomb craters. No wonder the Saxons named it after Grim, the Scandinavian god. The digging was done mostly with red-deer-antler picks, some of which have been found at the bottom of shafts. Another major find was an 11cm (4.3in) tall chalk 'mother goddess' figurine, buried with a pile of flint blocks and antlers.

Many people believe that flint mining was associated with the Windmill Hill culture from Avebury. It may be that they even started the practice. Unfortunately it seems that, unlike igneous stone axes, flints from different areas are difficult to characterise, and it has therefore proved hard to plot its distribution from source. If only it were possible to discover and positively identify Norfolk flints along the route then we could say for certain that the Greater Ridgeway was an

ancient trade route. But we can't. Maybe the archaeologists should look for Windmill Hill pottery coming north-east?

Just the other side of the railway line, we start to cross Roudham Heath. Here the agger on Peddars Way is clearly visible: only 30cm (1ft) high, but 9m (30ft) wide in places. It has been suggested that Boudicca's call to

Norfolk gives the impression of being quiet and relatively unpopulated. This hasn't always been the case. When Daniel Defoe came here: 'When we come into Norfolk, we see a face of diligence spread over the whole country; the vast manufactures carry'd on (in chief) by the Norwich weavers, employs all the country round in spinning yarn for them… Most of these towns are very populous and large; but that which is most remarkable is, that the whole country round them is interspers'd with villages, and those villages so large, and so full of people, that they are equal to the market-towns in other counties; in a word, they render this eastern part of Norfolk exceeding full of inhabitants.'

arms was met here on Roudham Heath. This was the place where they started their march to Colchester by heading, presumably along a path that became the Peddars Way, to Knettishall and on to Coney Weston.

The route continues through woodland sharing a path with the Hereward Way. After it opens out again, the route continues with the disused Thetford–Watton railway line L. Go over a road and continue straight on. The path then goes L and then R to reach another road and the village of Stonebridge. Turn R along the road and then fork L after the pub.

Stonebridge can make a useful break, as there's a pub (The Dog and Partridge). The village is thought to have got its name from the fact that a stone bridge crosses the old railway line. East Wretham Heath nature reserve, to the east, is primarily grassy heath, pine plantation (planted in Napoleonic times), meres and associated wildlife. Just beyond is Wretham Park where there was once a house designed by Sir Reginald Blomfield. It's now gone, and even the church of St Lawrence is in a state of ruin. The Hereward Way, incidentally, is a waymarked route across the fens from Oakham, near Rutland Water, via Ely to Brandon and the Brecklands. It's named after local hero Hereward the Wake.

We continue along this metalled lane with Brickkiln Covert L. Just after Galley Hill the army road bends L, while we continue by taking the R fork along a rough track.

The whole of this area is called Breckland. In all it covers about 78,000ha (300sq miles), straddling the Suffolk/Norfolk borderlands. It was so-named from areas of 'breck' or 'brake', bits of heathland intermittently broken up for cultivation in Neolithic times. The rather thin, sandy soils and low rainfall meant that it wasn't particularly good farmland but it was relatively easy to clear, simple to work and rich in flints. There are also numerous (and seemingly natural) shallow lakes or meres. The whole area is littered with barrows. As the heathland has never been ploughed in modern times, many stand proud in the landscape. At Little Cressingham one barrow excavated in Victorian times contained a skeleton complete with a dagger, spear, gold ornament and amber beads. There were also some fragments of three small gold boxes.

The deforestation started by the Neolithic peoples continued through to medieval times. Villages were restricted to the more fertile river valleys, while the 'uplands' reverted to heathland scrub. Daniel Defoe said that the area of the Brecklands was 'waste and thin of inhabitants'. This 'waste' appearance had been maintained by extensive sheep farming, gamebird rearing and, perhaps more notably, rabbit warrens. The area became quite famous for its rabbit 'farming' which started as far back as the twelfth century. It's said that rabbits were the only creatures that truly prospered here. Not only were they good to eat, but they also provided the fur used in Brandon (north-west of Thetford) to make top hats. The rabbits and their poachers also became the stuff of legend. There are said to be the ghosts of gamekeepers, killed by poachers, lurking around many a corner. And should you see a white rabbit with flaming eyes, you probably won't finish the walk.

Since those times, conifer forest has altered the character of much of Breckland. The Forestry Commission first arrived in 1922 and now owns over 20,000ha (50,000 acres). Thetford Forest is the largest lowland pine forest in Britain, comprised of Scotch and Corsican pine, Douglas fir and larch. The other big consumer of the 'wasteland' is the Ministry of Defence, who have been here since World War II. Although some villages were only 'temporarily' vacated, moving about 1,000 people, they mostly remain so. Evidence for this MOD activity will be seen all round for a while. Immediately west of the Peddars just here is the Stanford Battle Training Ground. It's all a bit reminiscent of Salisbury Plain, now roughly 350km (220 miles) behind us.

The track continues on a straight course past Thompson Water.

Thompson village is about 1.6km (1 mile) east from here (go R after passing Thompson Water). There's a fourteenth-century church built of knapped flint but, perhaps more relevantly for the hungry/thirsty walker, there's also the sixteenth-century thatched Chequers Inn.

In the middle of the nineteenth century, the River Issey was dammed and the reed-fringed Thompson Water formed, once a useful stop for drovers and shepherds making their way along the Peddars. Willie's Clump, with its memorial plaque to J.F. Wilson (see earlier), stands beside the track near the water. The smaller pools in these parts are known as 'pingos', formed in the last Ice Age when residual pockets of underground ice pushed the soil upwards to form small hillocks. When the ice melted these collapsed to form the craters that then became pingos. These are real wildlife havens, full of bogbean and water violet. The fringes of reed round the larger pingos and round Thompson Water are also good places to see sedge and reed warblers, and reed bunting.

Continue straight to reach the Merton Estate where the National Trail is forced to follow a route away from the Peddars. Luckily, as a National Trail, the superb waymarking makes route finding easy. On Sparrow Hill, we start with woods (and Merton Estate) R. The trail takes us L away from the Roman course, before bending back R to join and follow a clear path north. This crosses the Roman route to join some other tracks before continuing in roughly the same direction to pass Home Farm.

Merton has been home to the de Grey family since about 1337 and is currently owned by Lord Walsingham, who put a permitted path along this stretch of the Peddars. Merton Hall is based on a seventeenth-century house that was almost totally burnt down in 1956. It used to be surrounded by a typical eighteenth-century deer park that was produced by enclosing and landscaping a large area of Merton Common.

Just beyond Merton Park to the east (and just south of Watton) is Wayland Wood. This ancient woodland derives its name from the same source as Wayland's Smithy back on the Berkshire Downs – the Scandinavian god Wayland. The wood is associated with the murder of the Babes in the Wood, originally the subject of a sixteenth-century English ballad in which a small orphaned brother and sister were left in the care of their evil uncle. To get his hands on their inheritance, the uncle got two villains to lure them into the wood and do away with them. One couldn't do the deed, and killed the other instead. He left the children in the wood and promised to return. But he didn't, and the orphans died of hunger and thirst. The villain confessed his crime on the gallows by which time the evil uncle was already in gaol. Whether this story is true or not will probably never be known; the nearby Griston Old Hall has been identified as the evil uncle's house. It's said that, in 1879, the oak under which the babes died was struck by lightning and people came from miles around for mementoes. Wayland Wood is now owned by the Norfolk Naturalists Trust.

After the farm, the trail reaches a crossroads. Go L along a green lane. (Turn R here for Merton. Turn L there for Watton.)

Watton is about 3km (2 miles) east of the Peddars Way, and has bus links to Swaffham, shops and hotels. There's also a clock tower that dates from 1679 to commemorate the rebuilding of the town after a fire of 1673 that virtually raised the whole place. In World War II the town became home to one of the RAF bases, and there's a commemorative exhibition in The Old Officers Mess that's open on Sunday afternoons in the summer.

The green lane soon bends R to reach a road. Turn L to take a path that runs parallel with the road along the edge of fields into Little Cressingham.

Little Cressingham isn't a big place, but does have the White Horse Inn and a church, St Andrew's, that seems to have partially collapsed. The south-west tower fell some time in the eighteenth century, giving it the appearance of something out of a Gothic novel. There's a wind and water mill on the eastern road just out of the village. The system is apparently unique; two pairs of stones (on the first floor) are driven by power from the waterwheel, and two (on the third floor) by wind.

Stage 23: Little Cressingham to Castle Acre

Great Cressingham has a fine church (St Michael) and a priory, the latter dating from the sixteenth century and built inside the moat of an earlier manor house. The Windmill Inn has oak beams, a large garden and camping/caravanning facilities. The Scottish Arts & Crafts architect Robert Weir Schultz designed Pickenham Hall in Edwardian times.

Start:	Little Cressingham
Finish:	Castle Acre
Distance:	19.2km (12 miles)
OS:	Landrangers 144 Thetford & Diss, 132 North West Norfolk
Route Features:	Easy country
Information:	Tourist Information Centre: Swaffham (01760 722255); Swaffham Museum (01760 721230); Ecotech (01760 726100)

It's 19km (12 miles) from Little Cressingham to Castle Acre, and most of it is on country lanes. This obviously isn't ideal, but the country is very pleasant. Little Cressingham is reachable from Watton. Castle Acre has a small amount of accommodation and bus links to Swaffham and Fakenham. There's a convenient pub at North Pickenham and a Macdonalds on the A47. You should get to Castle Acre in time for some sightseeing.

In Little Cressingham, turn R at the pub crossroads. Continue over the next crossroads (turn L for Great Cressingham in 2km) and on along a road known as Caudle Hill. Some 4.5km from Little Cressingham, the lane crosses a more significant crossroads just after Hall Farm with Pickenham Hall to L behind the trees (turn L here for South Pickenham or R for Ashill in 3.2km).

About 1.5km after South Pickenham crossroads, the path takes a line parallel to the lane on the L behind a hedge (this is signposted). Shortly after, the route goes L into the valley and follows a zigzag course towards St Andrew's First School at North Pickenham. At the road, turn R to a T-junction. Turn R here for the centre of North Pickenham village or L to continue the walk.

Continue along the road to a junction. Go straight across and walk straight on. We are now back on the original course of the Peddars Way along 'Procession Lane'.

It has been suggested that this is called Procession Way (or Lane) because medieval pilgrims used to visit a religious hermit ensconced somewhere in North Pickenham. At one time there were thousands of pilgrims in this area, taking a course in a slight north-easterly direction towards Fakenham. This route, known as the Walsingham Way, was once incredibly busy for it was the pilgrimage route to Our Lady of Walsingham: 'England's Nazareth', as it became known, The shrine originated when, in 1061, Lady Richeldis decided to honour the Virgin Mary. Unusually, perhaps, Mary herself decided to help out and took the Lady 'in spirit' to Nazareth to show her where she'd been visited by the Archangel Gabriel. The Virgin then told Lady Richeldis to measure up the house and build one just like it in Walsingham. The Lady had this vision three times and even had the aid of some helpful angels in the construction of the shrine.

Norfolk is, in some quarters, famous for being the home of the American air force; Lakenheath and Mildenhall will perhaps forever be associated with it. North Pickenham was host to American B-24 Liberators during World War II. The airfield is just to the west of the village. After the war, the RAF's Thor ballistic missiles were based here. It then became a site for CND protest, and was dismantled and closed in the early 1960s. St Andrew's church is part medieval/part nineteenth century, and just nearby there's the freehouse Blue Lion pub. There's even a village shop.

continued on page 234

Hall Fm

Peddars Way & Norfolk Coast Path

BRECKLAND DIS

Windmill
Little Cressingham
PH
Threxton Hill
Wks
Oak Wood
Merton Common
Threxton Ho
Home Fm
Merto
Park

233

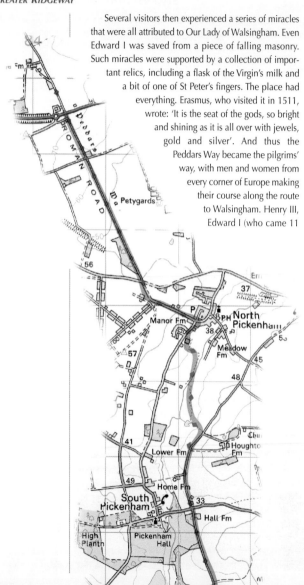

Several visitors then experienced a series of miracles that were all attributed to Our Lady of Walsingham. Even Edward I was saved from a piece of falling masonry. Such miracles were supported by a collection of important relics, including a flask of the Virgin's milk and a bit of one of St Peter's fingers. The place had everything. Erasmus, who visited it in 1511, wrote: 'It is the seat of the gods, so bright and shining as it is all over with jewels, gold and silver'. And thus the Peddars Way became the pilgrims' way, with men and women from every corner of Europe making their course along the route to Walsingham. Henry III, Edward I (who came 11 times), Edward II, Bruce of Scotland, Henry VI, Henry VII, and, even Henry VIII, all went on pilgrimage to Walsingham. The last few miles (from Houghton St Giles) were even walked barefoot. It must have made some of these villages along the Peddars busy and prosperous.

Shortly along the Procession Lane, we pass an old railway bridge (the Swaffham–Thetford line closed in 1964). Continue for 2.5km to reach a car park and the A47 (T). (Turn L for Swaffham in 2.5km.)

Whether Swaffham was on the original route of the Greater Ridgeway/Icknield Way is a matter of debate, although at least one source claims that there could be a line that follows the present-day A1065. Swaffham does act as a kind of local transport hub as well as an accommodation centre. It's a fine Georgian town that was largely rebuilt after a devastating fire in 1775. At the time, Swaffham was the market centre for a substantial area, and the rebuilding was duly lavish in keeping with its fashionable status. There were horse races and hare coursing on the heath. The Assembly Rooms were built with a flexible floor 'for the benefit of dancers', and there was a thriving theatre.

The north aisle of the church is associated with one John Chapman, aka 'the Pedlar of Swaffham'. He's also commemorated on a monument in the market place. John was a fourteenth-century pedlar who, it is said, had a dream that if he went to London he would find treasure.

South Acre Ford

235

About 10km (6 miles) east of Swaffham is Bradenham Hall and Park, noted principally as being the birthplace (in 1856) and home of the writer Rider Haggard. He wrote a series of ripping-yarn type books, and was an instant success and, in the tail end of Victoria's reign, a household name. The Hall is not open to the public but the gardens and arboretum are on two Sundays a month during the summer.

There he met a shopkeeper, who said that he had a dream of treasure buried in the Norfolk village of Swaffham in a pedlar's garden. Chapman hurried back home to dig the garden and there, under his tree, was a pot of money. Several versions then have it that our John gave thanks for his good fortune by funding the rebuilding of Swaffham church. His image is widely used about the town, including appearing on the town sign.

Continue straight on over the A47(T). (There's a trunk road service area to L here – complete with a MacDonalds!) This metalled lane crosses another disused railway (the King's Lynn–Dereham line) before bending L to reach a road. Turn R along the road for 250m and then turn L along Palgrave Road to Palgrave Hall. (Keep straight on for Sporle in just over 1km.)

Sporle, described as one of the most attractive villages in Norfolk, has a shop and, if you turn L in the centre, a pub, The Squirrel's Drey. There's also a small stream which runs along the side of the village street so that many of the houses effectively have a moat. Sporle church has a thirteenth-century tower with fifteenth-century battlements.

Pass Palgrave Hall and continue in the same direction to a road T-junction. Turn L. (Just to L here before the T-junction are all that remains of the village of Great

Stocks Green,
Castle Acre

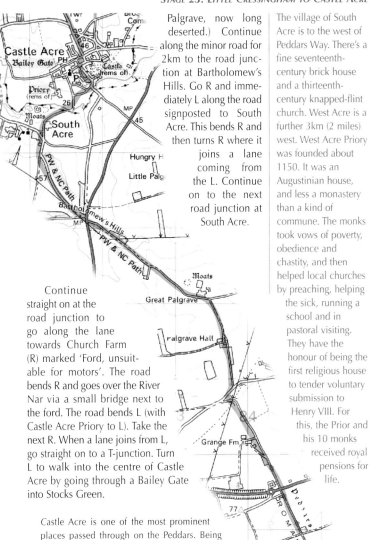

Palgrave, now long deserted.) Continue along the minor road for 2km to the road junction at Bartholomew's Hills. Go R and immediately L along the road signposted to South Acre. This bends R and then turns R where it joins a lane coming from the L. Continue on to the next road junction at South Acre.

The village of South Acre is to the west of Peddars Way. There's a fine seventeenth-century brick house and a thirteenth-century knapped-flint church. West Acre is a further 3km (2 miles) west. West Acre Priory was founded about 1150. It was an Augustinian house, and less a monastery than a kind of commune. The monks took vows of poverty, obedience and chastity, and then helped local churches by preaching, helping the sick, running a school and in pastoral visiting. They have the honour of being the first religious house to tender voluntary submission to Henry VIII. For this, the Prior and his 10 monks received royal pensions for life.

Continue straight on at the road junction to go along the lane towards Church Farm (R) marked 'Ford, unsuitable for motors'. The road bends R and goes over the River Nar via a small bridge next to the ford. The road bends L (with Castle Acre Priory to L). Take the next R. When a lane joins from L, go straight on to a T-junction. Turn L to walk into the centre of Castle Acre by going through a Bailey Gate into Stocks Green.

Castle Acre is one of the most prominent places passed through on the Peddars. Being roughly half way, it's also useful as a stop and/or recuperation point. Accommodation is a bit scarce,

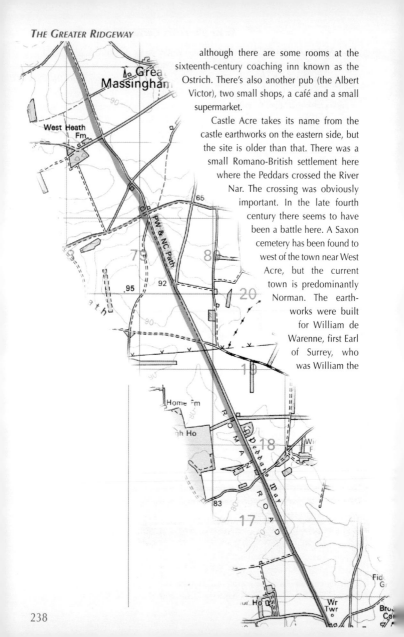

although there are some rooms at the sixteenth-century coaching inn known as the Ostrich. There's also another pub (the Albert Victor), two small shops, a café and a small supermarket.

Castle Acre takes its name from the castle earthworks on the eastern side, but the site is older than that. There was a small Romano-British settlement here where the Peddars crossed the River Nar. The crossing was obviously important. In the late fourth century there seems to have been a battle here. A Saxon cemetery has been found to west of the town near West Acre, but the current town is predominantly Norman. The earthworks were built for William de Warenne, first Earl of Surrey, who was William the

Conqueror's son-in-law. He had been a confidante of the Conqueror for some time and had fought alongside him at the Battle of Hastings. The Castle Acre site consists of a castle motte (based on a natural hill), an inner bailey and a larger outer bailey, in which the town was built. The castle was certainly here in 1086 as it was recorded in the Domesday Book. The first Earl's castle was more a fortified manor than a castle; it was the 3rd Earl, another William, who had the site substantially strengthened at the time of the civil wars of King Stephen (around 1140). In the thirteenth century a 50m (170ft) diameter round keep was built on top of the motte, said to be one of the largest in the country.

When the 6th Earl held the lands, Henry III visited several times while on pilgrimage to Walsingham. The seventh Earl was close to both Henry III and Edward I. He fought for Henry at Lewis in 1264 against the Barons,

The Bailey Gate, Castle Acre

The village of Castle Acre lies between the castle and priory. The heart of the place is Stocks Green, with its surrounding brick and flint houses. In fact, like many villages in this part of Norfolk, flint is used extensively as a building material in these late-Georgian houses. The overall effect is really nice. There's a sense of character here.

Caste Acre Castle

and again at Evesham in 1265. He joined Edward's invasion of Scotland in 1296 and was made Warden of the country. He was in the English forces that were routed by William Wallace at Stirling Bridge in 1297. The following year he helped Edward trounce Wallace at Falkirk. After the 6th Earl, the castle declined and was robbed for building stone. In 1615 Sir Edward Coke bought the estate. Coke was chief Justice to King James and he spent £60 repairing the ruins; said to be one of the earliest examples of private conservation work. The castle is still owned by his descendants but, since 1984, it's been looked after by English Heritage. The castle is open access without charge.

The first De Warenne and his wife also founded a Cluniac priory here, on the west side of town. Some of the Prior's rooms are still intact and contain displays of site finds. A Cluniac priory housed Benedictine monks whose aim was to 'return to the true spirit of religious community life' in a style according to St Benedict. In the twelfth century there were some 314 Benedictine colonies throughout Europe. The Abbot of Cluny (in Burgundy) was a prominent post in the Catholic church, second only to the Pope. Castle Acre housed about 25–35 monks. Until the Dissolution, the priory was very prosperous and owned some fairly large tracts of land around the village. It had also received support from numerous rich benefactors including several kings. Edward I and Queen Eleanor, for example, spent several weeks there in 1296. The Priory is also managed by English Heritage and is open all year round, although only Wednesday to Sunday in the winter months.

Stage 24: Castle Acre to Sedgeford

Start:	Castle Acre
Finish:	Sedgeford
Distance:	22.5km (14 miles)
OS:	Landranger 132 North West Norfolk
Route Features:	Easy country
Information:	Tourist Information Centre: Swaffham (01760 722255)

This section, to Fring and Sedgeford, has been described as dull. It's true that there's an awful lot of road; the first 5.5km (3.5 miles) from Castle Acre to a point known as Shepherd's Bush is entirely along a minor road. There is a verge path, but if you're unlucky, this is so muddy and generally dire that you end up staying on the road... So, do it on a sunny summer's day. Enjoy the bird song. Imagine the legionaries cursing the same dull plod along the road. Work out how much doing this ridiculous walk has cost you. Imagine how much cheaper it would be to have a holiday on a beach in Spain.

Castle Acre has bus routes to Swaffham and Fakenham. Sedgeford is actually about 2.5km (1.5 miles)

Great Massingham

from the route, but you can get buses into Hunstanton or Kings Lynn from there. There isn't a pub on the entire stretch (there is one at Great Massingham just off the route, but it's too far and comes too early), so a packed lunch is a must.

Turn R by the Albert Victor. The road then bends L. Walk past the small supermarket and on along the Great Massingham road for 5.5km. Eventually, this straight road bends R towards Great Massingham. There's a jauntily angled trig point to mark the spot which, I am told, marks the highest point on the Peddars. This is Shepherd's Bush. (Great Massingham is 1.5km further along the road.)

I've been along the Great Massingham road in both sunshine and rain. It seems ploddingly, leg-achingly long, whatever the weather. This whole, on what is called Great Massingham Heath, is littered with evidence of Stone Age man. There's a flint mine, and axes, scrapers and arrowheads are frequently found. Great Massingham has two rather nice village ponds surrounded by a fine variety of houses, with pub and shop between. In olden times there was a fair here to which farmers would bring cattle, driven all the way from Scotland, to be sold for fattening for the Michaelmas markets. Norfolk turkeys were also sold here and then taken to London. Little Massingham, a little further along, is home to the religious retreat of Massingham St Mary.

Back at the bend in the road, the Peddars Way continues

The Peddars Way on Harpley Common

straight on along an unmade track. Follow it over a series of minor roads to reach the much busier A148 at Harpley Dams near the Dogotel.

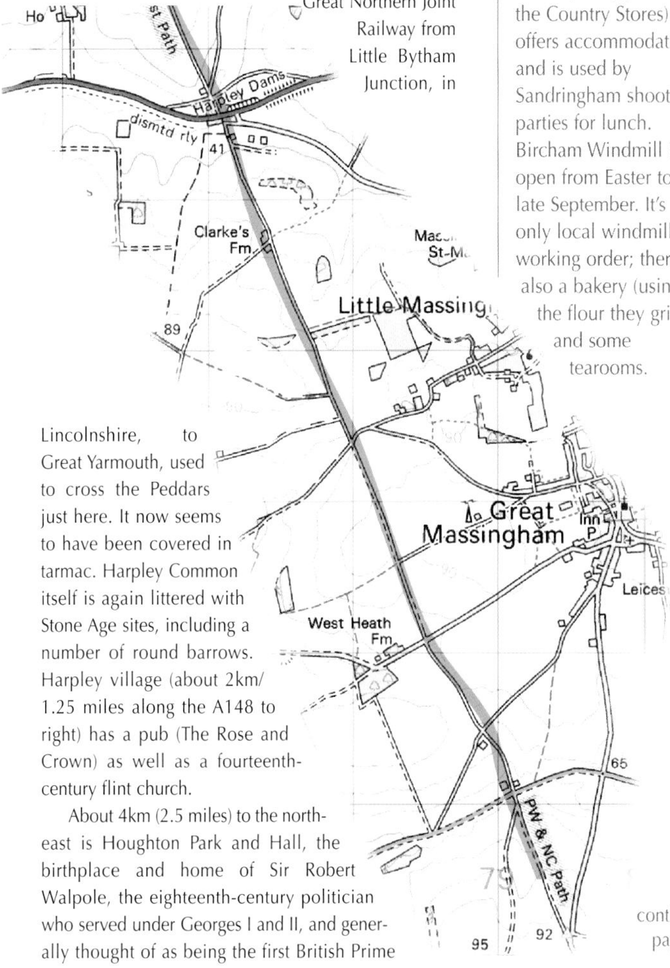

The old Midland & Great Northern Joint Railway from Little Bytham Junction, in

Great Bircham is a flint built village with a fourteenth century church. The Kings Head (just opposite the Country Stores) offers accommodation and is used by Sandringham shooting parties for lunch. Bircham Windmill is open from Easter to late September. It's the only local windmill in working order; there's also a bakery (using the flour they grind) and some tearooms.

Lincolnshire, to Great Yarmouth, used to cross the Peddars just here. It now seems to have been covered in tarmac. Harpley Common itself is again littered with Stone Age sites, including a number of round barrows. Harpley village (about 2km/ 1.25 miles along the A148 to right) has a pub (The Rose and Crown) as well as a fourteenth-century flint church.

About 4km (2.5 miles) to the north-east is Houghton Park and Hall, the birthplace and home of Sir Robert Walpole, the eighteenth-century politician who served under Georges I and II, and generally thought of as being the first British Prime

continued on page 244

243

Fring is a small estate village with a fourteenth-century church. At one time, this may have been an important junction as a Roman road leaves the Peddars Way here to go east to Great Walsingham and/or the Roman camp at Wighton. This route can be seen on OS maps from Barwick House (near Stanhoe) running east.

Minister. The Hall is built of grey, yellow and pink Whitby sandstone and is enormous but rather fine. Walpole started on the house in 1721, having it put up slightly south of an old one. To do this the village of Houghton was demolished and rebuilt further downhill, to form New Houghton where there are two rows of whitewashed semis together with almshouses and farmhouses. The park was filled with deer and peacocks and a church where Robert and his son Horace Walpole (a writer) are buried. The hall has been restored in recent years by the Marquis of Cholmondeley, who has installed 20,000 toy soldiers and has opened the place for visitors (on Thursdays and Sundays, and Bank Holiday Mondays, 1–5.30pm).

Cross the A148. Walk up the road opposite and then straight on up a track to R of some houses. The route continues straight over Harpley Common with Houghton Hall estate to R. Continue over two minor roads. Continue straight on over another two minor roads.

Continue straight on to cross another minor road and, after a further 1.25km, a second road at Fring Cross. Go straight on, uphill, along a path that after a further 1.5km reaches a field corner. Turn L, then R, to reach the B1454 at Littleport.

You can turn left here for Sedgeford in 2.5km (1.5 miles), although it's a bit further if you want the King William IV pub. Sedgeford is a small village, recorded in the Domesday Book, and lying in the fertile valley of the Heacham River. The flint-and-stone church is, partly at least, Saxon, and the site has been occupied since Neolithic times.

The Sedgeford Historical and Archaeological Research Project (SHARP), one of the biggest undertakings of its kind, holds annual digs, and frequent meetings and tours. The remains of a Saxon settlement and cemetery, a medieval manor house, and the site of a

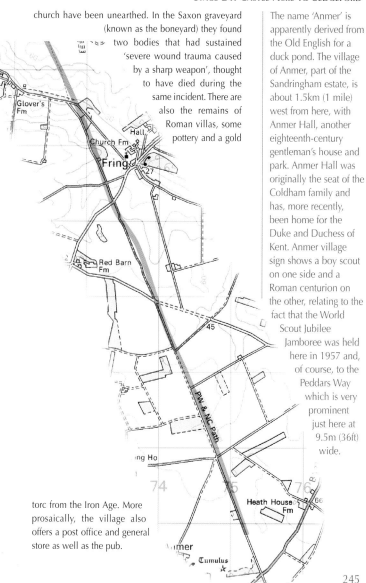

church have been unearthed. In the Saxon graveyard (known as the boneyard) they found two bodies that had sustained 'severe wound trauma caused by a sharp weapon', thought to have died during the same incident. There are also the remains of Roman villas, some pottery and a gold

The name 'Anmer' is apparently derived from the Old English for a duck pond. The village of Anmer, part of the Sandringham estate, is about 1.5km (1 mile) west from here, with Anmer Hall, another eighteenth-century gentleman's house and park. Anmer Hall was originally the seat of the Coldham family and has, more recently, been home for the Duke and Duchess of Kent. Anmer village sign shows a boy scout on one side and a Roman centurion on the other, relating to the fact that the World Scout Jubilee Jamboree was held here in 1957 and, of course, to the Peddars Way which is very prominent just here at 9.5m (36ft) wide.

torc from the Iron Age. More prosaically, the village also offers a post office and general store as well as the pub.

Stage 25: Sedgeford to Hunstanton

There are two schools
of thought about
Magazine Cottage.
One says that it's a
Victorian folly (which
is what it looks like).
The other has it as a
Royalists' ammunition
store during the Civil
War. You pays your
money…

Start:	Sedgeford
Finish:	Hunstanton
Distance:	14km (8.7 miles)
OS:	Landranger 132 North West Norfolk
Route Features:	Easy country
Information:	Tourist Information Centre: Hunstanton (01485 532610)

You'll be pleased to know that this short final stretch is altogether less plodding and more interesting than yesterday. The two ends can be readily linked by bus or taxi; there's an excellent pub at Ringstead, and then one at Holme for the first of the celebratory drinks.

If continuing from yesterday, turn R along the road, and then L into a drive leading to The Magazine Farm.

Our way continues along a grassy lane and over the long-gone Heacham-to-Wells railway line. For some reason, the National Trail now follows a path slightly to the R of the straight to a T-junction. Here turn L and then R to resume the actual route. Continue roughly straight on for just over 2km to reach a road called Peddars Way South. Go straight on and follow the road as it bends L and then R to reach the Gin Trap Inn in the centre of Ringstead.

Ringstead is the last village before Holme: a cause for joy (or sorrow) depending on the state of your feet. Iron Age artefacts found here include a pair of bridle bits that suggest that we're on a track that predates the Romans. At one time, Ringstead was known for its chalybeate spring (a source of water rich in irons). The spring was 2km (1.25 miles) west of the village, on Ringstead Downs. It's a part of the country that offers a last glimpse of some true chalk downland, which we've been following for nearly 580km (360 miles). Ringstead Downs represents an unusual landscape for north Norfolk, and the chalk grassland is now in the care of the Norfolk Wildlife Trust. About 2km (1.25 miles) east is Courtyard Farm, home of Lord Melchett, the former government minister and executive director of Greenpeace. He's had a very positive attitude to ramblers on his land and has created various new public rights of way across it. The Gin Trap Inn serves good beer (including their own) and food in sufficient quantity to sustain you to the end of the walk.

Pass the pub and go up the road past the church. The road bends R (straight on is signposted to Hunstanton) and then L. Continue along Peddars Way North, past an old windmill (L) and the end of speed limit signs to reach a bungalow (R – labelled as No 80). Go L along the path for about 400m and then R.

To the left here is sixteenth-century Hunstanton Hall and Park, owned by the L'Estrange family from the Norman Conquest until recent times. Sir Thomas L'Estrange of Hunstanton was a member of Henry VIII's court. Sir Roger L'Estrange was an early journalist and pamphleteer; he was a Royalist in the Civil War and was knighted for helping to discredit the Popish Plot (an alleged attempt by Jesuits to assassinate Charles II). The L'Estrange family have the hereditary title of Lord High Admiral of The Wash, giving them the right to claim anything out to sea for as far as a man on a horse can throw a spear. P.G. Wodehouse stayed at Hunstanton Hall in the 1920s, and apparently spent a good deal of his time punting on the moat. He also wrote *Money for Nothing* here, and used it for a number of scenes from his Wooster and Jeeves books. At the time of his stay, Charles L'Estrange was obsessed with breeding and showing Jersey cows. He also had a pigsty, complete with a black pig, which Wodehouse used to visit during his afternoon strolls.

Although presumably it must be nice and warm and calm sometimes, Holme beach is mostly a place for hardy folk; the sort who enjoy a good bracing British holiday in Arctic winds. Despite this it is strangely beautiful and enchanting, particularly on the salt marshes. The 223ha (550 acres) of sand dunes are managed by Norfolk Wildlife Trust, and within the reserve is the Holme Bird Observatory. More than 320 bird species have been seen here since 1962. The area is also rich in insects (notably dragonflies) and plants such as marsh orchid as well as the characteristic salt-marsh plants sea-blite and sea lavender.

There is a small entrance fee for the observatory reserve, but it's worth it.

Follow the field boundary between a line of bushes. Eventually this becomes a green lane and reaches the A149. Cross and go straight ahead towards the beach. After a short distance, pass a R turn (for central Holme-next-the-Sea). Before reaching the beach, cross a small bridge over the River Hun. Here, go L to join the Norfolk Coast Path with a caravan park R.

So here we are at Holme-next-the-Sea (pronounced 'Holum'). You might wish to consider it as the end of the walk. The village itself is just east of the Peddars, where you can celebrate your efforts in The White Horse Inn. We've reached the beach and the north-eastern shores of that expanse of water called The Wash. The Romans called it Metaris Aestuarium, and it's generally agreed merchant and military vessels would have left here for the coast of Lincolnshire and perhaps, even, York. There was certainly a signalling station here to communicate with the far coast, which on a clear day can be seen easily over to the left. How long the ferry continued to ply its trade is open to debate, although there is some evidence that one was still travelling from here or Thornham into medieval times.

During 1999, the Holme-next-the-Sea dunes hit the headlines for a different reason, when a wooden circle or 'henge' was found in the sands. Dated to 2050 BC, the henge consisted of the upturned stump of a huge oak tree encircled by some 56 posts from smaller oaks. The discovery was hailed by some archaeologists as one of the most exciting discoveries ever made in this area. They decided that it was a kind of ceremonial site, where bodies were laid out to speed decomposition and hasten the spirit to the afterlife. The sea had engulfed the circle (it was up to 48km/30 miles inland at the time it was built), and it was forgotten until the moving sands revealed it again. 'Seahenge' became infamous because English Heritage dug it up in order to protect it from being washed away. Modern druids and pagans, and to some extent locals from Holme, said that the timber circle was 'a gateway to the afterlife' and shouldn't be moved. But in the summer of 1999 it was taken to the

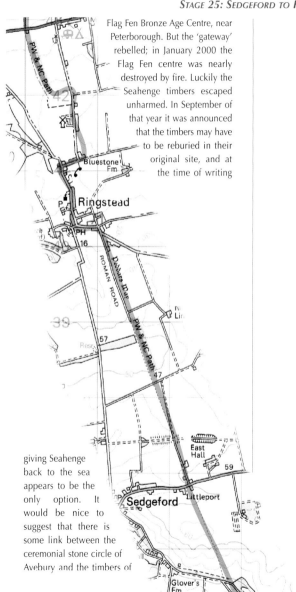

Flag Fen Bronze Age Centre, near Peterborough. But the 'gateway' rebelled; in January 2000 the Flag Fen centre was nearly destroyed by fire. Luckily the Seahenge timbers escaped unharmed. In September of that year it was announced that the timbers may have to be reburied in their original site, and at the time of writing

giving Seahenge back to the sea appears to be the only option. It would be nice to suggest that there is some link between the ceremonial stone circle of Avebury and the timbers of

Holme – and that somehow the Greater Ridge-way connects these two ritual sites? Maybe one day we might be able to demonstrate such a link. But for the present, we can only guess.

With the stream L and a caravan site R, follow the clear path through the outskirts of Old Hunstanton. At the end of this path, bear R along Golf Course Road to pass the clubhouse and car park. Continue up the road. At a junction turn R towards the beach. Turn L by a lifeboat shed. A path now goes along the cliffs to reach a large car park.

There are some fine views from up here. You can buy a drink, ice cream or something with Hunstanton written on it, and

enjoy this final amble into town. It's a spot to consider your achievement, or even to meet those disbelieving friends and relations who have come to see if you've

Memorial Chapel and Lighthouse, St Edmunds Point

Hunstanton as we see it today was invented in 1862 by Hamon L'Estrange (1840–1918) as a seaside resort at the end of the newly constructed railway line. Like a lot of old-fashioned seaside towns, it claims to be one of the sunniest places in the country. It's the biggest of the west Norfolk resorts, and the only East Anglian seaside town that faces west. It still has an air of Victorian gentility and 1950s style. It also has some wonderful 18m (59ft) high striped cliffs, made of beds of white chalk, red limestone and carstone. The centre of town is arranged round a 'green' that slopes to the sea. One thing I read said that the local carstone gives the place the quality of a sepia photograph. And it's true.

Hunstanton Cliffs

made it. The actual site of the car park is called St Edmund's Point. According to legend, it's here that King Edmund of the Angles landed in AD 855 and founded the village of Hunstanton. The king is shown on the town sign together with a wolf; after the Vikings defeated and decapitated him, a passing wolf guarded his head until it could be buried. Some 220 years after his death, his sanctified and mummified body was interned at Bury St Edmunds, which then became a major pilgrimage destination. What remains of a memorial chapel can be seen just beyond what remains of a lighthouse up here on St Edmund's Point. The chapel was built in 1272. A bell used to hang in the ruined doorway until it was stolen in 1966.

At the end of the car park, continue along a grassy stroller's path to reach the centre of Hunstanton, marked by a fine triangular green.

You could dawdle and rest. You could stay a few nights and just celebrate not having to walk any more. Or you could leave immediately. The favourite route appears to be bus to Kings Lynn from where trains will take you onwards.

Oh... well done!

ACCOMMODATION AND TRANSPORT

Things change so quickly that it is virtually impossible to make recommendations regarding either public transport or accommodation. I've been astounded, for example, by the number of pubs and shops that have disappeared from the villages along the route in the last five years. Luckily, accommodation and transport issues are now readily served by other means. The internet is a great resource for this, and if you're not on-line at home then check with your local library. Our tiny little local branch has two links and allows free access (including some tuition) for 30 minutes at a time, more than enough to sort out a hotel or a bus timetable.

For transport, and most particularly buses, you should look no further than www.pti.org.uk. This site seems to be becoming more comprehensive daily. You can find recommended routes as well as timetables. Alternatively, you may find the following telephone numbers useful:

Dorset: 01305 225165; Wiltshire: 08457 090899; Thamesdown: 01793 428428; Thames Travel: 01491 874216; Buckinghamshire (County Council): 01296 395000; Bedfordshire: 01234 228337; Hertfordshire: 08457 244344; Travel-Line East Anglia: 0870 6082608; Suffolk: 08459 583358 and Norfolk: 0845 3006116.

For accommodation you can refer to the many books published annually by, for example, the AA, the Good Guide people, and so on. These are usually stocked by public libraries. I also have *The National Trail Companion*, which gets updated regularly and which can be found in bookshops. It includes all four parts of our walk. I also use the internet, and any of the internet search engines will find something suitable. It is much more up to date and comprehensive than any book can be.

However, there are a number of books that relate specifically to the Greater Ridgeway route, and these are usually produced by the relevant associations. The biggest, of course, is the Ramblers' Association, who not only publish a general book, but also the *Ridgeway Information & Accommodation Guide*. The Ramblers can be found at: Ramblers' Association, 87–90 Albert Embankment, London SE1 7TW (tel: 0171 339 8500; fax: 0171 339 8501; e-mail: ramblers@london.ramblers.org.uk; web site: www.ramblers.org.uk).

The Wessex Ridgeway has no specific organisation attached to it, although the Dorset branch of the Ramblers Association does a pretty good job. You can look them up on www.dorset-ramblers.co.uk/. On the ground, the Wessex Ridgeway is looked after by Dorset Countryside, The Barracks, Bridport Road,

Dorchester, Dorset DT1 1RN (tel: 01305 250793; e-mail <u>dorset countryside-@ic24.net</u>).

The Ridgeway National Trail has its own office: National Trails Office, Cultural Services Dept, Holton, Oxford OX33 1QQ (tel: 01865 810224; fax: 01865 810207; e-mail: <u>mail@rway-tpath.demon.co.uk</u>). It shares a web site: <u>www.nationaltrails.gov.uk</u>. The National Trails Office sells a number of publications, badges and so on related to the Ridgeway. There's also the Friends of the Ridgeway, and they can currently be contacted c/o Peter Gould at 18 Hampton Park, Bristol BS6 6LH.

The Icknield Way Association publishes a route description and an accommodation list. They can be contacted c/o Mrs.Chris James, 56 Back Street, Ashwell, Baldock SG7 5PE (tel: 01462 742684), or via the Membership Secretary who is currently: Roy Wheeler, 19 Boundary Road, Bishops Stortford, Herts CM23 5LE.

The Peddars Way Association publishes information with regard to accommodation along the route including map, camp sites, shops and so on. The address is: 150 Armes Street, Norwich NR2 4EG (tel: 01603 623070).

For all the voluntary associations, it is important to realise that officers come and go. It is well worth checking the address and phone number of the current incumbent on the internet. Try looking on <u>www.gorp.com</u> or simply using a search engine.

The other great source of information is, of course, the Tourist Information Offices. Where they occur, I have included numbers in the appropriate place in the text. I never cease to be amazed by the helpfulness of the people at these places who seem to always dig out accommodation, a bus timetable, an opening time or a taxi number. The key difficulty is that many close 'out of season'.

DISTANCES

The distances between places along the Greater Ridgeway are here given as a guide only

Place	Distance		Place	Distance	
	Km	Miles		Km	Miles
Lyme Regis	0	0	Wendover	9.7	6.0
Wootton Fitzpaine	7.9	4.9	Wigginton	9.7	6.0
Thorncombe	8.4	5.2	Tring Station	3.2	2.0
Burstock	8.2	5.1	Ivinghoe Beacon	5.6	3.5
Beaminster	7.2	4.5	Dagnall	4.8	3.0
Hooke	9.7	6.0	Whipsnade	4.0	2.5
Lower Kingcombe	4.0	2.5	Dunstable Downs Park	2.4	1.5
Maiden Newton	4.8	3.0	Luton Leagrave	9.7	6.0
Sydling St Nicholas	4.0	2.5	Warden Hill	4.8	3.0
Cerne Giant's Head	9.7	6.0	Telegraph Hill	4.0	2.5
Bulbarrow Hill	12.1	7.5	Pirton	4.0	2.5
Shillingstone	8.0	5.0	Ickleford	4.8	3.0
Shroton	4.8	3.0	Letchworth Station	3.7	2.3
Ashmore	9.7	6.0	Baldock	4.3	2.7
Tollard Royal	3.2	2.0	Wallington	5.6	3.5
Ludwell	5.6	3.5	Sandon	4.8	3.0
Old Wardour Castle	5.6	3.5	Therfield	4.8	3.0
Hindon	9.7	6.0	Royston	4.0	2.5
Corton	8.8	5.5	Heydon	9.7	6.0
Heytesbury	3.2	2.0	Strethall	7.2	4.5
Warminster	7.2	4.5	Great Chesterford	4.0	2.5
White Horse	8.0	5.0	Linton	8.0	5.0
Coulston Hill	6.4	4.0	Balsham	6.4	4.0
West Lavington	8.0	5.0	Brinkley	9.7	6.0
Urchfont	8.0	5.0	Stetchworth	4.8	3.0
Devizes	8.0	5.0	Cheveley	4.8	3.0
Morgan's Hill	8.0	5.0	Gazeley	9.7	6.0
Avebury	8.8	5.5	Herringswell	6.4	4.0
Barbury Castle	9.7	6.0	Icklingham	6.4	4.0
Ogbourne St George	4.0	2.5	Barrows Corner	10.5	6.5
Liddington Hill	8.8	5.5	D House	4.8	3.0
Fox Hill	3.2	2.0	Euston	4.0	2.5
Uffington Castle	8.5	5.3	Knettishall	7.2	4.5
Sparsholt Firs	4.8	3.0	A11 Crossing	6.4	4.0
Manor Road Wantage	5.5	3.4	Stonebridge	3.7	2.3
Scutchamer Knob	6.8	4.2	Little Cressingham	12.9	8.0
Bury Down	2.4	1.5	North Pickenham	8.0	5.0
Lowbury Hill	7.2	4.5	A47 Crossing	3.2	2.0
Goring-on-Thames	6.4	4.0	Castle Acre	8.0	5.0
Mongewell	8.5	5.3	Shepherd's Bush	5.6	3.5
Nuffield	6.4	4.0	Harpley Dams	6.1	3.8
Watlington	8.7	5.4	Fring	10.8	6.7
Chinnor	9.0	5.6	Holme-next-the-Sea	9.7	6.0
Princes Risborough	8.5	5.3	Hunstanton	4.3	2.7

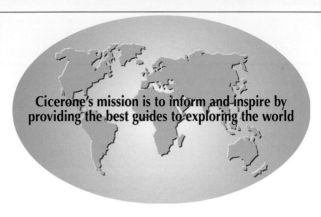

Cicerone's mission is to inform and inspire by providing the best guides to exploring the world

Since its foundation over 30 years ago, Cicerone has specialised in publishing guidebooks and has built a reputation for quality and reliability. It now publishes nearly 300 guides to the major destinations for outdoor enthusiasts, including Europe, UK and the rest of the world.

Written by leading and committed specialists, Cicerone guides are recognised as the most authoritative. They are full of information, maps and illustrations so that the user can plan and complete a successful and safe trip or expedition – be it a long face climb, a walk over Lakeland fells, an alpine traverse, a Himalayan trek or a ramble in the countryside.

With a thorough introduction to assist planning, clear diagrams, maps and colour photographs to illustrate the terrain and route, and accurate and detailed text, Cicerone guides are designed for ease of use and access to the information.

If the facts on the ground change, or there is any aspect of a guide that you think we can improve, we are always delighted to hear from you.

Cicerone Press
2 Police Square Milnthorpe Cumbria LA7 7PY
Tel:01539 562 069   Fax:01539 563 417
e-mail:info@cicerone.co.uk   web:www.cicerone.co.uk